New Approaches to Business, Human Rights and the Environment

Volume 1

The series 'New Approaches to Business, Human Rights and the Environment' contributes to the discussions which are highly relevant to legal and policy developments and meaningful changes in corporate practices in the area of business, human rights and the environment. This rapidly growing field encompasses many areas of law (e.g. private law, public law, EU law, international law, comparative law, environmental law, corporate law, securities law, etc.) and draws from other disciplines such as business/management studies, political economy and political science.

This series draws together legal research work from diverse authors in terms of disciplinary positioning, career stage, academic affiliation, gender and ethnicity. It offers new ideas and fresh perspectives on the interplay between business activities, the advancement of all human rights and environmental protection, including against climate change, which are key areas to sustainable development.

Unique Selling Points:

- Discusses highly relevant topics
- Focuses on business, human rights and the environment
- Offers an interdisciplinary approach

Shuma Talukdar
Editor

Law, Accountability, and Corporate Conduct

Case Studies from Asia, Africa, and Latin America

Springer

Editor
Shuma Talukdar
LexEd Research, Kolkata
Mahindra University
Hyderabad, Telangana, India

ISSN 2948-1333 ISSN 2948-1341 (electronic)
New Approaches to Business, Human Rights and the Environment
ISBN 978-3-032-28713-7 ISBN 978-3-032-28714-4 (eBook)
https://doi.org/10.1007/978-3-032-28714-4

This Springer imprint is published by the registered company Springer Nature Switzerland AG
The registered company address is: Gewerbestrasse 11, 6330 Cham, Switzerland

To the future generations and my 11-year-old twins, Chahkaar and Paiham

Acknowledgements

I extend my deepest gratitude to all the remarkable scholars who contributed to this volume. Their unwavering dedication, intellectual generosity, and the confidence they placed in me made this collective endeavour both enriching and rewarding.

I am particularly grateful to Nadia Bernaz, David Birchall, and Rachel Chambers, the series editors, for their invaluable guidance and constant support. I also wish to sincerely thank Laura Hofmann and Pradeep Kuttysankaran at Springer Nature for their exemplary editorial guidance and seamless administrative assistance throughout the publication process.

I would further like to acknowledge the contributions of the broader Springer team in bringing this project to fruition. My sincere appreciation also goes to the anonymous peer reviewers, whose insightful and constructive feedback significantly enhanced the quality of this work.

A special word of love and gratitude goes to my 11-year-old twins, who, despite their tender age, showed remarkable patience and understanding, often giving up precious time with me so that I could focus on my work. Above all, I owe a heartfelt debt of gratitude to my mother, whose blessings remain a constant source of strength and inspiration in all my endeavours.

Last but not least, I would like to thank Mahindra University, where I am currently pursuing my Ph.D.

Contents

Global and Regional Governance Challenge

List of Abbreviations

ABNT	Brazilian Association of Technical Standards
ADO	Declaratory Action of Unconstitutionality by Inaction
AFCFB	The ASEAN Fisheries Consultative Forum Body
AFI	Accountability Framework Initiative
AI	Artificial Intelligence
BELA	Bangladesh Environmental Lawyers Association
BFLLFEA	Bangladesh Finished Leather, Leather Goods, and Footwear Exporters Association
BHR	Business and human rights
BOD	Biochemical oxygen demand
BSCIC	Bangladesh Small Cottage Industries Corporation
BTA	Bangladesh Tanneries Association
CaC	Calcium carbide
CAC	Command and control
CETP/ETP	Effluent treatment plant
CLT	Consolidation of Labor Laws
CNJ	National Council of Justice
CS	Cabinet Secretary
CSDDD	Corporate Sustainability Due Diligence Directive
CSER	Corporate social and environmental responsibility
CSR	Corporate social responsibility
CSRD	Corporate Sustainability Reporting Directive
CVM	Brazilian Securities Commission
DoE	Department of Environment
EACC	Ethics and Anti-Corruption Commission
EEZ	Exclusive economic zones
EHRD	Environmental Human Rights Defenders
EIA	Environmental impact assessment
ELC	Environment and Land Court
ELRC	Employment and Labour Relations Court
EMCA	Environmental Management and Coordination Act

ESG	Environmental social governance
EU	European Unions
EUDR	EU Deforestation-Free Regulation
FAO	Food and Agriculture Organization
FEBRABAN	The Federation of Brazilian Banks
FIFA	Federation Internationale de Football Association
FKE	Federation of Kenya Employers
FLEGT	Forest Law Enforcement, Governance, and Trade
FPIC	Free prior and informed consent
FSB	Financial Stability Board
GDP	Gross domestic product
GHG	Greenhouse gas
HCV	High conservation value
HEQ	High environmental quality
HRW	Human Rights Watch
IACtHR	Inter-American Court of Human Rights
ICMA	International Capital Markets Association
IEIA	Integrated environmental impact assessment
IFRS	International Financial Reporting Standards
IPOA-IUU	International Plan of Action to Prevent, Deter, and Eliminate Illegal, Unreported, and Unregulated Fishing
ISPO	Indonesian Sustainable Palm Oil Certification
ISSB	International Sustainability Standards Board
IUU	Illegal, unreported, and unregulated
JSC	Judicial Service Commission
LGPD	General Data Protection Law
LLC	Limited Liability Company
LWG	International Leather Working Group
MPF	Federal Prosecutor's Office
NCPO	National Council for Peace and Order
NDPE	No Deforestation, No Peat, and No Exploitation
NECC	National Environmental Complaints Committee
NEMA	National Environmental Management Authority
NGO	Non-governmental organisation
OECD	Organisation for Economic Co-operation and Development AI Principles
PKKNK	Non-forestry timber utilization
PPE	Personal protective equipment
PUP	Plantation Business Assessment
QSE	Quality, safety, and environment
RAD	Annual Deforestation Report
RAJUK	Rajdhani Unnayan Kartripakhhya
REDD+	Reducing emissions from deforestation and forest degradation
RHE	Right to a healthy environment
RMG	Readymade garments

RSPO	Roundtable on Sustainable Palm Oil
RSPO	Roundtable Sustainable Palm Oil
SAPST	Société d'Aménagement et de Promotion de la Station de Taghazout
SASB	Sustainability Accounting Standards Board
SDG	Sustainable Development Goal
SEA	Strategic environmental assessment
SIPERIBUN	Plantation Licensing Information System
SUSEP	Superintendence of Private Insurance
TCFD	Task Force on Climate-Related Financial Disclosures
UK	United Kingdom
UN	United Nations
UNDP	United Nations Development Program
UNESCO	United Nations Educational, Scientific, and Cultural Organization
UNWTO	The World Tourism Organisation
VMS	Vessel monitoring system
VPA	Voluntary Partnership Agreement

List of Figures

List of Tables

Redefining Business: Integrating Human Rights, Sustainability, and Corporate Accountability

Shuma Talukdar

Abstract The intersection of business and human rights has emerged as a critical challenge in the evolving global economy. This introductory chapter introduces readers to the volume's theme, rationale, and structure, highlighting how it addresses key gaps in the literature on corporate accountability in the Global South. It focuses on case studies from Global South countries, Bangladesh, Brazil, Morocco, Indonesia, Mexico, Kenya, Thailand, and Latin America, and highlights the legal, regulatory, and ethical dynamics that are reshaping corporate accountability across diverse industries and geographic contexts. The chapter also justifies the selection of these countries and sectors. Taken together, these chapters suggest a multi-layered regulatory approach that integrates domestic legal frameworks, transnational sustainability laws, and corporate governance mechanisms. It concludes by outlining the distinctive contribution this volume makes to ongoing academic and policy debates.

1 Introduction and Background

1.1 Context and Rationale

The Global South, encompassing countries with lower economic development, plays a pivotal role in the global economy, particularly through its integration into international supply chains.[1] Multinational corporations often rely heavily on these regions for raw materials, manufacturing, and labour, which can lead to significant human rights challenges due to the weak or absent regulatory frameworks

[1] 1 Kano et al. (2020, p. 577).

S. Talukdar (✉)
LexEd Research, Kolkata, Mahindra University,
Hyderabad, Telangana, India

S. Talukdar (ed.), *Law, Accountability, and Corporate Conduct*, New Approaches to Business, Human Rights and the Environment 1,
https://doi.org/10.1007/978-3-032-28714-4_1

governing corporate human rights impacts. There are multiple reasons for this lapse; however, the most significant reason is the lack of "political will" that prioritises profit over people and planet.[2]

Some countries, however, such as India, have introduced mandatory environmental, social, and governance (ESG) reporting for the top 1000 companies in 2021 and corporate social responsibility (CSR) provisions in 2013, following the enactment of the UN Business and Human Rights (BHR) principles in 2011. Yet the extent to which ESG reporting and CSR provisions can genuinely hold businesses accountable remains debatable, as scholarship increasingly suggests that ESG is the latest version of CSR rather than a transformative shift.[3]

In the Global South, particularly, the tension between economic development and sustainability obligations creates a persistent dilemma in which states often prioritise growth over social and environmental protection.[4] This fraction is also reflected in the fact that the global ESG movement itself emerged partly as a response to persistent gaps in human rights protection within developing countries.[5] Ultimately, to deal with these frictions, several global governance frameworks emerged, starting with BHR, CSR, and the most recent ESG. Thus, BHR, CSR, and ESG are all deeply interconnected as they share the same fundamental dimensions of social control.[6] The implications ripple through global markets, shaping consumer ethics, corporate reputations, and international trade policies, thereby controlling businesses' social behaviour.[7]

BHR, shaped by the UN Guiding Principles (UNGPs) on Business and Human Rights, establishes a normative framework clarifying the responsibility of businesses to respect human rights, the duty of states to protect them, and access to remedy for the victims.[8] CSR traditionally refers to voluntary corporate initiatives that integrate social and environmental concerns into business operations.[9] ESG, by contrast, represents a market-based governance mechanism that translates social, environmental, and corporate governance concerns into measurable indicators used by investors, regulators, and corporations to assess corporate risk and performance.[10] While analytically distinct, these frameworks operate within the same ecosystem of corporate accountability. Consequently, the volume employs BHR, CSR, and ESG together, not as a separate analytical framework but as complementary layers of corporate governance, normative (BHR), ethical-voluntary (CSR), and market-regulatory (ESG), which collectively shape how corporate social behaviour

---

[2] Dev (2021, p. 151).

[3] Wang and Phillips-Fein (2023).

[4] Ma et al. (2025).

[5] Pargendler (2024).

[6] Schrempf-Stirling et al. (2022).

[7] Arnold (2010).

[8] Ruggie (2007).

[9] Baines (2009).

[10] Meiden and Silaban (2023).

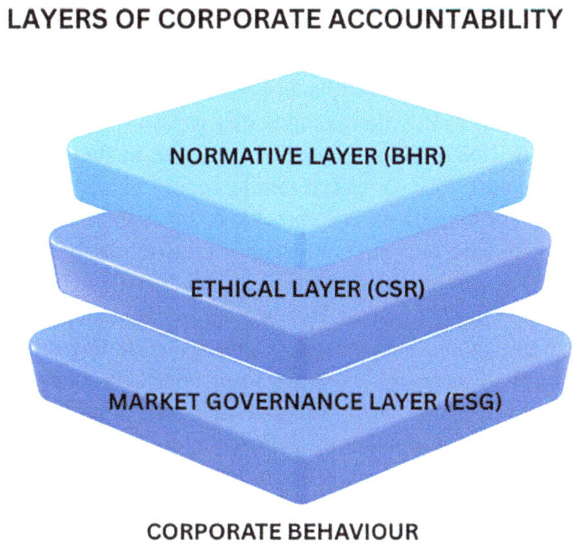

Fig. 1 Visual image of conceptual framework. Source: processed by author, 2026

is monitored, incentivised, and disciplined in transnational economic systems (see Fig. 1).

The absence of robust domestic legal frameworks, combined with an increasingly interconnected global business environment, makes the study of businesses' human rights impacts on developing countries significant. This volume is positioned explicitly within the field of BHR. By drawing on the UNGPs[11] and subsequent global debates on the responsibilities of different actors (states and businesses),[12] obstacles in accessing remedies,[13] and regulatory gaps,[14] the chapters frame sustainability and corporate accountability not as a voluntary commitment but as rights-based obligations. Each case study in this volume illustrates how BHR norms are interpreted, contested, or reinvented in Global South contexts, where legal pluralism, power asymmetries, and socio-economic vulnerabilities shape the real meaning of corporate responsibility.[15] For clarity, the term "human rights" in this volume includes both social and environmental rights, a position affirmed by the Supreme Court of India in several decisions.[16]

[11] United Nations (2011).

[12] Moon (2013).

[13] Rouas (2022).

[14] Thielbörger and Ackermann (2017, p. 44).

[15] Bennett (2025, p. 68).

[16] Gill (2012), Nyekwere et al. (2023) *also see* M.K. Ranjitsinh and Others v. Union of India (2024), May (2020).

1.2 BHR Failures V. Contrasting Good Practices

Instances of business-related human rights violence are most visible in developing countries, largely due to regulatory gaps—a reality that ultimately led to the formation of UNGPs. The Rana Plaza collapse in Bangladesh, which exposed the severe risks embedded in global textile supply chain, is a well-known example of how business operations can directly result in human rights abuses. Similar concerns arise in other sectors. For instance, tourism platforms such as Airbnb, Booking.com, and TripAdvisor list properties in Israeli settlements like Kfar Adumim, Shiloh, and Susya areas built on land taken from Bedouin communities.[17] These listings contribute to ongoing human rights concerns, including displacement, restricted access to essential services, and land loss, adversely impacting children and vulnerable groups. Such business practices raise serious ethical concerns for consumers, damage corporate reputations, and may prompt regulatory or trade policy responses, as seen when Airbnb delisted certain settlement properties in 2018.[18]

Conversely, some companies are actively promoting human rights, thereby strengthening their reputations and attracting ethically conscious consumers. For example, Eskom in South Africa supports gender equity and disability rights; CEMEX in Mexico promotes the inclusion of people with disabilities through its *Congruencia* program; MAS Holdings in Sri Lanka empowers rural women through its "Go Beyond" initiative; and ABB in Tanzania addresses human rights in rural electrification projects. These initiatives not only enhance public trust but also shape emerging standards for ethical and sustainable business conduct.[19]

Against this backdrop, this volume draws on the broader BHR framework to examine how businesses impact human rights and what responsibilities they bear. Focusing on case studies from Bangladesh, Brazil, Morocco, Indonesia, Mexico, Kenya, Thailand, and regions in Latin America, the volume highlights jurisdictions that play strategic roles in the global economy and possess diverse socio-economic contexts. These contexts are critical for understanding how corporate accountability, sustainability mandates, and human rights responsibilities operate in practice. Recognising that BHR challenges manifest differently across jurisdictions, sectors, and governance structures, the volume maintains methodological and regional diversity to capture the plural and context-dependent nature of business-related human rights impacts. The selection criteria of each country and sector in the volume are further discussed in detail in Sect. 3.1 of this chapter.

Beyond environmental and social harms, the volume also interrogates the digital and geopolitical dimensions of sustainability. As businesses adopt technologies, from AI infrastructure to new agribusiness models, the human rights implications multiply, demanding innovative legal responses. By engaging with soft laws (such as the UN Guiding Principles on Business and Human Rights), emerging

---

[17] Amnesty (2019).

[18] Amnesty (2019).

[19] The Global Compact (2024).

transnational regulatory frameworks (such as EU sustainability directives), local governance practices, and critical legal analysis, the chapters collectively offer a transnational legal understanding of how business and human rights challenges are evolving. Overall, the volume contributes to the existing BHR literature by identifying gaps in current scholarship and proposing a hybrid mechanism, such as community mobilisation, judicial activism, certification schemes, and transnational norms, to strengthen corporate accountability.

1.3 The Global South in Global Supply Chains

Multinational enterprises' dependence on Global South resources and labour is at the heart of today's complex value chains. For instance, in Bangladesh, the garment industry, a cornerstone of global fashion, faces persistent challenges such as worker safety and restrictions on union formation.[20] Similarly, Brazil, a major player in agribusiness and mining, contends with modern slavery and trafficking, with an estimated 369,000 Brazilians in slavery-like conditions in 2016.[21] These examples illustrate how supply chain dynamics in the Global South have direct repercussions for global business ethics and sustainability standards and how businesses have direct human rights impacts.

The human rights abuses in today's globalised world can easily cascade beyond national borders,[22] triggering political instability, migration pressures, and broader security concerns.[23] By examining these interconnected supply chain relationships, the volume reveals why strengthening corporate accountability in the Global South is essential for upholding international norms and achieving global development goals. This perspective provides more than geographical coverage; it introduces a distinct lens. Many Global South governments view global standards such as mandatory due diligence or ESG reporting both as tools for accountability and as external impositions shaped by Northern economic interests.[24] This notion is supported by the fact that labour conditions in the global value chain are deteriorating.[25] The compensation of the CEO, on average, increased by 940% from 1978 to 2018, whereas for labourers it is only 12%.[26] This tension between accountability, regulatory imposition, and labour welfare in the global value chain is central to understanding how BHR norms evolve. By foregrounding community perspectives, informal justice systems, and historical power imbalances, the chapters reveal alter-

[20] Baroi and Alam (2024, p. 31, 53).

[21] Emberson et al. (2022, p. 579)

[22] Young (2015, p. 2026).

[23] Vaughan and Lovatt (2021).

[24] Li and Xiang (2025).

[25] Raxer (2025).

[26] Bennett (2025, p. 71).

native legal imaginaries and challenge assumptions that global BHR standards are neutral or universally applicable.

1.4 Emerging Challenges in Business and Human Rights

As John Ruggie notes, the global regulatory landscape is marked by persistent regulatory gaps and challenges between corporate activity and human rights protection, especially in the Global South, where regulatory enforcement is weak or absent.[27] Labour exploitation, environmental degradation, and inadequate worker protections remain widespread problems where regulatory oversight is weak.[28] Reports such as UNDP's Business and Human Rights Progress document these trends, underscoring the need for robust legal and ethical frameworks.[29] The UNDP report 2024 specifically highlights that BHR challenges—such as unsafe working environment, child labour, gender-based violence, and clean water—can be effectively addressed only through strong legal enforcement and adherence to the rule of law.[30]

The 2024 report further demonstrated that strengthening the rule of law must be complemented by supporting businesses in implementing effective operational-level grievance mechanisms. Since stakeholder engagement in human rights due diligence remains a challenge for many companies, particularly those operating long and fragmented value chains, authoritative guidance on how to engage meaningfully with affected rights-holders is essential. Additionally, practical tools for conducting human rights due diligence in the financial sector, as well as access to contextualised human rights risk data, especially in conflict-affected contexts, are urgently needed.[31]

These reforms cannot remain confined to domestic jurisdictions alone. Many countries in the Global South continue to face challenges such as corruption and inconsistent law enforcement.[32] Therefore, developing global standards that are appropriately tailored to Southern contexts is essential to hold businesses accountable across borders. The term Southern used in this volume is to represent underdeveloped or developing Global South countries.

[27] Ruggie (2007, p. 834).

[28] Bridgeman (2008).

[29] UNDP (2024).

[30] UNDP (2024, p. 6).

[31] UNDP (2024, p. 130).

[32] Bridgeman (2008).

2 Rethinking Business: Rights, Regulations, and Real Impact

This section first outlines why global regulatory standards, including EU instruments and the UNGPs, are viewed differently from a Global South perspective. It then positions the volume within these debates by showing how each chapter responds to these tensions.

The Global South perspective offers a fundamentally different analytical lens in the transnational corporate accountability legal framework led by the Global North. While global standards, especially EU-led instruments, are often presented as strengthening corporate accountability, many scholars and states in the South question whether these frameworks genuinely promote justice or instead reproduce structural inequality.[33] For some, these standards will improve the labour and environmental conditions in the developing countries.[34] For others, this may risk the suppliers, especially small,[35] by altogether removing them from the supply chain.[36] Others anticipate contract termination risk because companies might like to avoid the high-risk countries.[37] The possibility of cascading the liability on the suppliers of the developing countries was also underscored in some studies.[38] The example of Brazil's resistance to certain extraterritorial regulations illustrates this tension.[39] Brazil's position reflects a broader pattern identified in Global South scholarship, where externally driven BHR standards are viewed simultaneously as instruments of accountability and as mechanisms that may reinforce global regulatory hierarchies. This is precisely the tension this volume seeks to explore through comparative empirical evidence.

A growing body of Global South scholarship has articulated systematic critiques of Western-led transnational corporate accountability mechanisms. As Debadatta Bose argues, many regulatory frameworks shaping contemporary BHR discourse are formulated within institutions in the Global North. They may therefore reproduce asymmetries in global economic governance rather than fully addressing them.[40] Scholars identify several key concerns. First, extraterritorial regulatory initiatives can function as de facto trade governance tools, imposing compliance burdens on suppliers in developing economies without corresponding participation in rule-making.[41] Second, the risk of regulatory displacement is highlighted, whereby multinational corporations might respond to heightened human rights due diligence

[33] Judijanto (2025a).

[34] Jäger et al. (2023), also see Thorens (2025).

[35] Judijanto (2025b).

[36] Wilhelm (2024).

[37] Mieszkowska (2024).

[38] Mieszkowska (2024).

[39] Bergman and Garphem (2025); also see da Silveira and de Oliveira (2025).

[40] Bose (2023).

[41] Krisch (2022).

obligations by withdrawing from high-risk jurisdictions, thereby undermining livelihoods and development opportunities in vulnerable economies.[42] Third, critics point to representation deficits, noting that many developing countries and affected communities have historically had limited influence in shaping the standards that govern their economic participation.[43] Finally, some scholars argue that BHR frameworks tend to prioritise corporate risk management over structural economic justice, leaving deeper issues of global inequality and development largely unaddressed.[44]

Beyond individual critiques of specific regulatory instruments, Global South concerns about Western-led BHR governance are also rooted in broader theoretical traditions within international law scholarship. One influential perspective comes from Third World Approaches to International Law (TWAIL), which argues that many international legal regimes, while formally universal, have historically reproduced structural inequalities between the Global North and South.[45] From this viewpoint, BHR frameworks developed largely within Northern institutions risk reinforcing asymmetrical regulatory authority, where standards governing labour, environmental protection, and corporate conduct are formulated in the North but implemented predominantly in Southern economies. Scholars drawing on TWAIL, therefore, question whether emerging regulatory regimes, particularly extraterritorial due diligence laws, may inadvertently reproduce patterns of economic dependency or regulatory dominance, even when framed as mechanisms for advancing human rights protection.[46]

A second line of critique emphasises the importance of regulatory pluralism and Southern governance practices. Scholars such as Morgan, Gomes, and Perez-Aleman note that corporate accountability in many Global South contexts often operates through hybrid arrangements that combine local populations, powerful civil societies, and state agencies.[47] From this perspective, Western-led corporate accountability frameworks may overlook locally embedded accountability mechanisms or impose compliance models that do not fully reflect the institutional realities of developing economies. These critiques, therefore, do not reject BHR norms outright; rather, they call for governance approaches that recognise diverse legal traditions, development priorities, and local knowledge systems. Incorporating these perspectives is essential for understanding why globally celebrated corporate accountability frameworks may still be contested within Global South scholarship.

In that case, UNGPs are also not without criticism. It is criticised grossly for failing to make corporations accountable,[48] giving access to remedies to rightsholders,

---

[42] Narula (2019).

[43] Bose (2025).

[44] Leite (2023).

[45] Darian-Smith (2000).

[46] Dehbi and Martin-Ortega (2026).

[47] Morgan et al. (2016).

[48] Wolfsteller and Li (2022).

and also criticised based on process, whereby developing countries were excluded from certain consulting meetings.[49] Therefore, unpacking these debates is essential for understanding why rules that are universally "good" are contested in Global South scholarship. These limitations reinforce the broader point that neither soft-law framework nor hard-law EU instruments fully resolve South concerns about fairness, representation, and regulatory equity.

These debates underscore why a fresh, context-sensitive re-examination of BHR is urgently needed, one that goes beyond universal claims and engages deeply with the lived experience of the South. This volume critically examines how rising global and local demands for sustainable, rights-respecting business practices are reshaping the corporate landscape, particularly in sectors with elevated human rights risks. Against the backdrop of intensified stakeholder scrutiny and evolving legal frameworks such as the EU's Corporate Sustainability Reporting Directive (CSRD) and Corporate Sustainability Due Diligence Directive (CSDDD), it explores how emerging regulatory expectations are challenging the traditional profit-first model.[50] Through rich comparative case studies from Bangladesh to Brazil and Kenya to Thailand, it investigates how both transnational and domestic legal tools interact with local governance innovations, revealing complex zones of convergence, conflict, and opportunity in the pursuit of meaningful corporate accountability.

Taken together, the chapters in this volume illuminate distinct yet interconnected dimensions of BHR challenges in the South. The Bangladesh and Mexico chapters foreground the struggles of local and Indigenous communities confronting environmental degradation and weak regulatory enforcement, while the Kenya chapter explores certification governance as a site where competing public and private standards intersect. The Brazil chapter highlights judicial activism as a unique Global South pathway for advancing corporate accountability, and the Indonesia chapter examines how deforestation and external regulatory pressures, particularly from the EU, reshape domestic governance. Morocco advocates for ethical governance and more inclusive stakeholder participation in the eco-tourism industry. Thailand's analysis of labour migration and illegal, unreported, and unregulated (IUU) fishing exposes the vulnerabilities of migrant workers in high-risk supply chains, and the Latin America chapter adds a novel frontier by revealing how AI infrastructure imposes disproportionate ecological burdens on Southern ecosystems. Collectively, these chapters challenge the North assumption that BHR and sustainability standards operate neutrally across contexts;[51] instead, they show how power asymmetries, colonial legacies, regulatory gaps, and socio-economic conditions shape how global norms are received, contested, or reinvented.[52] By rooting each analysis in specific legal, cultural, and political realities, the volume demonstrates that South

[49] Rasche and Waddock (2021).

[50] Abnett (2025).

[51] Gonzalez (2015).

[52] Judijanto (2025a).

perspectives are not peripheral contributions but essential analytical vantage points for understanding the evolving landscape of business and human rights.

By grounding its analysis in Global South orientation, the volume offers a much-needed corrective to business and human rights discourse often dominated by Global North narratives. It not only generates fresh empirical insights on corporate resistance, greenwashing, socialwashing, and enforcement loopholes but also introduces a multi-layered regulatory model that combines binding law, civil society engagement, and ethical business conduct. Crucially, the volume maps new alignments between global standards like the Global Reporting Initiative and local accountability mechanisms, charting a path towards truly transformative sustainability practices. Engaging with the debates on how BHR norms are interpreted, resisted, and reconfigured across diverse Global South contexts, the volume returns to its central claim: that meaningful BHR reform cannot be universalised without sustained engagement with the Global South knowledge system, governance practices, and lived realities.

3 Methodology and Approach

3.1 Selection Criteria

Cases and sectors in the volume were chosen according to clearly articulated criteria to ensure both relevance and diversity. First, the study prioritised industries that contribute at least 3% of global exports to capture high-impact sectors.[53] Second, regulatory salience was assessed by identifying jurisdictions in which sustainability regulations have been newly adopted or contested, ensuring that cases illustrate evolving legal norms.[54] Third, the volume included documented community-level impacts, such as major environmental incidents or human rights litigation, to ground analysis in empirical significance.[55] Finally, geographic and sectoral diversity guided selection to include at least one case from South Asia, Southeast Asia, Africa, and Latin America and across industries ranging from agribusiness to digital infrastructure.[56]

The geographical diversity of the case studies is intentional and reflects the comparative methodology adopted in this volume. Rather than focusing on a single regional model, the study examines how BHR norms are interpreted and implemented across different governance contexts in the Global South. Each country was therefore selected as an illustrative case representing a distinct BHR challenge. For instance, Bangladesh for its supply chain labour rights and environmental harms;

---

[53] Seawright and Gerring (2007/2008, p. 4).

[54] Seawright and Gerring (2007/2008, p. 4).

[55] Crowe et al. (2011).

[56] University of Twente (n.d.).

Brazil for judicial activism and hybrid ESG regulations; Mexico for highlighting conflicts between extractive industries and Indigenous rights; Kenya for demonstrating the growing influence of certification and standards-based governance; Indonesia for reflecting deforestation concerns and the impact of EU-driven due diligence regulations; Thailand for representing emerging practices in transnational enforcement; Morocco for ESG and BHR implementation gaps; and, lastly, Latin America for technological infrastructure and new environmental risks. Together, these cases illustrate how BHR norms are being reinterpreted and adapted across varied South-oriented analyses.

The diversity of the volume is not intended to produce a uniform regional model but rather to reveal how BHR norms are adapted, contested, and operationalised in different institutional environments. The comparative breadth, therefore, allows the study to capture a wider spectrum of regulatory responses and governance innovations emerging across the Global South.

It is also noteworthy that readers may observe that several chapters foreground environmental harms. This emphasis reflects the empirical reality that environmental degradation often constitutes the primary pathway through which corporate activities affect social and economic rights. As argued by Chiara Macchi, climate change engages both the state duty to protect and the corporate responsibility to respect, as articulated under pillar I and pillar II of the UN Guiding Principles on Business and Human Rights, respectively.[57] She further notes that recent policy and judicial developments indicate the emergence of "climate due diligence" as an evolving dimension of HRDD obligations for both states and corporations. Macchi therefore advocates a holistic approach to HRDD that integrates principles from human rights law, climate law, and environmental law.[58] Accordingly, while environmental protection and business and human rights have traditionally operated through distinct legal frameworks, this volume intentionally brings them together to reflect the integrated manner in which communities experience corporate impacts in practice.

3.2 *Interdisciplinary Methods (Legal Analysis, Fieldwork, Interviews)*

The volume adopted a deliberately plural methodological approach. Several chapters employ legal doctrinal analysis, examining statutes, case law, and international treaties to map corporate obligations and identify enforcement gaps. Complementing this, some of the contributions integrated empirical fieldwork, such as site visits to tanneries, plantations, or data centres, observation of compliance practices, and

[57] Macchi (2021, p. 94).

[58] Macchi (2021, p. 94).

local governance arrangements, thus providing first-hand information.[59] These chapters also draw on semi-structured interviews with workers, government officials, and civil society actors, using purposive sampling to capture diverse perspectives on human rights mandates. Additionally, policy review of national action plans, corporate sustainability reports, and NGO assessments provided documentary evidence to triangulate and contextualise findings.[60]

At the same time, other chapters, such as those focusing on Brazil and Kenya, rely primarily on doctrinal and policy-oriented analysis without empirical components. Taken together, the volume thus reflects methodological plurality, bringing together doctrinal, empirical, policy-analytic, and context-sensitive approaches. Accordingly, the chapters do not follow a single template or uniform method. Some chapters rely on doctrinal or policy-oriented analysis, others use grounded case studies, and some examine sectoral developments within a broader regional context (e.g. AI infrastructure in Latin America). The themes identified later in the chapter function as organisational lenses rather than strict methodological or substantive categories.

3.3 Analytical Framework: Legal Pluralism and Community Agency

Legal pluralism is applied as an analytic lens, recognising that two or more legal systems (state, customary, transnational) coexist and interact within each case setting.[61] This framework enables the volume to trace how transnational laws are negotiated, appropriated, or contested alongside local norms and practices. Centring community agency, the studies examine how affected populations mobilise collective action, draw on social capital, and invoke both formal and informal dispute resolution mechanisms to assert rights and seek remediation.[62] Together, these lenses reveal the structural justice dimensions of business and human rights, highlighting power asymmetries and pathways for inclusive regulatory reform.

The term "communities" refers here to the right-holders, the affected local groups living near sites of corporate activity, including Indigenous peoples, workers' collectives, and other socially or culturally distinct groups whose lives and livelihoods are directly shaped by business operations.[63] Their role is framed not only as right-holders but also as governance actors whose knowledge systems, norms, and practices interact with formal BHR standards. The communities in the

---

[59] Crowe et al. (2011).

[60] University of Twente (n.d.).

[61] Swenson (2018).

[62] Luloff and Bridger (2003).

[63] McDonnell (2023).

chapters are not merely passive victims but central right-holders.[64] Their involvement activates the third pillar of the UNGPs: access to remedy. By examining Indigenous communities in Mexico, fishing communities in Thailand, palm-oil-affected groups in Indonesia, or leather-sector workers in Bangladesh, the volume shows how communities operationalise BHR norms by using courts, protests, customary norms, and transnational advocacy networks. This grounds BHR in lived realities rather than corporate reporting.

3.4 Limitations and Scope

This study focuses on eight Southern contexts and selected industries, which, while diverse, cannot exhaustively represent all regions or sectors; generalisability is therefore circumscribed by geographic and sectoral scope. While the mixed-methods approach fosters triangulation, the reliance on purposive sampling and case study depth over breadth introduces potential selection bias, which future studies could address through larger comparative designs.

4 Structure of the Volume

Thematically, the book is organised around three broad areas: environmental justice and corporate accountability, ESG standards and sector-specific governance, and global and regional governance challenges. These themes are not intended as rigid or mutually exclusive categories; rather, they serve as heuristic frameworks to help readers navigate the chapter's diverse methods, case types, and regulatory concerns. Not all chapters directly engage with all three themes, and some (such as the analysis of AI governance in Latin America) take the form of regional or sectoral studies rather than traditional case studies.

4.1 Theme I: Environmental Justice and Corporate Accountability

In the first theme, environmental justice and corporate accountability, the book highlights the detrimental environmental and social consequences of corporate practices in industries such as leather production in Bangladesh, floriculture in Kenya, and mining in Mexico. These chapters illustrate how marginalised communities often bear the brunt of environmental degradation and human rights abuses,

---

64 Kemp and Vanclay (2013).

as well as the barriers they face in seeking justice and remediation. By focusing on the lived experiences of affected populations, this theme underscores the urgent need for corporate accountability and responsive legal systems to support environmental justice particularly in the Global South.

4.2 Theme II: ESG Standards and Sector-Specific Governance

The second theme, ESG standards and sector-specific governance, explores ESG agenda and key challenges in its implementation in Brazil. It also examines the application of ESG frameworks within specific industries, such as palm oil in Indonesia and tourism in Morocco. These chapters assess how different sectors incorporate or struggle to incorporate ESG principles amid regulatory, economic, and operational challenges. They delve into the role of national and international standards, self-regulation practices, and certification schemes in encouraging sustainable practices and ethical corporate behaviour. By presenting sector-specific insights, this theme reveals the challenges and potential of ESG implementation and the need for tailored governance strategies that consider the unique pressures within each industry.

4.3 Theme III: Global and Regional Governance Challenges

The third theme, global and regional governance challenges, expands on the fragmented regulatory landscape and its implications for the Global South. This section investigates issues like illegal fishing in Thailand and the environmental impact of AI in Latin America, showing how weak regulatory frameworks and lack of cohesive global standards often allow corporations to bypass environmental and social obligations. The chapters here argue for stronger international cooperation and cohesive regulatory approaches to address cross-border challenges, prevent corporate exploitation of regulatory loopholes, and strengthen local governance capacity.

5 Chapter Overview

5.1 Bangladesh: Tanneries, Judicial Orders, and Coordination

The volume starts with a case study by Masrur Salekin and Mahbuba Kamal of Bangladesh's leather industry. In Bangladesh, the court-ordered relocation of Hazaribagh's polluting tanneries to a new Savar estate (2017) aimed to protect the Buriganga River but without effective cross-sector planning. Post-relocation, untreated tannery waste has flowed into the Dhaleshwari River, effectively shifting the pollution burden.[65] Industry leaders resisted closure, citing the leather sector's economic importance (Bangladesh earned about $1107.35 million from leather exports in 2023, and officials feared collapsing a million-dollar industry).[66] This case shows that judicial directives alone, without concurrent environmental infrastructure (e.g. functioning effluent plants) and stakeholder coordination, can simply relocate problems. Sustainable outcomes require integrated regulations that balance economic livelihoods with real pollution controls and community needs. This case study, encompassing all three pillars of the UNGP, highlights weak state protection mechanisms in Bangladesh, the failure of corporate actors in adopting environmental safeguard measures, and the lack of effective remedies for the affected communities.

The chapter navigates the tension between economic development and environmental protection in Bangladesh. Highlighting systemic issues such as climate vulnerability, industrial pollution, and weak regulatory enforcement, the chapter calls for integrating environmental justice principles into development strategies, strengthening institutional frameworks, and enhancing community participation. It also draws on international human rights and environmental norms to propose a rights-based, inclusive framework for sustainable growth.

5.2 *Kenya: Community-Centric Floriculture and ESG Standards*

The third chapter is a sectoral study from Kenya, an emerging market deeply integrated into global trade; the country stands out as a leading exporter of cut flowers, particularly to European markets, where sustainability and ethical sourcing are increasingly prioritised. Kenya's flower farms illustrate how centring workers and communities strengthens both social and economic goals. Major growers (often EU and US export oriented) have invested in local welfare: offering fair wages, health and education initiatives, and active community development programmes. For example, one large farm employs 2000 people, which amounts to 80% of the residents. The firm also funded schools, clinics, and scholarship programmes. Such practices reflect the Kenya Flower Council's social criteria and demonstrate "investment in community development to enhance the welfare of both employees and local communities".[67] These real-world successes align with evolving BHR norms and ESG regulations. Under the EU's CSRD, companies must disclose on human rights and supply chain due diligence, and the upcoming EU CSDDD will require identifying and addressing adverse human rights impacts even outside Europe. In

---

[65] Salekin and Kamal (2026).

[66] Zaman (2024).

[67] Muriuki Sharon (2026).

Kenya's case, empowering communities and integrating them into business (rather than sidelining them) show how BHR frameworks and corporate practice can reinforce each other, promoting inclusive growth while meeting global market standards. This study shows how corporate responsibility (UNGP pillar II) can integrate community welfare, aligning business incentives with social rights.

The study analyses environmental and social issues in the floriculture industry while detailing the legal infrastructure governing ESG compliance, including labour laws, environmental assessments, and corporate governance norms. Furthermore, it evaluates the roles of courts and tribunals in disputes related to business and human rights and highlights Kenya's alignment with international obligations, particularly its compliance with EU sustainability directives. The author of the chapter, Muriuki Sharon, ultimately concludes that sustainable floriculture in Kenya demands robust legal compliance, active corporate responsibility, and meaningful engagement with both local communities and global regulatory expectations.

5.3 *Mexico: Mining Spill, Top-Down Failures, and Participatory Justice*

The fourth chapter presents a case study from Mexico, one of the world's key manufacturing and mining hubs. Mexico's 2014 tailings spill in the Sonora/Bacanuchi River basin exposed the limits of a strictly top-down approach. Initial remediation plans (e.g. a trust fund for clean-up) were implemented without meaningful local input, leading affected communities to sue. The Supreme Court of Mexico ultimately intervened: in a landmark decision, it held that community participation is a constitutional right in environmental matters. As the court noted, the clean-up process "was not transparent. It did not consult with the affected people" and "did not grant any participation to the affected communities". This 2019 ruling (amparo) forced the redesign of the clean-up with community oversight. It resonates strongly with the principles of the Escazú Agreement, which Mexico has ratified: Escazú enshrines access to information, public participation, and justice in environmental decision-making.[68] The ruling strengthens UNGP pillar III by affirming access to justice and participatory rights as constitutional human rights. Mexico's mining case thus underlines that public participation is central to environmental justice and that when communities are included (not excluded), remediation agreements are stronger and more legitimate.

[68] Ramos Gómez and Ramos Gómez (2026).

5.4 Brazil: Biodiversity, Inequality, and Judicial Enforcement

The fifth chapter is a study from Brazil, a major agribusiness and mining hub. Brazil struggles with modern slavery, with 369,000 people in slavery-like conditions in 2018, and environmental degradation, particularly affecting Indigenous rights, as per the UK government's report.[69] Brazil's megadiversity and social inequalities make robust BHR norms and ESG governance both vital and challenging. Brazil is globally unparalleled in biodiversity, hosting roughly 15–20% of the world's species.[70] It also has vast cultural diversity (200+ Indigenous peoples) and many poor, rural communities that depend directly on those ecosystems.[71] In this context, Brazil's courts have become pivotal BHR enforcers by decolonising ESG investment. For instance, in July 2022 the Supreme Federal Court (STF) found the government failed in its constitutional duty to protect the Amazon and climate, ordering activation of the Climate Fund to finance deforestation control.[72] The STF even confirmed that international environmental treaties (e.g. UNFCCC, Paris, CBD) now have "supranational status", effectively placing them above ordinary legislation.[73] In practice, this empowers courts to require executive action on environmental agreements. The county illustrates judicialisation of BHR norms, reflecting accountability theory in action, where courts become central enforcers of human rights obligations.

Despite these judicial advances, Brazil still grapples with corruption and climate vulnerability. Decades of systemic graft (e.g. *Lava Jato*) have eroded trust and governance; Brazil ranked 94th out of 180 on the latest Corruption Perceptions Index. Such weakness hampers BHR norms. At the same time, the climate crisis is already hitting Brazil's economy: reports note that extreme weather events are growing more frequent (e.g. record floods in Rio Grande do Sul in 2023–2024, endangering infrastructure and incomes).[74] Brazilian authorities themselves stress the need for resilience: a central bank forum explicitly called for "developing an economy resilient to extreme natural events… and protecting the most vulnerable social groups". Together, these factors mean Brazil's ESG strategy must emphasise transparency, anti-corruption measures, and disaster resilience alongside environmental protection.[75]

The chapters start Brazil's ESG trajectory, evolving from voluntary commitments to binding obligations. While the first part highlights Brazil's systemic challenges and the judiciary's proactive role in advancing environmental protections,

---

[69] Gonzalez de Oliveira (2019).

[70] Huet and Neveux (n.d.).

[71] Survival (n.d.).

[72] PSB et al. v. Brazil (on Amazon Fund) *"Partido Socialista Brasileiro (PSB), Partido Socialismo e Liberdade (PSOL), Partido dos Trabalhadores (PT) e Rede Sustentabilidade v. União Federal"*

[73] Adriana Sá Leitão Di Pasquale (2024).

[74] Bauer and Martins da Rosa (2026).

[75] Bauer and Martins da Rosa (2026).

the subsequent section provides a detailed account of specific legal instruments and institutional mechanisms, such as Associação Brasileira de Normas Técnicas (ABNT's) PR2030 and PR2060 and financial sector regulations that have formalised ESG principles across sectors. Together, these dimensions illustrate how Brazil is crafting a hybrid model of self-regulation, legal mandates, and judicial oversight to align corporate behaviour with constitutional and international sustainability standards.

5.5 *Morocco: Taghazout Bay and the Gap between Rhetoric and Reality*

The sixth chapter is a study from Morocco, an emerging market increasingly integrated into global trade. Exemplifying the Taghazout Bay tourism project in Morocco, the chapter highlights how ESG promises can outpace practice. Academic analyses observe that Moroccan development plans have historically prioritised growth, "contributing to the boom of mass tourism" *at the expense of* social and environmental considerations. In Taghazout, a luxury surf-resort development (about $1 billion investment in hotels, apartments, and infrastructure) was launched with eco-tourism branding. Yet local reports warn that villages like Tamraght and Aourir saw homes bulldozed and businesses disrupted to make way for the project. Critics emphasise the disconnect: for example, Moroccan surfers and activists stress that the communities "must have a voice" in developments that affect their livelihoods.[76]

Using a longitudinal case study approach involving semi-structured interviews and document analysis, the authors Rachid El Bazzim and Hassan EDMAN reveal a significant gap between official sustainability rhetoric and actual practices. Despite the resort's eco-tourism branding and various sustainability certifications, persistent challenges, such as inadequate waste management, pressure on water resources, and limited engagement with local communities, highlight the shortcomings in current ESG integration. These findings emphasise the urgent need for stronger ethical governance and more inclusive stakeholder participation to ensure that Morocco's tourism development truly aligns with sustainable and rights-respecting principles.

The case exposes the gap between branding and substantive human rights due diligence, reaffirming critiques of "ESG-washing" within transnational BHR debates. It illustrates that putting sustainable tourism slogans on a project is not enough: genuine community integration, access to decision-making, and safeguarding local resource use must be ensured to translate ESG *rhetoric into reality*. The case exemplifies how, in developing economies, ESG investments ignore human rights dimensions.

[76] Bazzim and EDMAN (2026).

5.6 *Indonesia: Palm Oil, Certification, and Regulatory Harmonisation*

The seventh chapter presents a study of Indonesian palm oil, a key player in global agribusiness and mining, which faces persistent challenges in labour practices and corporate accountability. Indonesia's palm oil sector shows how ESG standards and law can work together but also clash without coordination. The government enforces environmental rules (moratoria on forest clearing, licensing requirements, a *mandatory* certification called ISPO), while industry and NGOs push voluntary schemes like the Roundtable on Sustainable Palm Oil (RSPO). These dual systems have created complexity: many companies (especially smallholders) had to choose between Indonesian Sustainable Palm Oil (ISPO) and the RSPO certifications, slowing overall compliance. The authors note this overlap impedes progress, as of late 2022 only 25% of plantations were ISPO certified and 16.6% RSPO certified.[77] Highlighting regulatory incoherence, weak enforcement, and difficulties in harmonising environmental and social frameworks, the authors advocated harmonising ISPO and RSPO requirements to ensure broad participation, transparency, and traceability.

The study also underscores how external policy instruments, notably the EUDR, influence domestic governance by introducing stringent due diligence and risk assessment requirements. In effect, Indonesia's experience suggests that while certification and oversight can advance environmental and social goals, policy alignment is crucial: regulatory and voluntary standards must be integrated to avoid conflicting obligations and to scale up sustainable practices.[78]

5.7 *Thailand: Fisheries Reform, Inclusion, and Cooperation*

The eighth chapter is a case study of Thailand, another key global manufacturing and export hub, which has taken significant steps in advancing BHR norms. Thailand's overhaul of its fishing industry provides a case of inclusive governance delivering sustainability. After receiving an EU "yellow card" (warning) in 2015 for illegal, unreported, and unregulated (IUU) fishing, Thailand embarked on wide-ranging reforms, such as the implementation of vessel monitoring systems (VMS), port inspections, and catch documentation schemes.[79] By 2019, a joint Thai-EU press briefing credited Bangkok's success to broad legal and management changes covering new fisheries laws, vessel monitoring, catch traceability, and enforcement implemented with stakeholder input.[80] The EU Fisheries Commissioner noted that Thailand now has "one of the most effective systems for combating IUU fishing in

[77] Cetera and Hawari (2026).

[78] Cetera and Hawari (2026).

[79] European Commission (2015).

[80] ASEAN (2019).

the region", serving as a model for its neighbours. Thailand leveraged partnerships: it worked closely with EU advisors and, as ASEAN Chair, pushed a regional agenda on sustainable fishing and labour standards.[81]

While these reforms have marked a significant step towards aligning national practices with international standards, they have also faced resistance from powerful commercial fishing operators, leading to disruptions in seafood supply chains and employment patterns. This inclusive, cooperative approach in Thailand shows how combining domestic reforms with international and community collaboration can turn a compliance crisis into a lasting sustainability achievement. The chapter thus highlights the need for a balanced approach, one that combines robust legal enforcement and international cooperation with socio-economic considerations, to achieve sustainable fisheries management and uphold human rights within the seafood sector.

5.8 Latin America: AI Governance and Environmental Costs

The ninth chapter is a sectoral and regional study of Latin America. In Latin America, the environmental dimensions of cutting-edge technologies are coming into focus. The chapter critically examines the environmental impacts of AI in Latin America, focusing on how unchecked expansion in data infrastructure and resource use contributes to ecological harm. AI development relies on vast data centres and advanced chips, whose production depends on minerals (copper, lithium, rare earths, etc.) often mined in Latin American rainforests and mountains. Critically, much of AI's "hardware supply chain" is concentrated in ecologically fragile regions of Latin America.[82]

The global surge in demand for these critical minerals is already driving deforestation, water pollution, and biodiversity loss in mining areas.[83] Experts warn that without governance, AI will amplify resource extraction impacts; calls are growing for sustainability safeguards. For example, recent policy literature emphasises that AI governance must enforce transparency and hold tech companies accountable for environmental externalities (energy use and mining impacts). Turning to the environmental risk of AI, the study evaluates the effectiveness of global AI governance frameworks, such as the EU AI Act and UNESCO recommendations, which often lack enforceable environmental provisions. Through an analysis of 77 Latin American AI legislative proposals, the study finds growing but inconsistent efforts to integrate environmental protections. The study further found that by forging regional AI policy frameworks, for instance, incentives for clean data centres and

[81] Kaewtong et al. (2026).

[82] Smart and Labrin (2026).

[83] Smart and Labrin (2026).

cross-border sustainability standards for mining inputs and energy, Latin American countries could turn a liability into leadership.[84]

Accordingly, it calls for Latin American nations to take a leading role in shaping AI governance that prioritises sustainability and social justice. Such coordinated action would align with global initiatives (e.g. the EU's AI Act) while ensuring the region's rich resources and communities are protected as AI grows.

5.9 Conclusion: Synthesising Insights

The last chapter of the volume, the concluding chapter, synthesises the cross-cutting insights gained from different case and sectoral studies and identifies three unifying themes that emerge across the volume: (1) the centrality of affected communities and Indigenous governance systems in shaping the meaning of remedy and accountability; (2) the role of Southern courts, regulators, and civil society actors in reshaping the contours of due diligence, environmental protection, and labour rights; and (3) the need for global BHR norms to incorporate regional diversity, knowledge systems, and histories of inequality if they are to be genuinely effective. By bringing these strands together, the conclusion argues that truly transformative BHR standards require shared governance where Global South experiences, norms, and practices are integral to defining what corporate accountability means in theory and in practice.

6 Final Remarks

By placing Global South case studies at the centre, the volume reframes corporate accountability as a transnational, negotiated, and co-developed process rather than a one-directional transfer of norms from North to South. Across the chapters, a blend of doctrinal analysis, policy critique, sectoral governance studies, and grounded fieldwork demonstrates how BHR standards acquire meaning only when interpreted and adapted within specific southern legal, political, and socio-economic contexts. For instance, Chap. "Taking Seriously the Right of Local Communities to Participate in Environmental Decisions in the Context of Damages caused by Mining"'s doctrinal unpacking of the Escazú Agreement is brought to life in Chap. "The Siege Closes on Self Regulation, Public Rules and Judicial Precedents to Implement ESG Standards in Brazil"'s on-the-ground study of Kenyan floriculture; judicial activism in Brazil, Indigenous governance in Mexico, certification systems in Kenya, fisheries reform in Thailand, and community-based monitoring in Indonesia each show how BHR norms are locally reshaped, contested, or expanded.

[84] Smart and Labrin (2026).

These contributions challenge the assumption that the Global South merely complies with standards authored in the Global North. Instead, the volume reveals how Southern courts, communities, regulators, and civil society actors actively reinterpret due diligence, environmental rights, and labour protections, contributing to "co-development" and exposing blind spots in Northern regulatory assumptions.

The "co-development" referred here means plural, iterative, and participatory processes through which global standards, such as the UNGPs, EU sustainability directives, reporting frameworks, or certification schemes, interact with domestic laws, community agency, Indigenous norms, and regional governance practices. As the concluding chapter of the volume elaborates, new standards emerge through these frictions and negotiations: courts expand the meaning of remedy; communities redefine participation; regulators hybridise public and private norms; and local governance systems supply concepts of justice that global frameworks overlook. By synthesising lessons from all chapters, the conclusion underscores that truly transformative BHR reform requires co-produced and context-sensitive approaches that incorporate diverse Southern experiences, knowledge systems, and accountability practices.

This introductory chapter, therefore, positions the volume as a bridge between local struggles for justice and global regulatory innovation. Part I lays out environmental justice cases; Part II examines sector-specific ESG challenges; and Part III analyses supranational and regional governance frameworks. Ultimately, the volume calls for a shared governance future in which legal, ethical, and environmental standards are co-developed through inclusive, pluralistic processes that reflect the realities of the Global South. We encourage practitioners, policymakers, and civil society actors to build on these insights by piloting multi-stakeholder roundtables, strengthening participatory mechanisms, and facilitating cross-border data sharing to advance equitable corporate accountability.

References

Abnett K (2025) EU changes to sustainability law risk company lawsuits, legal scholars say. https://www.reuters.com/sustainability/cop/eu-changes-sustainability-law-risk-company-lawsuits-legal-scholars-say-2025-05-09. Accessed 7 July 2025

Amnesty (2019) Chapter 5: Human rights violations | five case studies. https://wwwamnestyorg/en/latest/campaigns/2019/01/chapter-5-case-studies/. Accessed 1 July 2025

Arnold DG (2010) Transnational corporations and the duty to respect basic human rights. BEQ 20(3):371–399

ASEAN (2019) Joint Communiqué of the 52nd ASEAN Foreign Ministers Meeting Bangkok, 31 July 2019. https://aseanorg/wp-content/uploads/2021/01/CIRCULATE-Joint-Communique-of-the-52nd-AMM-FINALpdf. Accessed 4 July 2025

Baines T (2009) Integration of corporate social responsibility through international voluntary initiatives. IJGLS 16(1):223–248

Baroi RA, Alam T (2024) The impact of manufacturing costs paid by global clothing brands on the safety and well-being of workers in the Bangladesh garment industry. Dissertation, Vaasa University of Applied Sciences

Bauer L, Martins da Rosa RS (2026) The siege closes on self regulation, public rules and judicial precedents to implement ESG standards in Brazil. In: Talukdar S (ed) Law, accountability, and corporate conduct, this volume. Springer Nature, Cham, Switzerland
Bazzim RE, Edman H (2026) Ethical issues and the applicability of environmental, social and governance (ESG) standards in the Moroccan tourism industry: the case of the seaside resort Taghazout Bay (Agadir). In: Talukdar S (ed) Law, accountability, and corporate conduct, this volume. Springer Nature, Cham, Switzerland
Bennett EA (2025) Labour justice in the global economy and global economic governance: a broad overview with focus on the ILO and CSR. In: Berger A, Brandi C, Kollar E (eds) Justice in global economic governance: normative and empirical perspectives on promoting fairer globalisation. Edinburgh University Press, pp 66–86
Bergman L, Garphem S (2025) EUDR: green facade or real change?: A qualitative study of how unilateral environmental policies affect Brazil, viewed through the lens of climate imperialism
Bose D (2023) Decentring narratives around business and human rights instruments: an example of the French devoir de vigilance law. BHRJ 8(1):18–42
Bose D (2025) Are there humans in human rights due diligence? Available at SSRN 5316055
Bridgeman (2008) Narrowing the accountability gap: toward a new foreign investor accountability mechanism. GIELR 20(2):187–236
Cetera K, Hawari A (2026) Smart regulation in palm oil governance: enhancing the implementation of ESG principles in Indonesia. In: Talukdar S (ed) Law, accountability, and corporate conduct, this volume. Springer Nature, Cham, Switzerland
Crowe S, Cresswell K, Robertson A, Huby G, Avery A, Sheikh (2011) The case study approach. BMC Med Res Methodol. https://doi.org/10.1186/1471-2288-11-100
da Silveira IG, de Oliveira SEMC (2025) The impacts of the European Union deforestation-free regulation (EUDR) on the Brazilian Agri-food system: global governance, regulatory sovereignty, and climate justice. RP3 Rev Pesqui Polít Públicas 1(3)
Darian-Smith E (2000) Structural inequalities in the global legal system. LSR 34(3):809–828
Dehbi F, Martin-Ortega O (2026) Human rights and environmental due diligence regulation: Eurocentrism and unintended consequences in supply chains in Africa. In: Handbook on business, human rights, and the environment in Africa. Springer Nature Switzerland, Cham, pp 321–340
Dev S (2021) Business and human rights: alternative approaches to transnational regulation. Annu Rev Law Soc Sci 17:139–158. https://doi.org/10.1146/annurev-lawsocsci-113020-074527
Di Pasquale ASL (2024) Addressing the relationship between climate, justice, and conflict: towards a peace-oriented transition?
Emberson C, Pinheiro SM, Trautrims A (2022) Adaptations to first-tier suppliers' relational antislavery capabilities. Supply Chain Manag 27(4):575–593
European Commission (2015) EU acts on illegal fishing: yellow card issued to Thailand while South Korea & Philippines are cleared. https://ec.europa.eu/newsroom/mare/items/22708#:~:text=After%20a%20thorough%20analysis%20and,force%20behind%20good%20ocean%20governance. Accessed 10 July 2025
Gill GN (2012) Human rights and the environment in India: access through public interest litigation. ELR 14(3):200–218
Gonzalez CG (2015) Environmental justice, human rights, and the global south. SCJIL 13:151
Gonzalez de Oliveira T (2019) Business and human rights and modern slavery: a comparative analysis between the Modern Slavery Act (2015) and the Brazilian Law. Dissertation, University of Essex
Huet JM, Neveux G (n.d.) Biodiversity in Brazil: a fundamental concern for European companies. https://wwwbearingpointcom/en-in/insights-events/insights/biodiversity-in-brazil/. Accessed 11 July 2025
Jäger J, Durán G, Schmidt L, Bruckner S (2023) Expected economic effects of the EU corporate sustainability due diligence directive (CSDDD). Verlag Arbeiterkammer, Vienna

Judijanto L (2025a) Green Néo-colonialism or sustainable trade: EUDR's equity implications for global south smallholders. IJES 11(11s):588–599

Judijanto L (2025b) Smallholders at the crossroads: barriers to EUDR compliance and equity in palm oil supply chains. ARACÊ 7(7):38202–38223

Kaewtong S, Kongmuang P, and Jehpong P (2026) Illegal Fishing in Thailand's Food Industry. In: Shuma Talukdar (ed) Law, Accountability, and Corporate Conduct, this volume. Springer Nature, Switzerland

Kano L, Tsang EWK, Yeung HW (2020) Global value chains: a review of the multidisciplinary literature. JIBS 51(4):577–622

Kemp D, Vanclay F (2013) Human rights and impact assessment: clarifying the connections in practice. Impact Assess Proj Apprais 31(2):86–96

Krisch N (2022) Jurisdiction unbound: (extra)territorial regulation as global governance. EJIL 33(2):481–514

Leite M (2023) Beyond buzzwords: mandatory human rights due diligence and a rights-based approach to business models. BHRJ 8(2):197–212

Li Z, Xiang Y (2025) Domestic mandatory human rights due diligence laws as global business and human rights regulation. Am Univ Int Law Rev 40(2):319–416

Luloff AE, Bridger JC (2003). https://wwwresearchgatenet/publication/288395080_Community_Agency_and_Local_Development. Accessed 29 June 2025

M.K. Ranjitsinh v. Union of India (2024) SCC OnLine SC 570.

Ma Y, Loh L, Yin ZJ (2025) Integrating economics, environment, social, and governance (EESG): a more comprehensive sustainable framework. IGD 4(1):100199

Macchi C (2021) The climate change dimension of business and human rights: the gradual consolidation of a concept of 'climate due diligence'. BHRJ 6(1):93–119

May JR (2020) The case for environmental human rights: recognition, implementation, and outcomes. Cardozo Law Rev 42:983

McDonnell K (2023) Epistemic injustice and remedy: can BHR ever really 'centre' rights holders? AJHR 29(1):84–102

Meiden C, Silaban A (2023) Exploring the measurement of environmental performance in alignment with environmental, social, and governance (ESG): a qualitative study. Inf Sci Lett 12(9):2287–2297

Mieszkowska J (2024) The unintended consequences of the EU corporate sustainability due diligence directive. Am J Int Law 118:291

Moon S (2013) Respecting the right to access to medicines: implications of the UN guiding principles on business and human rights for the pharmaceutical industry. HHR 15(1):32–43

Morgan G, Gomes, Perez-Aleman (2016) Transnational governance regimes in the global south: multinationals, states and NGOs as political actors. Revista de Administração de Empresas 56(4):374–379

Narula (2019) Enforcing higher labor standards within developing country value chains. JIBS 50(9):1622–1635

Nyekwere EH, Nnawulezi U, Adiyatma SE, Balarabe K, Rouf MA (2023) Constitutional and judicial interpretation of environmental laws in Nigeria, India and Canada. LSLR 7(2):905–958

Pargendler M (2024) The global south in comparative corporate governance. ECGI Working Paper Series in Law

Ramos Gómez RA, Ramos Gómez AE (2026) Taking seriously the right of local communities to participate in environmental decisions in the context of damages caused by mining. In: Talukdar S (ed) Law, accountability, and corporate conduct, this volume. Springer Nature, Cham, Switzerland

Rasche A, Waddock S (2021) The UN guiding principles on business and human rights: implications for corporate social responsibility research. BHRJ 6(2):227–240

Raxer X (2025) Tackling labor exploitation in global supply chains. https://supplychainreport.org/tackling-labor-exploitation-in-global-supply-chains/. Accessed 24 November 2025

Rouas V (2022) Corporate accountability and access to justice in international and European legal frameworks. In: An assessment of litigation and regulatory responses in European civil-law countries. University of London Press, London
Ruggie JG (2007) Business and human rights: the evolving international agenda. Am J Int Law 101(4):819–840
Salekin M and Kamal M (2026) Balancing economic growth and environmental justice: the challenges of Bangladesh's leather industry. In: Talukdar S (ed) Law, accountability, and corporate conduct, this volume. Springer Nature, Cham, Switzerland
Schrempf-Stirling J, Van Buren HJ III, Wettstein F (2022) Human rights: a promising perspective for business & society. Bus Soc 61(5):1282–1321
Seawright J, Gerring J (2007/2008) Case-selection techniques in case study research: a menu of qualitative and quantitative options. http://www.stevendroper.com/CaseSelection.pdf. Accessed 7 July 2025
Sharon M (2026) An Analysis of Kenyan Laws Affecting Environmental and Social Governance on and for the Floricultural Industry. In: Talukdar S (ed) Law, Accountability, and Corporate Conduct, this volume. Springer Nature, Switzerland
Smart S, Labrin DR (2026) AI, environmental damage, and regulatory divides: fragmented governance and the Latin American response. In: Talukdar S (ed) Law, accountability, and corporate conduct, this volume. Springer Nature, Cham, Switzerland
Survival (n.d.) The Brazilian indigenous people. https://www.survivalinternational.org/tribes/brazilian. Accessed 11 July 2025
Swenson G (2018) Legal pluralism in theory and practice. Int Stud Rev 20(3):438–462. https://doi.org/10.1093/isr/vix060
The Global Compact (2024) Business leader initiative on human right. https://wwwundporg/sites/g/files/zskgke326/files/2024–04/5-%20Guide%20intergate%20HR%20in%20Business%20managementpdf. Accessed 10 June 2025
Thielbörger P, Ackermann T (2017) A treaty on enforcing human rights against business: closing the loophole or getting stuck in a loop? IJGLS 24(1):43–79. https://doi.org/10.2979/indjglolegstu.24.1.0043
Thorens M, Bernaz N, Hospes O (2025) Advocating for the EU corporate sustainability due diligence directive against the odds: strategies and legitimation. JCMS 63(2):606–623
UNDP (2024) UNDP rule of law and human rights global programme — 2024 Annual Report. https://rolhr.undp.org/annualreport/2024/assets/files/Annual-Report-2024.pdf#page=151.11. Accessed 02 December 2025
United Nations (2011) UN guiding principles on business and human rights. https://digitallibrary.un.org/record/720245?ln=en. Accessed 23 November 2025
University of Twente (n.d.) How to select cases? https://wwwutwentenl/en/bms/m-store/step-by-step-guide/getting-started/Methodology/CaseSelection/. Accessed 6 July 2025
Vaughan J, Lovatt J (2021) Business in conflict-affected and high-risk contexts. https://www.bsr.org/en/reports/business-in-conflict-affected-and-high-risk-contexts#:~:text=Business%20activity%20in%20high%2Drisk%20contexts%20may%20exacerbate%20conflict%2C%20corruption,kleptocracy%2C%20and%20undermining%20economic%20development. Accessed 23 November 2025
Wang ML. Phillips-Fein K (2023) Environmental, social, and corporate governance: a history of ESG standardization from 1970s to the present. Thesis. Colombia University
Wilhelm M (2024) Mandatory due diligence legislation: a paradigm shift for the governance of sustainability in global value chains? JIBP 7(4):459–465
Wolfsteller R, Li Y (2022) Business and human rights regulation after the UN guiding principles: accountability, governance, effectiveness. HRR 23(1):1–17
Young EA (2015) Universal jurisdiction, the alien tort statute, and transnational public-law litigation after 'Kiobel'. DLJ 64(6):1023–1127
Zaman AU (2024) Look back at 2023 for understanding Bangladesh's leather sector performance. https://www.textiletoday.com.bd/look-back-at-2023-for-understanding-bangladeshs-leather-sector-performance. Accessed 4 July 2025

Shuma Talukdar is a corporate lawyer and governance professional with over 18 years of cross-sectoral and multi-jurisdictional experience across shipping, energy, infrastructure, and development. She holds dual master's degrees in Business Law and Public Administration and is currently pursuing a Ph.D. in law at Mahindra University, India. She is the co-founder of LexEd Research, a policy-oriented think tank. Her scholarship engages with sustainability law, corporate accountability, transnational law, and global governance, with a particular emphasis on Global South perspectives. Talukdar is the co-editor of *Judicial Responses to Climate Change in the Global South* (Springer Nature, 2023). She has presented her research at leading global institutions, including the Asian Institute of Technology, Max Planck Institute, Sutherland School of Law, UC Berkeley, University of Canberra, and University of Hamburg, and has published widely with leading international publishers.

Environmental Justice and Corporate Accountability

Balancing Economic Growth and Environmental Justice: The Challenges of Bangladesh's Leather Industry

Masrur Salekin and Mahbuba Kamal

Abstract The leather and leather goods industry is one of the prominent sectors of Bangladesh's economy. It is the second-largest export sector after ready-made garments (RMG). The leather tannery industry contributes significantly to economic growth in Bangladesh, but its origin in Hazaribagh, Dhaka, discharged untreated effluent into the Buriganga River and exposed workers and nearby communities to toxic conditions till its relocation. Responding to public interest litigation by Bangladesh Environmental Lawyers Association (BELA), the Supreme Court ordered the relocation of tanneries to a new industrial estate in Savar. Against this backdrop, this chapter investigates how Bangladesh's judiciary, state agencies, and tannery owners have managed the relocation process and the interaction between environmental justice, sustainable development, and the business and human rights (BHR) framework in the Global South. Applying a qualitative method and socio-legal methodology, it shows that relocation has transferred rather than eliminated environmental harm: pollution has shifted from the Buriganga to the Dhaleshwari amidst persistent infrastructural and regulatory failures, while many workers and residents have suffered job losses, reduced incomes, and deteriorating living conditions. It argues that judicial environmental activism without a sustainability approach, in the absence of robust state and corporate human rights due diligence, risks producing new "sacrifice zones" in the name of environmental protection. The chapter concludes by outlining how judicial reasoning, administrative practice, and corporate conduct in Bangladesh's leather sector could be realigned with integrated environmental justice and BHR standards.

M. Salekin (✉)
Bangladesh Judicial Service, Dhaka, Bangladesh

M. Kamal
University of Birmingham, Birmingham, UK

S. Talukdar (ed.), *Law, Accountability, and Corporate Conduct*, New Approaches to Business, Human Rights and the Environment 1,
https://doi.org/10.1007/978-3-032-28714-4_2

1 Introduction

Dhaka, the capital of Bangladesh, is a city that is known for both development as well as flaws of development—often failing to strike the balance of sustainability between environmental justice and business and human rights (BHR). The industries here grew alongside the city itself on the banks of the Buriganga River.[1] Among various sectors, the leather processing industry, commonly referred to as "tannery", is one of the oldest and has been thriving at the Hazaribagh (can be translated as Place of Thousand Gardens)[2] in Dhaka since 1965, from as early as the revolution of leather processing activities from developed to developing nations began.[3] Historically rooted in the colonial era, the leather sector surged in the 1980s and 1990s,[4] fuelled by export policies and cheap labour in Hazaribagh's tanneries. This industrial area has been steadily developed since then and makes Hazaribagh the main centre for leather processing in the country, with the presence of 95% of Bangladesh's tanneries till its relocation in Savar.[5] The Hazaribagh tannery area encompasses approximately 50 acres of land,[6] consisting of over 270 tanneries in 2013.[7] With the rapid growth of the global market's demand for top-quality leather products, the leather industry's potential in Bangladesh's economy has been consistently important. Crushed leather, polished leather, leather apparel, and footwear account for approximately 95% of the leather and leather goods produced in Bangladesh.[8] In 2024–2025, Bangladesh exported 1.06 billion US dollars worth of leather.[9] Moreover, the contribution of the export-oriented leather sector to the gross domestic product (GDP) is estimated to be 0.35%.[10] The leading markets for these leather products include Germany, Italy, France, the Netherlands, Spain, Russia, Brazil, Japan, China, Singapore, and Taiwan.[11] The expansion of export markets through the leather sector also enhances job opportunities. After ready-made garments (RMG), the leather sector represents over 3% of the total exports of the country.[12]

This prosperity also casts a long shadow. Although economic growth and development due to the leather industry labour rights appear to be influential for the country, it is responsible for massive environmental degradation and human rights

[1] Hossain (2008, p. 2).

[2] Shakil (2014, p. 2).

[3] See Karn and Harada (2001, pp. 483–496).

[4] For more details see Rakib (2020, pp. 170–172).

[5] See Huq (2000, pp. 22–28).

[6] See The European Union's INSPIRED Program for Bangladesh (2013).

[7] Rouf et al. (2013, p. 155).

[8] Ibid.

[9] See World Footwear (2025).

[10] See Reza (2022, p. 51).

[11] Ibid.

[12] Reza (2022, p. 51).

violations, leading to environmental injustice. In 1965, as the tannery industries in Hazaribagh began to prosper, it was considered a peripheral area of Dhaka City according to the growth conditions noted in 1950.[13] By 1990, it had evolved into one of the central industrial activity hubs of Dhaka City, and the urban expansion extended past the Hazaribagh area across the Buriganga River. By 2010, Hazaribagh had become located nearly at the heart of Dhaka City.[14] While this sector has been making a considerable contribution to Bangladesh's economy, the unregulated and haphazard growth of this industrial area has been increasing its impact on the physical environment. The toxic leather processing operation ultimately transformed the area into a brownfield.[15] There had not been an establishment of either a central or individual effluent treatment plant (CETP/ETP) for the treatment of liquid and solid waste generated from leather processing. Furthermore, there has been a lack of regulation concerning the use of harmful chemicals associated with this industry.[16] Neither government nor non-government organisations have made any efforts to implement an environmentally friendly tanning process in the Hazaribagh region.[17] According to statistics provided by the Department of Environment (DoE), 95% of the tannery industries have been developed in an unplanned manner within the congested areas of Hazaribagh.[18] For decades, tanneries in Hazaribagh have poisoned the Buriganga River with untreated waste, negatively branding the area among the globe's most toxic sites. To protect the environment and prevent human rights violations in the Hazaribagh tannery, the judiciary of Bangladesh mandated the relocation of the tannery from Hazaribagh to Savar, through the case of *Dr Mohiuddin Farooque v. Bangladesh* (Writ Petition No. 891 of 1994).

Although the judiciary's approach to protect the environment is commendable, this chapter argues that unlike other judiciaries of Asia and the Pacific, which promote sustainable development,[19] the judiciary of Bangladesh failed to consider the principle of sustainable development in the case of the tannery relocation. Subsequently, unfinished effluent treatment facilities and neglected worker needs such as housing, healthcare, and job security sparked new challenges. Amidst the backdrop, the importance of this research lies in the judiciary's approach to uphold sustainability in the context that Bangladesh is a densely populated country with limited resources and environmental rights in the Constitution are not enforceable for the Court. This chapter follows a qualitative method and socio-legal theoretical approach, highlighting the nexus of environmental justice and business and human rights through sustainable development.

---

[13] Bhowmik (2013, p. 108).

[14] Ibid.

[15] For more detail see Shams et al. (2009, pp. 123–137).

[16] See Kashem and Singh (1999, pp. 347–361).

[17] See Shams et al. (2008).

[18] Azom et al. (2012, p. 153).

[19] For more detail see Preston (2005).

This chapter critically assesses the tannery relocation project's implementation, the failure of inter-agency coordination, and the mismanagement that has resulted in the Savar Tannery Industrial Estate becoming an example of less effective environmental intervention by the judiciary, highlighting the nexus of environmental justice and business and human rights through sustainable development.

2 Conceptual Framework

Sustainable development is one of the most important elements of environmental governance.[20] The concept was first made popular by the World Commission on Environment and Development (WCED) in 1987.[21] It refers to "development that meets the needs of the present without compromising the ability of future generations to meet their needs".[22] Since it was first articulated, sustainable development used to consider two pillars, such as economic development and environmental protection, until 1995, when social development became part of sustainable development at the World Summit for Social Development.[23] According to the Summit statement:

> We are deeply convinced that economic development, social development and environmental protection are interdependent and mutually reinforcing components of sustainable development, which is the framework for our efforts to achieve a higher quality of life for all people.…We also recognize that broad-based and sustained economic growth in the context of sustainable development is necessary to sustain social development and social justice.[24]

Interconnectedly, the concept of environmental justice also situates environmental issues as part of a broader social issue.[25] It advocates that costs and benefits arising from the application of environmental laws have to be evenly distributed among the individuals to whom such laws apply.[26] By doing so, it prohibits social, spatial, and temporal imbalance in the consumption of national resources and pollution.[27] Goodland established the classical notion of environmental sustainability. According to him, for a project related to urban development to be environmentally sustainable, it must incorporate decisions made by the local social community as key stakeholders, the project's economic viability, and the local environment's capacity to

---

[20] See Hunter et al. (2015).

[21] See WCED (2987).

[22] Atapattu and Rosing (2025, p. 451).

[23] Ibid.

[24] Ibid.

[25] Doorey (2017, p. 225).

[26] Ibid.

[27] Ibid.

assimilate changes.[28] Developed by Bowley and others, the framework for engaging the engagement of stakeholders through the well-known urban planning framework is known as the Social Theories of the City.[29] This nexus between sustainability and BHR has been developed in recent years. Particularly, the guiding developments have been the United Nations (UN) Guiding Principles on Business and Human Rights (UNGP) 2011 and the 2012 UN Rio+20 Sustainable Development Conference.[30]

In 2011, the UN Human Rights Council endorsed the "Protect, Respect and Remedy" framework of 2008[31] and the UNGP,[32] which placed joint duties of states and the private sector regarding business and human rights. This framework is mainly based on three general principles: first, the state duty to protect human rights; second, the corporate responsibility to respect human rights; and third, shared responsibility of both actors to facilitate access and put in place remedy mechanisms to effectively address human rights violations.[33] Meanwhile, the 2012 Rio+20 set the stage for the development of green economy policies, agreed to establish a process for Sustainable Development Goals (SDG) linked to the Post-2015 Development Agenda expected to be released by September 2015 through its action plan document, "The Future We Want".[34] These frameworks reflect the relationship between the environment and human rights in the BHR context, and sustainability can be considered their common ground.

For the purpose of this chapter, the concept of sustainable development vis-à-vis the judiciary's approach particularly concerns the precautionary principle. The precautionary principle offers direction for the creation and implementation of international environmental law in situations where scientific uncertainty exists.[35] The aim is to prompt decision-makers to weigh the potential harmful impacts of their actions on the environment before engaging in those actions.[36] A significant shift is seen in the transfer of the burden of proof. Traditionally, the responsibility to prove that an activity does or is likely to result in environmental harm falls on the individual opposing the activity.[37] However, when the precautionary approach is utilised, the burden of proof shifts to the individual who intends to carry out the activity, requiring them to demonstrate that it will not harm the environment.[38] This means that the

[28] For more detail see Goodland (2005).

[29] Bhowmik (2013, p. 94).

[30] Mooney (2015, p. 1143).

[31] Special Representative of the Secretary-General, Rep. on Human Rights and Transnational Corporations and Other Business Enterprises, U.N. Doc. A/HRC/8/5 (2008).

[32] Special Representative of the Secretary-General, Rep. on Human Rights and Transnational Corporations and Other Business Enterprises, U.N. Doc. A/HRC/17/31 (2011).

[33] United Nations (2011, p. 1).

[34] Mooney (2015, p. 1144).

[35] For more details see Razzaque (2000, pp. 17–18).

[36] Ibid.

[37] Ibid.

[38] Ibid.

polluter or the state responsible for pollution must prove that their actions and the emission of specific substances will not have adverse or significant effects on the environment prior to receiving permission to release potentially harmful substances and proceed with the proposed activity.[39]

In Bangladesh, the court assessed the gravity of environmental damage to establish the necessity for a precautionary approach. However, the criteria for such damage were not analysed nor were they recognised as part of customary law. In certain instances, Indian courts aimed to bypass the strict rules and standards of evidence and causation, choosing instead to apply the precautionary principle as a component of customary law.[40] Unlike the Indian Supreme Court, the judges in Bangladesh were less inclined to adopt the precautionary principle as an aspect of international customary law. Nevertheless, both judicial systems acknowledge that the Rio Declaration of 1992 carries "persuasive value" and that both India and Bangladesh have signed the Declaration. However, the judiciary in Bangladesh maintains that an international treaty, once signed by a country, is always subject to ratification and can only be enforced as law once enacted by its legislature.[41] Although most recent environmental laws have incorporated the precautionary principle, the court may choose not to implement this principle if the case before them does not relate to any of the relevant legislation.[42] Nevertheless, the role of the judiciary has been vital in promoting environmental governance as it upholds the rule of law and ensures a fair balance between environmental, social, and developmental issues.[43]

The Hazaribagh tannery litigation discussed later in this chapter illustrates this cautious judicial stance. The High Court correctly recognised the severe, ongoing pollution of the Buriganga and ordered strict measures, including relocation of the tanneries and possible closure of non-compliant units. However, it did not explicitly invoke the precautionary principle nor did it require the state or tannery owners to demonstrate that the proposed Savar Tannery Industrial Estate and its central effluent treatment plant would sufficiently prevent new significant pollution of the Dhaleshwari River or avoid creating new risks for surrounding communities. In other words, judicial attention focused on addressing existing, visible environmental damage but did not systematically anticipate and prevent foreseeable harms at the relocation site—a central concern of the precautionary approach.

---

[39] Ibid.

[40] Vellore Citizen's Welfare Forum, (1996) 5 SCC 647 at 658; Taj Trapezium case, (1997) 2 SCC 353; M. C. Mehta (Badkhal and Surajkhal Lakes Matter) vs Union of India, (1997) 3 SCC 715; S. Jagannath case, (1997) 2 SCC 87; M. C. Mehta (Tanneries) Case (1997) 2 SCC 411.

[41] See Razzaque (2000, pp. 17–18).

[42] Ibid.

[43] See Preston (2005).

3 Environmental Degradation in the Hazaribagh Tannery and Demand for Relocation

3.1 Uncontrolled Operation and Environmental Pollution

The tannery waste in Hazaribagh and its vicinity is severely contaminated and poses a significant threat to the environment. More than 95% of the leather produced in Bangladesh undergoes chrome tanning.[44] In the Hazaribagh region, there are no facilities for treating waste, recycling chemicals, or reusing water and wastewater from the tanning industry, which usually contains chromium, dissolved lime, hydrogen sulfide, dyes, oils, organic materials, suspended solids, and more.[45] Besides, the tanning process demands a large quantity of chromium powder and solution—a hazardous chemical for the environment.[46] Chromium levels were detected at rates up to 20 times higher, with the average concentration being 10 times above the acceptable limit.[47] A study indicates that the average readings for other water quality parameters, such as pH, electrical conductivity, alkalinity, dissolved oxygen, biochemical oxygen demand, chemical oxygen demand, chloride, suspended solids, total dissolved solids, nitrites, nitrates, phosphorus, and sulfate, also exceed the national standards for discharge into surface water bodies.[48] An estimated analysis indicates that approximately 15,800 m^3 per day of wastewater, exhibiting a biochemical oxygen demand (BOD) load of 17,600 kg per day alongside elevated chromium concentrations, is discharged by the tannery industries located in Hazaribagh.[49] Consequently, it can be concluded that these effluents from various tanneries have a detrimental impact on human health, aquatic ecosystems, plant life, and the overall environment.[50] Moreover, the solid waste produced during leather processing, such as animal fleshings, trimmings, and sludge, presents considerable disposal difficulties. Poor waste management practices may result in soil contamination and other environmental risks. The leather sector further adds to air pollution due to the release of volatile organic compounds and particulate matter during tanning processes. These emissions present health hazards to both workers and surrounding communities.[51]

---

[44] For more details see Rouf et al. (2013, pp. 155–166).

[45] Ibid, p. 155.

[46] See Nath et al. (2009, pp. 227–234).

[47] Rouf et al. (2013, p. 165).

[48] Ibid.

[49] Ibid, p. 155.

[50] Ibid.

[51] Ibid.

3.2 Adverse Health and Safety Impact

Workers in the leather industry in Bangladesh frequently endure dangerous working environments, as extended exposure to harmful chemicals results in numerous health complications.[52] The chemicals created discoloured ponds and lakes of hazardous waste in residential neighbourhoods, posing significant risks to the individuals who live and work in the tanning district.[53] The majority are experiencing chronic respiratory issues, skin disorders, and even damage to the nasal septum. Tannery employees characterise their work environments as hot, odoriferous, unsanitary, and, in some instances, inadequately lit. They have faced illnesses or injuries related to their jobs. They endure skin ailments. They have dealt with respiratory issues, hand injuries, leg injuries, fractured waist, and episodes of dizziness. Furthermore, they experience discomfort due to the heat.[54]

Tanning involves a variety of chemicals, and some of these can pose serious health risks if appropriate safety measures are not followed. A 2012 report by Human Rights Watch indicates that around 20 chemicals are typically present in each of the 3 stages of leather processing.[55] Some workers directly handle these chemicals without using protective gloves, aprons, or boots, or they may breathe in fumes in poorly ventilated areas without wearing masks.[56] Such exposure can be harmful to health. For instance, sodium sulfide, sulfuric acid, and formic acid can irritate or damage the tissues and membranes of the eyes, skin, and respiratory system. Breathing in vapours of sulfuric and formic acid can lead to lung oedema, which is the build-up of fluid in the lungs.[57] Short-term exposure to sodium carbonate can irritate the eyes, skin, and respiratory system, while repeated exposure may result in dermatitis and even perforation of the nasal septum. Sodium metabisulfite is also highly irritating to the gastrointestinal tract, and inhalation can lead to reactions akin to asthma.

The chemicals utilised by tannery workers during the tanning process, especially in the "wet blue" phase, release gases such as hydrogen sulfide, sulfur dioxide, and ammonia. Breathing in hydrogen sulfide for short periods can lead to unconsciousness, lung oedema, and impacts on the central nervous system. High concentrations of this gas can be fatal. Ammonia gas can also damage the tissues and membranes of the eyes, skin, and respiratory system, with inhalation of elevated levels possibly causing lung oedema. Additionally, prolonged exposure to sulfur dioxide can provoke asthma attacks in individuals who have asthma.[58] A research study reveals that 47.3% of tannery employees lack sufficient awareness of the impacts of tannery

---

[52] See Rahman et al. (2014, pp. 57–76).

[53] Ibid.

[54] See Lanteigne (2010)

[55] See Human Rights Watch (2012, pp. 41–70).

[56] Ibid.

[57] Ibid.

[58] Ibid.

waste, while 70.5% of those surveyed do not know the regulations regarding the use of hazardous chemicals in the leather processing sector.[59] A primary reason for this is that many workers are either uneducated or have limited education. Owners of the plants fail to offer training for their employees, which results in a lack of knowledge about health and safety in the leather industry.[60] Only 15.2%, 11.6%, and 7.1% are seen using masks, aprons, and gloves, respectively, during work, with 66.1% not adopting any protective measures at all due to a lack of knowledge and inadequate access to personal protective equipment; the majority do not adhere to the regulations set forth for the leather processing industry.[61] Many suffer from health issues even before entering the industry. Economically disadvantaged tannery workers are unable to follow health regulations, leading to a range of long-term health problems.[62]

3.3 Death of the Buriganga River

All the liquid waste transported by the drains of the city corporations is dumped in the low-lying areas of Hazaribagh. The solid waste (small fragments of leather, surplus fat, flesh, and hair) is heaped along the streets in front of the tanneries. In the end, both these liquid and solid wastes find their way into the Buriganga River, which is the lifeline of Dhaka City. Prior to 1988, the low-lying areas of Hazaribagh frequently experienced flooding from the Buriganga River, and tannery wastes were discharged directly into the river. Following the significant flood of 1988, the government constructed the Dhaka Protection Embankment.[63] Consequently, the waste no longer flowed directly into the river but was obstructed by the embankment and, during the monsoon season, became mixed with rainwater and spread to the nearby residential areas. In 1996, four pumps were set up at the section of the embankment located in the low-lying areas of Hazaribagh to drain water into the Buriganga, and, ultimately, the tannery waste is also discharged into the river.[64] The harmful leather tanning industries situated along the banks of the Buriganga River in Hazaribagh have become a major threat to the environmental sustainability of Dhaka. Due to the waste produced by tanneries, the living conditions in the Hazaribagh leather industrial area have drastically worsened over the decades. The aquatic life in the Buriganga River has significantly declined, leaving around 2 million people living near Hazaribagh and the Buriganga vulnerable because of this deteriorated environment.[65] The primary cause of pollution in the Buriganga River is the discharge of

[59] Garai (2014, p. 281).

[60] Ibid.

[61] Ibid.

[62] Ibid.

[63] Bhowmik (2012, p. 3).

[64] Ibid.

[65] Arias-Barreiro (2010, pp. 471–475).

untreated liquid waste from tannery industries located in Hazaribagh. The chromium that is released from the tanneries in Hazaribagh has polluted the waters of the Buriganga. These tanneries used to produce 7.7 million litres of liquid waste and 88 million tons of solid waste every day.[66] They are discharged into the rivers, gutters, and canals that run alongside the roads of Hazaribagh. Toxins are also leaching into groundwater.[67] A substantial number of research studies have been carried out to assess pollution levels and health risks in this area.[68] All of these studies have expressed a similar viewpoint regarding the severe effects on both surface and groundwater, as well as the considerable health risks faced by the population in contact with these conditions. Supporting this assertion, this region was classified among the "world's top ten worst places for toxicity" in 2013.[69] Such toxicity and pollution have led to the degradation of the Buriganga River.

3.4 The Demand for Relocation of Tanneries to Savar

The demand for relocation of tanneries from Hazaribagh has been a persistent issue since the early 1990s, driven by environmental concerns and urban planning needs. *Dr Mohiuddin Farooque v. Bangladesh* (Writ Petition No. 891 of 1994), a public interest litigation filed by Dr. Mohiuddin Farooque, Secretary General, Bangladesh Environmental Lawyers Association (BELA), highlighted the issue of the relocation of the tannery of Hazaribagh.[70] In the Master Plan for Dhaka, Rajdhani Unnayan Kartripakkha (RAJUK) identified Hazaribagh's 84 acres, hosting 270 tanneries, as a "spontaneous residential area" unsuitable for toxic industries. Discussions on relocation began in earnest on 31 July 1991, when the Ministry of Industries addressed the problem concerning the Hazaribagh tannery. Despite years of talks since 1989, no progress has materialised. Tannery owners continued advocating for an ETP, while the DoE pressed for relocation. The DoE was again tasked with finding a site and conducting an econo-technical survey, alongside hastening an ETP proposal. Finally, on 23 October 2003, Bangladesh Small Cottage Industries Corporation (BSCIC), the Bangladesh Finished Leather, Leather Goods and Footwear Exporters Association (BFLLFEA), and the Bangladesh Tanneries Association (BTA) signed a trilateral agreement to relocate to Savar. Despite this, tannery owners resisted, citing costs and logistical challenges, and so no relocation occurred during this period. The 1991–2002 era underscores a cycle of commitments and failures, reflecting conflicting interests and weak enforcement, leaving

[66] Azom et al. (2012, p. 153).

[67] Lanteigne (2010).

[68] See Mizan et al. (2020), Anawar et al. (2000), Zahid et al. (2006).

[69] See Afp Geneva (2013).

[70] *Dr Mohiuddin Farooque v. Bangladesh* (2003) 55 DLR (HCD) 69 and subsequent orders (HCD 23 June 2009; HCD 6 March 2017; HCD 24 August 2017).

Hazaribagh's environmental and health crises unaddressed. The agreement stipulates that the tanneries located in Hazaribagh must be moved to a designated leather estate that includes a CETP.[71] As outlined in the memorandum of understanding of the trilateral treaty, a location at Chandra Narayanpur within Savar thana, positioned along the banks of the Dhaleshwari River, was chosen for the establishment of the new tannery estate.[72] The relocation of the tannery was finalised in order to ensure the planned development within the "Tannery Industry Town" by setting up the CETP.[73]

4 Role of Judiciary in Relocation of Tannery Industry in Bangladesh

In 1994, the BELA initiated a Writ Petition (Writ Petition No. 891 of 1994) to seek redress for the pervasive pollution affecting air, water, soil, and the environment, attributed to 903 industrial entities, including the tanneries situated in Hazaribagh.[74] A rule was promulgated on 6 June 1994, addressing pollution issues within Bangladesh. This rule was subsequently affirmed through a judgement and order dated 15 May 2001. Following a comprehensive review of pertinent facts, laws, and the perspectives of all relevant stakeholders, the Honourable Court, in its judgement dated 15 July 2001, mandated the Director General of the Directorate of Environment to ensure that industrial establishments classified as "Red" under Rule 7 of the Environment Conservation Rules, 1997, implement adequate measures to mitigate pollution within one year from the date of receiving the judgement. The Court also emphasised on establishment of new industrial units and factories with adequate and sufficient measures to control pollution, as required under the provisions of the Bangladesh Environment Conservation Act of 1995 and the rules of 1997. Furthermore, the Court required a compliance report to be submitted within 6 weeks thereafter. However, the concerned authority failed miserably in doing so. In this judgement, there was no mention of Hazaribagh tannery relocation or closure. However, the Court considered the decision of the Supreme Court of India on the question of water pollution caused by the tanneries in discharging their effluent in the river.[75] In this case, the Supreme Court of India ordered the setting up of primary treatment plants, failing which it directed the closure of the concerned tanneries and K. N. Singh, J. held as follows:

> This Court issued notices to them but in spite of notices many industrialists have not bothered either to respond to the notice or to take elementary steps for the treatment of industrial

---

[71] Rabbani (2009, pp. 319–338).

[72] Bhowmik (2013, p. 193).

[73] See Shakil et al. (2016, pp. 126–137).

[74] *Dr Mohiuddin Farooque v. Bangladesh* (2003) 55 DLR (HCD) 69.

[75] *M.C. Mehta v. Union Of India & Ors* (1988) AIR (SC) 1037.

> effluent before discharging the same into the river. We are therefore issuing the directions for the closure of those tanneries which have failed to take minimum steps required for the primary treatment of industrial effluent. We are conscious that closure of tanneries may bring unemployment, loss of revenue, but life, health and ecology have greater importance to the people.[76]

In this case, the Indian Supreme Court identified that the closure of tanneries may affect tannery workers due to job loss, but it prioritised environmental protection over economic development.

Later on, after the judgement of 2001 on Writ Petition No. 891 of 1994, the court order dated 28 April 2009, both the respondents and the petitioner were instructed to submit reports detailing the actions taken to implement the directives outlined in the judgement dated 15 July 2001. They were required to submit these reports within 1 month, with further proceedings scheduled for 1 June 2009. In response, reports were submitted by both the respondent and the petitioner, sworn on 1 June 2009. However, these reports were submitted significantly later than expected and are highly unsatisfactory. They revealed a troubling and alarming state of environmental pollution in Bangladesh, particularly in and around Dhaka City. Since 2001, the conditions of the Buriganga River have deteriorated significantly and have become almost unrecognisable. It no longer resembled a river but had instead turned into a large drainage channel.

In June 2009, Syeda Rezwana Hasan, Advocate for the petitioner and current Adviser for Environment, Forest and Climate Change to the Interim Government of Bangladesh, submitted before the Court that the tanneries in Hazaribagh were the most significant and harmful contributors to toxic pollution. She claimed that this location was the most contaminated area within the Dhaka Metropolitan City, and initiatives had been underway since 1991 to move and relocate these tanneries. Furthermore, she pointed out that the entire tannery area is classified as a Red category, yet the owners had not installed ETPs, which violates relevant environmental laws and earlier judgements of this case.[77]

On 23 June 2009, A division bench of the Hon'ble High Court Division of the Supreme Court of Bangladesh asserted that while recognising the significant number of workers in the tannery industry, it was crucial to consider the potential crisis stemming from their redundancy due to the possible closure of such industry resulting from non-compliance with required ETPs. The Court stated:

> As such, on balance we are left with no alternative but to implement the provisions of law strictly. We have to take the risk of redundancy of few thousand workers to save the city and its 12 million inhabitants. Otherwise, the future of this country will be seriously jeopardized (para. 13).[78]

---

[76] Ibid, para. 21.

[77] *Dr Mohiuddin Farooque v. Bangladesh* (2003) 55 DLR (HCD) 69.

[78] *Dr Mohiuddin Farooque v. Bangladesh* (Writ Petition No. 891 of 1994) (HCD Order 23 June 2009).

Subsequently, the Court issued an order mandating the relocation of the tanneries from Hazaribagh by 28 February 2010 and required the regulation of their operations with necessary pollution control devices, ETPs, and proper sanitary landfills.[79] It also mentioned that failing to relocate the industry would result in a shutdown.[80] However, the Court did not impose any duty on the tannery owners to respect or protect tannery workers' rights or to meet the workers' needs caused by this tannery relocation. On 6 March 2017, in light of the tanneries' intentional delays in moving from Hazaribagh to the Tannery Industrial Estate in Savar, the Court directed that the Director General of the DoE promptly utilise all legal powers under Sections 4 and 4A of the Environment Conservation Act 1995, to ensure the complete cessation of all production activities in the remaining non-compliant tanneries in Hazaribagh.[81] Though the Court noted that 43 out of 155 tanneries of the Hazaribagh were relocated by 2017, it neither evaluated the socio-economic impact of relocation suffered by the tannery workers nor the environmental impact of this tannery relocation.

Therefore, the judiciary of Bangladesh prioritised the relocation of the Hazaribagh tannery to Savar to protect and address environmental degradation. However, it did not fully consider the potential environmental consequences of this relocation nor did it take into account the impact on the tannery workers, their families, and their concerns. Additionally, the Court overlooked the possible economic gains or losses associated with this decision.

5 New Challenges of Tannery Relocation

5.1 Negative Response from Tannery Owners and Workers

The willingness of tannery owners to relocate to the proposed Savar tannery complex, along with their existing machinery, presents a complex situation that contrasts with the government's decision. Research findings indicate that 82% of the surveyed tannery owners are not inclined to move to the proposed tannery complex.[82] Conversely, only 18% of the respondents expressed a willingness to relocate, albeit under specific conditions.[83] This pronounced reluctance clearly reflects a rejection of the government's policy to transfer tanneries from Hazaribagh within the tannery owners' community. These owners contend that the government has persistently blamed them for environmental pollution and degradation in Hazaribagh

[79] Ibid.

[80] Ibid.

[81] *Dr Mohiuddin Farooque v. Bangladesh* (Writ Petition No. 891 of 1994) (HCD Order 6 March 2017).

[82] Bhowmik (2013, p. 104).

[83] Ibid.

and has also refrained from providing financial assistance to establish an environmentally sustainable leather processing system and CETP in Hazaribagh.[84] This situation has coerced them into considering relocation. Initially, these owners were resistant to moving; however, due to encountering numerous bureaucratic obstacles related to their business, they ultimately felt compelled to reconsider their position.[85]

Because it is not only about relocating the physical infrastructure of the tannery but also about the relocation of the people associated with the day-to-day business of the industry, tannery workers have expressed concerns about relocating to Savar due to inadequate facilities.[86] There is a shortage of housing, as well as limited access to educational and medical services.[87] Workers, along with supportive organisations such as the Tannery Workers Union, have raised their concerns multiple times. The majority of employees stated that they would only agree to move if essential amenities such as housing, healthcare, schools, madrasas, and mosques were provided.[88] However, they also mentioned a willingness to relocate to Savar if their tannery makes the move. Most of the workers have migrated from various districts of Bangladesh to Dhaka for employment in tanneries and leather factories.[89] They feel obligated to consider the move to Savar due to a lack of job alternatives. Others have indicated that they would only be open to relocating if the basic conditions and facilities meet their needs.[90]

5.2 *Review of Relocation Plan and Environmental Sustainability*

Efforts have been made by various governments across the world to implement top-down relocation initiatives for the leather processing industry, such as in Tamil Nadu, India;[91] Cairo, Egypt;[92] and Mexico,[93] yet all of these have proven unsuccessful. The reasons behind these failures can be traced back to Goodland's classical notion of environmental sustainability. The evaluation of the Hazaribagh tanneries' relocation initiative from the perspectives of urban planning and environmental economics clearly indicates that the project lacks justification in terms of sustainability.

[84] Ibid.

[85] Ibid, p. 105.

[86] See Theuws and Sandjojo (2015, p. 24).

[87] Ibid.

[88] Ibid.

[89] Ibid.

[90] See Theuws and Sandjojo (2015).

[91] See Kennedy (1999, pp. 1673–1691).

[92] See Bartone and Benavides (1997, pp. 3–21).

[93] See Blackman (2000, pp. 4–14).

According to the classic definition of environmental sustainability,[94] and the contemporary challenges in urban planning aimed at achieving sustainable development, any urban planning endeavour should ensure that waste emissions remain within the local environment's assimilative capacity, avoiding unacceptable deterioration of its future capacity to absorb waste to achieve environmental sustainability.[95]

The relocation plan for the Hazaribagh tanneries did not satisfy these criteria since it has been determined that the proposed site for the relocated tanneries would be limited in its ability to manage waste, as the Dhaka structure plan designates it as a flood flow zone with a flood retention pond. Additionally, in Hazaribagh itself, where the absorptive capacity has already been compromised, the redevelopment of residential areas and the execution of the project will significantly harm the local environment. The social framework proposed by Goodland also underscores the project's failure, as the majority of tannery owners are unwilling to relocate or finance the construction of the CETP and landfill site at the suggested location. The lack of cooperation from this actively engaged local community and key stakeholders has not facilitated sustainability at all. Furthermore, analysing the unsuccessful tannery relocation projects globally in comparable situations reveals that due to the tannery owners' strong reluctance, issues related to workforce, property, and finances in relocating the Hazaribagh tanneries have become another failure in Bangladesh.[96]

Most importantly, the relocation process suggests that the Court did not fully operationalise sustainable development and precautionary reasoning in its orders. The judgement concentrated on removing existing sources of pollution from Hazaribagh, but it did not require prior assessment of Savar's environmental assimilative capacity, the reliability of the CETP, or the socio-economic consequences for tannery workers and nearby residents. From a BHR perspective, this meant that significant environmental and social risks were left unexamined and unmitigated.

6 Assessment of the Aftermath of Tannery Relocation

The relocation of the tannery has significantly impacted the livelihoods of workers.[97] There were 186 tanneries in Hazaribagh before the move, but since 2017, about 71 factories have ceased production.[98] The Savar tannery industry has struggled to maintain expected employment levels, leading to job losses and forcing many individuals into unfamiliar work. Not all workers secured jobs at the new

---

[94] See Goodland (1995).

[95] See Campbell (1996).

[96] For more details see Bhowmik (2013, pp. 93–119).

[97] Sarker and Akter (2018).

[98] Bangladesh Labour Foundation (2021).

Savar tannery.[99] The research findings show a detrimental change in livelihoods for Hazaribagh residents. After relocation, as many as 30% became unemployed and migrated from the area. Many have also not received their dues after the lay-off.[100]

Part-time or contractual workers also have had difficulty finding jobs in Savar, with only about 20% obtaining employment there and just 1% remaining at the old tannery in Hazaribagh for post-production tasks. Workers at Savar face challenges, including transportation issues and conflicts with local employees, complicating their work experience. Heavy traffic in Dhaka makes it hard for those with distant workplaces to stick to strict schedules, often leaving early and returning late, reducing time with families.[101] A staggering 92% of workers stopped their children's education to generate income, and women's specific needs are neglected at Savar.[102] The insufficient management of human resources in the tannery sector exacerbates the conditions for workers.[103] Moreover, numerous tannery owners experienced significant financial losses.[104] Some tanneries had to shut down due to insufficient opportunities to relocate to Savar, leading to unpaid wages for labourers. Labour groups protested for justice as promised by the authorities. The government aimed for environmental sustainability in relocating tanneries but failed to consider alternatives and conduct adequate research on risks and socio-economic impacts.[105] Due to the new environment and lack of facilities in Savar, production suffered, and workers' salaries were compromised. Conditions were better in Hazaribagh a few years prior.[106]

Furthermore, in Jamjam City, adjacent to Savar tannery industries, residents face severe challenges due to unpleasant odours and an unsuitable living environment.[107] Many well-off tenants have left, leading to increased vacancies and a decline in land prices, as owners are forced to rent to less suitable tenants for economic reasons.[108] This decline in residential demand has halted the development of civic facilities, worsening community standards.[109] Meanwhile, the Dhaleshwari River suffers from pollution due to industrial waste—turning into another Buriganga—compromising fish habitats and forcing fishermen to relocate or find alternative livelihoods. The lack of ETPs exacerbates the situation, with untreated waste creating health hazards for locals and further deteriorating water quality.[110] In addition, the relocation of the

[99] Sarker and Akter (2018).

[100] See Iqbal et al. (2023).

[101] See Iqbal et al. (2023).

[102] Bangladesh Labour Foundation (2021).

[103] Iqbal et al. (2023, p. 36).

[104] Ibid.

[105] Human Rights Watch (2012).

[106] Iqbal et al. (2023, p. 37).

[107] Department of Environment (2018, p. 77).

[108] Ibid.

[109] Ibid.

[110] Department of Environment (2018, p. 101).

tannery greatly affected the people of Hazaribagh, as a significant number of them worked at the tannery. After the move, the price for both sublet and shared accommodation fell from 1500 taka to 1000 taka.[111] Many individuals connected to the tannery sector intended to relocate from Hazaribagh to be closer to their new jobs. Furthermore, the rent for single rooms and smaller apartments decreased from 6000 taka to 5000 taka and from 15,000 taka to 10,000 taka, respectively.[112] This drop in rental rates is due to families leaving the area and a decrease in the daily earnings of those who remain. On the other hand, the rent for upscale apartments in the chosen locality has risen.[113]

There is a common belief that the Hazaribagh area has been "cleaned" following the relocation of tanneries; this perception may stem from the slightly higher dissolved oxygen levels recently detected in the nearby Buriganga River.[114] A research study analysing the soil has confirmed that this assessment might not be accurate and that mitigation measures are essential to make the area safe for habitation.[115] It is crucial to implement soil remediation strategies before commencing any residential or commercial development projects. Some cost-effective and environmentally friendly remediation methods include phytoremediation (with or without chelating agents), the immobilisation of heavy metals using chemical agents, and soil washing with chemical solutions.[116] The move of tanneries from Hazaribagh to the Savar leather industrial park was intended to reduce environmental harm. However, the transition has faced setbacks and insufficient infrastructure, resulting in varied outcomes. The relocation process encountered difficulties, including the incomplete establishment of the CETP and the lack of adequate waste management facilities. At present, approximately 40,000 m^3 of waste are generated daily by tanneries in Savar. However, the CETP's daily treatment capacity in this area is 25,000 m^3. As a result, the excess 15,000 m^3 of waste is being discharged into the Dhaleshwari River untreated.[117] The operations of the Savar tannery are currently causing significant pollution and affecting both environmental and social quality of life. In the future, these effects could become irreversible and incredibly challenging to address effectively.[118]

---

[111] Iqbal et al. (2023, p. 35).

[112] Ibid.

[113] Ibid.

[114] See Mizan et al. (2020).

[115] Ibid.

[116] See Mizan et al. (2020).

[117] See Rony (2022).

[118] Department of Environment (2018, p. 121).

7 Recommendations

The analysis of the Hazaribagh tannery relocation demonstrates that a judicially driven environmental intervention, pursued in the name of pollution control, can reproduce environmental injustice and undermine BHR commitments when it is not embedded in a broader governance framework. This section sets out two analytically grounded recommendations arising from the case study.

7.1 Sustainable Development within Judicial Reasoning

Although the Court rightly treated the Buriganga's degradation because of Hazaribagh tannery as a major public concern and prioritised environmental protection in the tannery relocation litigation, the judgement and subsequent orders paid limited attention to how environmental benefits and burdens would be divided across different stakeholders nor to the long-term implications for tannery workers' livelihoods and the new host community in Savar. This judicial intervention was a formal justice for "the environment" but, in practice, delivered harm from one river and community to another. From an environmental justice context, this aftermath reflects a narrow scope of environmental protection, detached from questions of equity, participation, and recognition. From a sustainable development perspective, it demonstrates the negative outcome of ignoring socio-economic dimensions in environmental protection objectives.

This case, therefore, teaches that future judicial interventions in Bangladesh should expressly take into consideration sustainable development in addition to environmental justice as interpretive principles, not merely as background rhetoric. In other words, while considering remedies such as relocation or closure of industrial estates, the Courts may review three criteria. Firstly, how the burdens and benefits of the order will be divided between different groups; secondly, whether affected workers and local communities have been consulted; and thirdly, whether there are mechanisms to mitigate the risk of creating new "sacrifice zones" in the receiving area. Also, the judiciary, while promoting environmental rights via judicial activism, needs to consider an intersectionality approach by focusing on substantiated issues associated with the environment, i.e. labour rights of the workers and the industrial development. As the constitutional reform notion is at its peak in Bangladesh after the political transition in July 2024, and the Constitution Reform Commission and environmental law researchers are strongly advocating for constitutionalising the environment right,[119] the government may go an extra step by adopting an intersectional approach instead of enforcing a blanket environmental right. Recent scholarships have shown how existing constitutional and statutory frameworks, including "national interest" clauses in core environmental legislation,

[119] Salekin et al. (2025).

have enabled severe ecological degradation despite the presence of nearly 200 environmental laws in Bangladesh, effectively normalising ecocidal practices in the name of development.[120] And, albeit, the judicial activism can play an important role in this move through judicial reasoning that would meet both international environmental law and contemporary BHR standards, which prioritise non-discrimination and community participation.

7.2 *Integrating Human Rights Due Diligence in Relocation and Industrial Policy*

The Hazaribagh-Savar case underscores the absence of structured human rights due diligence (HRDD) in the design and implementation of the relocation project. Recent work on climate-related harms in Bangladesh has argued that, following the ICJ Climate Advisory Opinion on obligations of states in respect of climate change, due diligence functions as a concrete standard of conduct rather than a loose political aspiration.[121] These debates demonstrate that international due diligence can be operationalised domestically in different environmental settings and that it has a clear human rights dimension: States must anticipate foreseeable risks, regulate private actors accordingly, and protect affected communities.

The resulting job losses, disruption of education, gender-specific vulnerabilities, and deterioration of living conditions demonstrate that the relocation did not adequately anticipate, let alone mitigate, adverse human rights impacts. Under the BHR framework, and particularly the UN Guiding Principles on Business and Human Rights, both state agencies and companies are expected to identify, prevent, mitigate, and account for adverse human rights impacts linked to business activities. In a context such as Bangladesh's leather sector—where environmental risks, labour precarity, and informality intersect—relocation processes are precisely the kind of intervention that requires structured HRDD.

In the context of the leather industry, this suggests the need for a tannery sector due diligence framework that combines state obligations with corporate human rights due diligence. The harms documented in this chapter—continued pollution of the Dhaleshwari, malfunctioning treatment infrastructure, job losses, and deteriorating living conditions—were not unforeseen accidents but outcomes that could reasonably have been anticipated before and during relocation. From a state due diligence perspective, public authorities should have assessed whether Savar's environmental assimilative capacity, the design and operation of the CETP, and the broader regulatory regime were sufficient to prevent significant harm to rivers, workers, and local residents. From a BHR perspective, tannery owners and associated companies should have carried out human rights due diligence to identify,

[120] See Abid (2024).

[121] Abid and Rahman (2026).

prevent, and mitigate adverse impacts on health, work, housing, and the environment across their operations and value chains. Accordingly, this chapter recommends that future reforms in Bangladesh's leather sector be framed explicitly as joint exercises in state and corporate due diligence.

8 Conclusion

The judicially mandated relocation of the Hazaribagh tanneries to Savar was framed as a corrective measure to protect the Buriganga River, but this chapter has shown that, in practice, it reconfigured rather than resolved environmental harm. Pollution was displaced to the Dhaleshwari and surrounding communities, while many tannery workers and residents experienced loss of livelihood, deteriorating living conditions and new health risks. The relocation thus exemplifies how a narrow, techno-centric vision of "environmental protection", focused on removing a visible source of contamination, can reproduce environmental injustice when it ignores questions of distribution, recognition, and participation.

Analysed through a business and human rights lens, the case also reveals the limits of relying on judicial activism without embedding it in a broader governance and due diligence framework. The Court's orders did little to operationalise the state duty to protect or corporate responsibility to respect, treating compliance with environmental law as an end in itself rather than part of ongoing human rights due diligence. In light of emerging climate and human rights jurisprudence, including the growing emphasis on state and corporate due diligence obligations, the Hazaribagh-Savar experience stands as a warning against "green" interventions that externalise social and ecological costs onto already marginalised groups or the working class.

More broadly, the chapter contributes to debates on responsible and irresponsible business in the Global South by demonstrating that judicial environmental interventions can themselves become drivers of injustice if they are not informed by sustainable development, environmental justice, and BHR principles together. While the analysis is grounded in a single sector and country, the dynamics it traces—judicially ordered relocation, infrastructural failure, regulatory fragmentation, and weak human rights safeguards—are likely to recur in other industrial contexts. Future research could therefore compare similar relocation projects across sectors and jurisdictions, to test how far integrating environmental justice and human rights due diligence into judicial reasoning and state policy can prevent the creation of new "sacrifice zones" in the name of sustainability.

References

Abid FA (2024) When 'National Interest' leads to Ecocide: The Unseen Constitutional Violation of Environmental Laws in Bangladesh. Oxford Human Rights Hub. https://ohrh.law.ox.ac.uk/when-national-interest-leads-to-ecocide-the-unseen-constitutional-violation-of--environmental-laws-in-bangladesh/. Accessed 29 November 2025

Abid FA and Rahman M (2026) Constitutionalising Climate-Resilient Agriculture in Bangladesh: Salinity, Food Security and State Responsibility after the ICJ Climate Advisory Opinion. In Kapasia N, Roy A, Rahaman M, Chouhan P(eds), Climate Change and Agricultural Challenges Solutions for Sustainable Livelihood. Springer (in press).

Afp Geneva (2013) Hazaribagh on list of most polluted spots. The Daily Star. https://www.thedailystar.net/news/hazaribagh-on-list-of-most-polluted-spots. Accessed 10 February 2025

Anawar HM et al (2000) Environmental exposure assessment of chromium and other tannery pollutants at Hazaribagh area, Dhaka, Bangladesh, and health risk. J Environ Chem 10(3):549–556

Arias-Barreiro CR (2010) Ecotoxicological characterisation of tannery wastewater in Dhaka, Bangladesh. J Environ Biol 31:471–475

Atapattu S, Rosing M von (2025) Chapter 31 - The Paris Agreement and human rights: Is sustainable development the "new human right"?. In: Rosing M von (eds), The Sustainability Handbook, Volume 1: The Body of Knowledge around Substantial Sustainability Innovation. Elsevier, pp 445–463

Azom MR et al (2012) Environmental impact assessment of tanneries: a case study of Hazaribag in Bangladesh. Int J Environ Sci Dev 3(2):152–156

Bangladesh Labour Foundation (2021) Gap analysis report on shifting tannery industry from Hazaribagh to Savar, Dhaka. Bangladesh Labour Foundation https://blfbd.com/gap-analysis-report-on-shifting-tannery-industry-from-hazaribagh-to-savar/. Accessed 10 January 2025

Bartone CR, Benavides L (1997) Local management of hazardous wastes from small-scale and cottage industries. Waste Manag Res 15:3–21

Bhowmik AK (2012) Environmental sustainability vs. political decision: a review of the Bangladesh leather processing industry relocation plan. In: The 2nd world sustainability forum. MDPI, Basel, Switzerland. https://doi.org/10.3390/wsf2-00885

Bhowmik AK (2013) Industries' location as jeopardy for sustainable urban development in Asia: a review of the Bangladesh leather processing industry relocation plan. Environ Urban Asia 4(1):93–119

Blackman A (2000) Making small beautiful - lessons from Mexican leather tanneries and brick kilns. Small Enterp Dev 11:4–14

Campbell S (1996) Green cities, growing cities, just cities?: Urban planning and the contradictions of sustainable development. J Am Plan Assoc 62:296–312

Department of Environment (2018) Environmental impact study of two Tannery Estates on the Buriganga and the Dhaleshwari Rivers. Department of Environment, Ministry of Environment, Forest and Climate Change, Government of the People's Republic of Bangladesh. https://doe.portal.gov.bd/sites/default/files/files/doe.portal.gov.bd/page/1f58f60a_51d9_46c0_9fa1_79b7b565db05/2020-10-01-13-04-437e7423b2266d269cc021ed8f6e921f.pdf. Accessed 19 January 2025

Doorey DJ (2017) Just transitions law: Putting labour law to work on climate change, Journal of Environmental Law and Practice 30(2):201–239

Garai J (2014) Environmental aspects and health risks of leather tanning industry: a study in the Hazaribag area. Chin J Popul Resour Environ 12(3):278–282. https://doi.org/10.1080/10042857.2014.910875

Goodland R (1995) The concept of environmental sustainability. Annu Rev Ecol Syst 26:1–24

Goodland R (2005) Strategic environmental assessment and the World Bank Group. International Journal of Sustainable Development and World Ecology 12(3): 245–255

Hossain S (2008) Rapid urban growth and poverty in Dhaka City. Bangladesh e-J Sociol 5:1–24

Human Rights Watch (2012) Toxic tanneries: the health repercussions of Bangladesh's Hazaribagh leather. Human Rights Watch. https://www.hrw.org/reports/bangladesh1012_brochure_web_0.pdf. Accessed 8 December 2024
Hunter et al (2015) International Environmental Law and Policy. 5th edn. Foundation Press
Huq SI (2000) Critical environmental issues relating to tanning Industries in Bangladesh. In: Naidu et al (eds) Towards better management of soils contaminated with tannery waste. Australian Centre for International Agricultural Research. AgEcon Search Proceedings of a Workshop held in Coimbatore, India, 31 January–4 February 1998. ACIAR Proceedings, 88:22–28
Iqbal A et al (2023) Environmental and socio-economic impact assessment in Hazaribag area of Dhaka for tannery relocation. Int J Soc Sci Econ Rev 5(1):29–39. https://doi.org/10.36923/ijsser.v5i1.184
Karn SK, Harada H (2001) Surface water pollution in three urban territories of Nepal, India and Bangladesh. Environ Manag 28:483–496
Kashem MA, Singh B (1999) Heavy metal contamination of soil and vegetation in the vicinity of Industries in Bangladesh. Water Air Soil Pollut 115:347–361
Kennedy L (1999) Cooperating for survival: tannery pollution and joint action in the Palar Valley(India). World Dev 27:1673–1691
Lanteigne D (2010) Colours of water: Bangladesh's leather tanneries. Our World. https://ourworld.unu.edu/en/colours-of-water-bangladeshs-leather-tanneries. Accessed 10 December 2024
Mizan A et al (2020) Environmental and health risks of metal-contaminated soil in the former tannery area of Hazaribagh, Dhaka. SN Appl Sci 2:1915. https://doi.org/10.1007/s42452-020-03680-4
Mooney L (2015) Promoting the rule of law in the intersection of business, human rights, and sustainability. Georgetown Journal of International Law 46(4):1135–1150
Nath K et al (2009) Phytotoxic effects of chromium and tannery effluent on growth and metabolism of Phaseolus mungo Roxb. J Environ Biol 30:227–234
Preston B (2005) The Role of the Judiciary in Promoting Sustainable Development: The Experience of Asia and the Pacific. Asia Pacific Journal of Environmental Law 9(2&3):109–211
Rabbani MG (2009) Environmental risks in Dhaka: present initiatives and the future improvements. In: Shaw R et al (eds) Urban risk reduction: an Asian perspective, Community, environment and disaster risk management, vol 1. Emerald Group, Leeds, pp 319–338. https://doi.org/10.1108/S2040-7262(2009)1
Rahman MM et al (2014) Occupational health hazards of tanners at Hazaribagh tannery industries of Dhaka city in Bangladesh. Soc Sci Rev 31:57–76
Rakib MA (2020) Export trend of the leather industry of Bangladesh: challenges to sustainable development. BUFT J Bus Econ 1:163–187
Razzaque J (2000) Access to environmental justice: role of the Judiciary in Bangladesh. Bangladesh J Law 4(1&2):1–25
Reza MH (2022) The ins and outs of the leather industry in Bangladesh. Journal La Bisecoman 3(2):49–58
Rony MH (2022) Relocation of tannery industry and its aftermath. Daily Observer. https://www.observerbd.com/news/393149. Accessed 10 January 2025
Rouf MA et al (2013) Characterization of effluents of leather industries in Hazaribagh area of Dhaka city. Bangladesh J Sci Ind Res 48(3):155–166
Salekin M et al (2025) Greening the post-July Aspired Constitution through Pro-activism. Judicial Administrative Training Institute Journal 24:69–92
Sarker AR, Akter S (2018) Impact of human resource management practices on the working life of tannery workers in Bangladesh. Dhaka Univ J Manag 12(1):161–170
Shakil SH (2014) Multi-actor partnership for environmental governance: an investigation from the perspective of Bangladesh. Dissertation, University of Manchester
Shakil SH et al (2016) Stakeholder debate in policy implementation: an evaluation of Bangladesh leather processing industry relocation policy. Bangladesh E-J Sociol 13(1):126–137

Shams KM et al (2008) Chromium contamination from tannery wastes in the soils of Hazaribagh area in Dhaka City, Bangladesh, and aspects of its phytoremediation. Geophys Res Abstr 10

Shams KM et al (2009) Soil contamination from Tanne wastes with emphasis on the fate and distribution of tri- and Hexavalent chromium. Water Air Soil Pollut 199:123–137

The European Union's INSPIRED Program for Bangladesh (2013) Technical report leather sector. EU Inspired. http://euinspired.org.bd/docs/grant_scheme/INSPIRED%20-%20Leather%20Sector%20Report%20-%20Jan%2013.pdf. Accessed 20 Nov 2024

Theuws M, Sandjojo V (2015) Mapping of the tannery and leather sectors in Bangladesh. Stichting Onderzoek Multinationale Ondernemingen (SOMO). https://cbsg-bd.org/control-panel/pages/pdf/Mapping-of-the-tannery-and-leather-sectors-in-Bangladesh.pdf. Accessed 10 January 2025

United Nations. (2011). Guiding principles on business and human rights: Implementing the United Nations "Protect, Respect and Remedy" Framework. Office of the United Nations High Commissioner for Human Rights.

World Footwear (2025) Bangladesh: leather and non-leather footwear exports on the rise in 2024–2025. https://www.worldfootwear.com/news/bangladesh-leather-and-non-leather--footwear-exports-on-the-rise-in-2024-2025/10737.html#:~:text=Overall%2C%20the%20total%20value%20of%20leather%20exports,was%20driven%20primarily%20by%20the%20footwear%20segment. Accessed 29 November 2025

Zahid A et al (2006) Evaluation of aquifer environment under Hazaribagh leather processing zone of Dhaka city. Environ Geol 50:495–504

Masrur Salekin is a legal scholar and judicial professional with over 19 years of experience as a judge, researcher, and academic. His research interests include environmental law, constitutional law, and law and development. He holds a Ph.D. in Law from the University of Galway and an LL.M. in International Law and Development from the University of Nottingham, UK. He has received prestigious scholarships, including the Hardiman Research Scholarship and the Chevening Scholarship, and has published widely in leading journals.

Mahbuba Kamal is an LL.M. in Human Rights candidate at the University of Birmingham, UK, and a recipient of the Chevening Scholarship 2025–2026. She holds an LL.B. (Hons.) from BRAC University, Bangladesh, and has been an Open Society University Network (OSUN) Exchange Scholar at Central European University, Austria. She currently serves as a research assistant at the Birmingham Law School and is a founder of Bangladesh Society of International Law. Her academic work focuses on human rights, international law, and environmental justice.

An Analysis of Kenyan Laws Affecting Environmental and Social Governance on and for the Floricultural Industry

Muriuki Sharon

Abstract Kenya's placement in East Africa, its infrastructural developments, and its wealth in human resources have made it a hub for multinationals. One of the major areas where such investments have been made is the flower-growing sector, which has become a pillar of Kenya's economy. The continuing effects of this industry include employment and social and environmental concerns. Many have been set up along water bodies and rely on casual labor provided on daily or seasonal contracts. The application of environmental impact assessment (EIA) laws in the setting up of flower farms and the hiring and termination of employment services has led to litigation in the NEMA Tribunal, the Environment and Land Court (ELC), and the Employment and Labor Relations Court (ELRC). Case law shows that many employers default on the provisions of Sections 35–49 of *the Employment Act, No. 11* of *2007* as well as Sections 58–107 of the *Environmental Management and Co-ordination Act.* This chapter aims to highlight the Kenyan laws on the processes of environmental impact assessment and hiring, engaging, and termination of employee services, the environment, and other laws affecting corporate governance. The chapter concludes that due process plays a central role and should be expressly provided for in the contracts and guidelines of every company including multinational companies.

1 Introduction

On May 1, 2020, Kenyan media reported that a consignment of flowers dubbed "Flowers for Hope" was sent by the government of Kenya to the United Kingdom and distributed to frontline workers battling the COVID-19 pandemic. The donation caused an uproar when online users accused the government of ignoring the welfare of Kenyan workers fighting the pandemic, causing the president to comment that

M. Sharon (✉)
The Biodiversity Circle, Portland, OR, USA

S. Talukdar (ed.), *Law, Accountability, and Corporate Conduct*, New Approaches to Business, Human Rights and the Environment 1,
https://doi.org/10.1007/978-3-032-28714-4_3

this was a good marketing strategy as it would lead to more orders of Kenyan flowers once the pandemic was over (Too, 2020).[1] The floricultural industry is Kenya's fourth contributor of foreign exchange after diaspora remittances, tourism, and tea exports.[2] It also employs both large- and small-scale farmers. The applicability of the European Union's positions on Corporate Sustainability Reporting Directive (CSRD) and Corporate Sustainability Due Diligence Directive (CSDDD) in Kenya's floricultural industry requires the outlining of Kenya's business human rights (BHRs) legal structure, noting that a great percentage of these exports find their way into the EU's retail market. The legal awareness and strict implementation of these BHRs are the starting point of adherence to the CSDDD and CSRD, avoiding legal and social responsibility pitfalls.

1.1 Industry Background

Kenya is one of the world's leading exporters of cut flowers. According to the Kenya Flower Council, Kenya is the world's third-largest producer of cut flowers after Colombia and Ecuador, exporting to over 60 destinations globally.[3] The European Union imports about 48% of Kenya's flowers (Kenya Flower Council 2024). Other major importers include Japan, Australia, and the United Arab Emirates (Kenya Flower Council 2024). The horticultural industry and the sale and export of flowers are a substantive contributor to Kenya's economy. The Kenya horticulture sector is a key part of the agricultural industry[4] which is a major contributor to the gross domestic product. In 2018, flowers contributed KSh 113 billion, amounting to 74% of the horticultural sector. The promotion, development, and regulation of the Kenyan horticultural industry are managed by the Horticultural Crops Directorate.[5] The export of flowers by both national and multinational companies is a major contributor to global trade in terms of goods and employment, where it has been noted that transnational corporations account for 80% of global trade.[6] The uproar over health workers' welfare and labor rights governance with flowers as a denominator

[1] See report by Too Emmanuel (2020) titled 'Stop Social Media Nonsense! When former President Uhuru scolded Kenyan social media users' uproar over flowers sent to the UK during the Covid -19 pandemic'.

[2] See report by The Star Newspaper (2020) titled 'Kenya Sends 300 Bouquets of Flowers to the UK for Compassion and to Protect Farm Jobs'.

[3] Read the Kenya Flower Council Report (2024) titled 'From Kenya with love'.

[4] See the report by Kenya's Agriculture and Food Authority. (2024) titled 'Overview of Horticultural Crops Directorate'.

[5] This is done through the *Agricultural and Food Authority Act, Act No 13* of 2013, and the *Crops Act, Act No 16 of 2013*. This chapter will incorporate the provisions of these Acts in ESGs, complimentary to other Laws of Kenya which the chapter substantively addresses.

[6] Read Macchi Chiara (2022). Business, Human Rights and the Environment: The Evolving Agenda.

opened another page in Kenya's floricultural business-human rights pyramid of labor, business, and governance.

1.2 Background of the Study

In June 2022, the Federation of Kenya Employers (FKE)[7] published a member's briefing note[8] sensitizing its members on environmental and social governance (ESG) and its implications on enterprises. The briefing note notes that there has not been the prioritization of ESG by many businesses in Kenya, though there has been a noticeable change in recent times. The briefing note cites ESG investing as investments in companies with strong records on environmental, social, and governance issues. This chapter uses the areas cited in the briefing note to identify legal instruments and procedures of ESG governance and implementation in Kenya. The briefing note provides the background of the study as the floricultural industry is a major employer in Kenya in terms of land usage and management, employment, transport, and social systems.

1.3 Objectives

This study aims to identify and highlight Kenya's floricultural industry's ESG governance with regard to:

(a) Environmental laws on carbon reduction emissions, efficient usage of resources, limitation of waste reduction and recycling, and compliance with environmental regulations
(b) Social issues such as workplace safety, decent work, diversity and inclusion, and employee data safety
(c) Governance including salaries, board compositions, shareholder voting rights, and business policies on bribery and corruption

1.4 Study Methodology

The FKE briefing note provides the case study for this chapter. Its provisions on ESG will be analyzed through various laws and judicial precedents as well as international legal instruments due to the importance of the international market

[7] The Federation of Kenya Employers is an association of corporate bodies doing business in Kenya.
[8] Read the Federation of Kenya Employers' Members Briefing Note. (2022). 'ESG and its implications for Kenyan Enterprises'.

to Kenya's economy as well as Kenya's duties and responsibilities to comply with international legal instruments it has ratified over the years. In addition, it is worth noting that the Kenyan legal system operates on a hierarchy of laws where the constitution is supreme and subsequently the laws that are promulgated under it. It is also premised on the principle that ignorance of the law is not a defense and thus necessitating an investigation of laws that would affect the ESG industry.

2 Previous Research

This section looks at scholarly and scientific works on environmental, business, and human rights, social and governance actions, and structures of the flower-growing sector in Kenya.

2.1 *Floriculture and Business Human Rights*

Studies in business human rights (BHRs) are tri-focused on (i) the negative impacts of business on human rights, (ii) prevention and redress, and (iii) accountability of BHR violators.[9] Due to climatic conditions, much of the world's cut flowers are grown in the Global South and exported to the Global North. The Global South also provides labor while the Global North provides monetary resources, sustaining the trade. In a 2008 study, it was noted that profits are invested in headquarters outside the floricultural growing country.[10] The profits come at the expense of the health of the workers in such farms.

2.2 *Environmental and Human Health Challenges*

Previous research shows that flower farms have consumed more water than the surrounding communities in Naivasha, one of the leading floricultural areas in Kenya.[11] The flower farms rely on water from Lake Naivasha and underground water sources drilled into the ground. Amayi (2021) notes that there is a disparity in how the flower farms dispose of their hydro waste compared to other residents of the area

[9] See Rao Madhura and Bernaz Nadia (2020).

[10] See Donohoe Martin (2008).

[11] Read Amayi Kaleha (2021).

whose water waste disposal is poor and inefficient. Floriculture has been cited for the reduction of food crop-growing areas leading to malnutrition, water reduction due to irrigation pollution, pesticide poisoning, and human health complications (Donohoe 2008, 165–169).

2.3 Locating and Contextualizing the European Union's Positions on CSRD and CSDDD

A large percentage of Kenya's floricultural products are exported to the European Union.[12] This means that floricultural companies growing, exporting, and selling flowers to Europe are subject to the European Union's positions on CSRD and CSDDD. CSRD aims at transforming the European Union into a modern, resource-efficient, and competitive economy with no emissions of greenhouse gases by 2050.[13] In addition, it aims to protect, conserve, and enhance the EU's natural capital as well as protect the health and well-being of its citizenry (E.U. 2024). It aspires to have its citizens transition into a sustainable economic system. Floricultural companies are required to disclose certain undertakings to meet CSRD standards. They include reorienting capital flows toward sustainable investments to achieve sustainable growth, managing financial risks stemming from climate change, resource depletion, and environmental degradation, and fostering transparency in financial and economic activities (E.U. 2024).

Floricultural companies are expected to foster sustainable and responsible corporate behavior anchored in human rights in their operations and corporate governance to align with the CSDDD.[14] This is expected to benefit EU citizens, companies, and developing nations by introducing corporate diligence duties for corporations and their directors. CSDDD is to be enforced through administrative supervision by state-designated authorities and civil liability by way of an award for damages for failure of compliance with the duties imposed. Having established the CSRD and the CSDDD, this chapter looks at the legal framework anchoring these directives and reports in Kenya. This legal awareness is important because of the multiplicity and sometimes duality of laws and rules over the same subject.

---

[12] See Note 3 on Kenya's exports to the EU.

[13] See the European Union's legal database.

[14] See the European Commission's Corporate Sustainable Due Diligence Directive aimed at Fostering Sustainability in Corporate Governance and Management Systems.

3 Kenya's Executive Governance Structure

The Kenya governance structure is divided between the national and county governments. National functions are the responsibility of the national government, while devolved functions are carried out by county governments.[15] The objects and principles of devolved governments include giving the right of self-governance to the people, enhancing the participation of the people in exercising the powers of the state, and making decisions that affect them. They involve the right of communities to manage their affairs and provide the rights and interests of minorities and promote economic and social development, equitable sharing of national and local resources, and decentralization of state organs. In implementing environmental and social governance (ESG) obligations, floricultural companies ought to bear in mind the roles of these branches of governance, especially on national and county laws and enforcement of laws regarding the environment, employment, data protection, equality, transport, and land administration.

4 National Legislation and Devolved Governance Laws

The Parliament of Kenya consists of the National Assembly and the Senate.[16] They have legislative authority derived from the people at the national level.[17] The role of the National Assembly is to represent the people of various constituencies and special interests, deliberate and resolve issues concerning the people, allocate revenue between the levels of government, and declare wars and extend of states of emergency.[18] The role of the Senate is to approve bills concerning the counties, allocation of national revenue to the counties, and oversight of public officials.[19] At the county level, every county consists of a county executive and a county assembly.[20] The county assembly consists of members elected by registered voters in wards and seats allocated to special groups to ensure equity. County assemblies make laws for the effective performance and function of the county government and oversight of the county executive committees and approve plans for the management and exploitation of a county's resources and the development of the county's infrastructure

[15] Constitution of Kenya, 2010. For the provision on governance, see Article 11.

[16] See Article 94 of the Constitution of Kenya, 2010 on the role of Parliament.

[17] The Parliament manifests the diversity of the nation, represents the will of the citizens, and exercises their sovereignty; it has a duty to protect the Constitution.

[18] Read Article 94 more on the role of the legislature and its powers.

[19] Read more on the supervisory powers of the Senate including motions on impeachment of county governors.

[20] See Article 177 on membership of county assembly and particular provisions on diversity and inclusion.

and institutions.[21] County executive committees implement county legislation, implement national legislation at the county level, manage and coordinate functions of county administration, prepare proposed legislation, and report to the county assembly on county matters.[22] Floricultural companies can participate in public participation exercises on legislation concerning the county under Article 196 of the Constitution.

5 Adherence with the Provisions of the Companies Act and Other Laws Regarding Commercial Entities and Employee Benefits

The Companies Act[23] is an act of the Parliament relating to the incorporation, registration, operation, management, and regulation of companies. It also provides for the appointment and functions of auditors. From the onset, floricultural companies should be aware of the function and regulations regarding the allocation of shares, trade, holding of annual general meetings, subsidiary companies, the release of annual financial statements, preservation of records, and various offenses that can occur when the law is contravened. The Act contains provisions for employee share schemes, which are schemes that encourage or facilitate the holding of shares in a company by bona fide employees or former employees of the company, its subsidiaries, or its holding company.[24] In addition, there are provisions for the creation of a pension scheme to provide benefits consisting of a pension, lump sum, benefits, and gratuity to be given upon retirement or death of employees or former employees.[25] Due to the international business and export of flowers, the companies should familiarize themselves with foreign companies' regulations, voting rights, and liquidation of such companies, whose processes are provided in the statute. Further afield, they should also comply with the payment of taxes due to the national government and levies due to the county governments as well as awareness of tax breaks available.

---

[21] Article 185 expounds on resource management powers of the county assemblies.

[22] See Article 183 of the Constitution of Kenya.

[23] See Cap 486, Laws of Kenya.

[24] See Section 3 of the Companies Act.

[25] I recommend Section 3 for further details on these labor rights.

6 Legal Provisions and Judicial Decisions on the Environment

The Kenya legal system's rulings, judgments, declarations, and orders come from issue jurisdiction-specific tribunals, the magistrates' courts, the High Court, the Environment and Land Court, the Employment and Labor Relations Court, the Court of Appeal, and the Supreme Court of Kenya. The legal system is founded on the common law system of its former colonizer. It draws its legal foundations and referrals from its constitution,[26] acts of the Parliament, judicial precedents, customary laws, and international laws, among others. This section addresses Kenya's legal system and its holding on the provisions of the FKE briefing note.[27]

6.1 *Constitutional Foundations on the Environment*

The right to a clean environment is founded on the Constitution of Kenya, 2010, which provides for the right to a clean and healthy environment that is protected for the present and future generations.[28] The Constitution further provides that the state is obligated to ensure sustainable utilization of the environment, maintain forest cover, ensure intellectual property rights concerning indigenous plants and knowledge, encourage public participation regarding the conservation of the environment, protect genetic resources, establish environmental impact assessment procedures, and eliminate harmful acts to the environment.[29] The Constitution obligates every person to cooperate with state organs to ensure the protection and conservation of the environment to ensure sustainable development.[30] This thus obligates flower companies to ascribe to the law to ensure environmental protection. The enforcement of environmental rights can be instated by any person seeking orders to prevent, stop, and discontinue activities harmful to the environment, compel public officials tasked with environmental protection to act, and seek compensation for harm done to the environment.[31]

[26] This chapter recognizes the supremacy of the Constitution. In the discourse on laws, it limits itself to acts of the Parliament and judicial decisions where legal procedures and outcomes are addressed.

[27] Mentions are made with regard to laws published as the 'Kenya Law Reports' (KLR) and itemized by KLR in Chapters.

[28] The supremacy of the Constitution with regard to the right to a health environment is generational, and this continuity should be in all floricultural plans.

[29] See Article 69 of the Constitution of Kenya.

[30] Tree cover, biodiversity, impact assessments, and utilization of resources are some of the duties of the state that floricultural companies may be subject to through laws and rules.

[31] See Article 70 of the Constitution.

6.2 *Land Acquisition, Ownership, and Usage*

Floricultural companies are usually set up in areas where water and good soil are abundant. The constitution obligates every person to ensure that the holding, usage, and management of land are equitable, efficient, productive, and sustainable. Land in Kenya can be public, private, or communally owned. In establishing the companies and building facilities, national and multinational flower companies find themselves affected by the three types of land ownership in Kenya. Thus, these companies need to familiarize themselves with land acquisition procedures, registration, and usage processes.

Public land is defined to include all government forests and all rivers, lakes, and water bodies as provided for by statute, the land between low and high water marks, and land that is not communally or privately owned. Thus, a company that is using water from lakes and rivers and affecting national forests should be aware of licenses and limitations of public land usage. They should also be aware of the administration of public land at the county and national level. Unalienated land, land transferred by sale, reversion, or surrender, land in which no individual or community interests can be established legally, and land where an heir cannot be identified vest in county governments and are administered by the National Land Commission.[32]

Community land is land held by communities identified by way of ethnicity, culture, and common interests. These lands gain legal status when they are registered in the names of a group of representatives, transferred to a specific community through a legal process, or declared to be community land by an act of Parliament. Private land is defined as land that is held by persons, such as companies and individuals in freehold or leasehold terms or declared to be so held through a statute.[33] On ownership of land by non-Kenyan citizens, the courts have held that the right to property under Article 40 is subject to limitations imposed by Article 65, which limits the right of non-Kenyan citizens to hold land on a leasehold tenure not exceeding 99 years.[34]

6.3 *Contracts and Consents Regarding Dealings in Land*

All agreements and contracts regarding land transactions must be in writing. No suit shall be brought upon a contract in land unless the contract is in writing, has been signed by all the parties thereto, and has been attested/witnessed by a party who was present during the making of the contract.[35] This is buttressed by the provisions of

[32] Further reading recommended of Article 70 above.

[33] See Article 64 of the Constitution.

[34] See Petition No 19 and 291 of 2016 (Consolidated) Malindi Law Society and 12 Others-v- The Attorney-General and 2 Others (2021).

[35] See Section 3 of the Law of Contract Act, Cap 23, Laws of Kenya.

the Land Registration Act, which further provide that signatures, thumbprints, and electronic signatures must be affixed and signed before an attorney, magistrate, judge, or notary public.[36] The importance of contracts in environmental governance is crucial because companies may find themselves seeking easements, leases, or licenses from surrounding communities.

Consent from local land boards is required when dealing with agricultural land. Such consent must be gained and approved before ownership changes.[37] Applications to the land control boards must be in the prescribed forms and done within 6 months of agreeing. Consent can be denied when the division of agricultural land reduces local husbandry and the general productivity of the land. In urban areas, floricultural companies must ensure that land rates are paid to the relevant authorities, such as the national government, county government, and tax authorities. Change of user licenses must be obtained on some properties. They must also ensure registry and physical searches and visits so as not to interfere with rivers, forests, and general vegetation of the area.

6.4 Provisions of the Agriculture and Food Authority Act

The Agriculture and Food Authority Act defines agriculture to include the cultivation of crops and horticultural products.[38] The statute governs the Crops Act 2016. The Agriculture and Food Authority and the National Land Commission advise the Cabinet Secretary (CS) in charge of agriculture to come up with land development guidelines that are implemented by respective county governments. The Cabinet Secretary makes general rules on the preservation, utilization, and development of land by prescribing how owners and occupiers manage their land in line with good estate management. The rules also govern good husbandry, control, and prohibition on the cultivation of land, advice on crops to be grown, construction of buildings, and other works on agricultural land. The Cabinet Secretary also provides for conditions or exemptions on the usage of agricultural land.[39] This law further provides the Cabinet Secretary with powers to prohibit, regulate, and control agricultural activities such as firing, clearing, or destruction of vegetation if such acts lead to the protection of agricultural land and prevent degradation, protect water sources, and preserve the soil and its fertility.

---

[36] Section 44 of the Land Registration Act, Cap 300, Laws of Kenya.

[37] Section 6 of the Land Control Act, Cap 302 Laws of Kenya.

[38] See Section 2 of the Act which is Chap. 317, Laws of Kenya. It is a statute to provide for the consolidation of laws on the regulation and promotion of agriculture, establish the Agriculture and Food Authority, and define the roles of the national and county governments in agriculture excluding livestock production.

[39] See Section 2 of the Agriculture and Food Authority Act.

6.5 *Principles on the Management and Administration of Agricultural Land under the Crops Act*

Section 4[40] of the Crops Acts provides the following four principles an entity or company engaged in horticultural farming should be aware of:

(a) The communal function of agricultural land and that ownership has a social responsibility.
(b) Landowners and lessees of agricultural land should make the land productive in a sustainable and environmentally friendly manner.
(c) The ability of the state to acquire such land for public purposes or public interest under Article 40 (3)[41] of the Constitution.
(d) State regulations on the use of the land in the interest of land order, public morality, and public health and or land use planning under Article 66[42] of the Constitution.

The Crops Act applies to scheduled crops listed in the First Schedule[43] of the statute which includes various types of flowers and applies to all agricultural land, whether privately or communally owned, land owned by cooperative societies, community associations, or farmers and farmers organizations. It is worth noting that a company acquires the status of a legal person once it has been incorporated.

6.6 *The Environment and Land Court*

The Environment and Land Court Act was enacted in 2011 to give effect to Article 162(2) (b) of the Constitution.[44] This was to create a superior court with pecuniary and territorial jurisdictional powers regarding the environment and the use, occupation, and title to land.[45] The Act establishes the Environment and Land Court (ELC)

---

[40] Read Crops Act, No 13 of 2016, Laws of Kenya.

[41] This Article addresses the protection of the right to property and provides limitation to this right including instances where land can be compulsorily acquired by the state for public purposes or interests. Compensation and access to the legal process are guaranteed as constitutional rights.

[42] Parliament is empowered to legislate regulations that ensure that investments in state-regulated properties and land usage benefit the local communities and their economies.

[43] See the list of crops in the First Schedule which is subsidiary legislation to explain and make procedures and terms clear.

[44] The Environment and Land Court Act is itemized as *Act No 19 of 2011* on the Laws of Kenya register. It has been amended over the years as the laws progresses. The Act also contains rules and regulations related to the structure and governance of the Court.

[45] Recommended further reading of the Environment and Land Court Act as well as other land acts on physical and legal possession of land.

under Section 4.[46] It is a superior court of equal status to the High Court. The ELC hears and determines matters regarding environmental planning and protection, climate issues, land usage title, tenure, boundaries, rates, rents, valuations, compulsory acquisition of land by the government, land administration and management, contracts, and agreements, whether concerning public, private, or community land, as well as redress when the right to a clean environment occurs.[47] The Act empowers the Court to order and grant interim and permanent orders, injunctions, compensation, specific performance, restitution, declarations, and costs. The Court also has appellate jurisdiction to hear disputes from tribunals such as the National Environment Tribunal and rulings and judgments from the magistrates' courts concerning land and the environment. Knowledge of the ELC court and pecuniary jurisdiction of disputed matters should be clear to avoid dismissal of suits due to want of jurisdiction.

6.7 *The Role of the Magistrates' Courts*

The magistracy in Kenya runs from the Resident Magistrates' Court to the Chief Magistrates' Courts. They are established by the Magistrates' Court Act[48] which provides for their jurisdiction, procedures, and appellate processes. The Magistrates' courts hear and settle criminal and civil matters as governed by the statute. In civil matters, jurisdiction is limited either in terms of pecuniary or territorial jurisdiction. The Chief Magistrates Court is limited to matters not exceeding 20 million Kenya shillings, 15 million shillings for the Senior Principal Magistrates Courts, 10 million for the Principal Magistrates Courts, 7 million for the Senior Resident Magistrates Court, and 5 million for the Resident Magistrate Court.[49] It is with these jurisdictional caps that the magistrates' courts are empowered to hear and determine claims related to employment and labor relations, as well as land and environment cases.[50] Cases filed in these courts can range from environmental planning and protection, climate issues, land use planning, title, tenure, boundaries, rates, rent, valuation, mining and minerals, compulsory acquisition of land, land use administration, and land management. The jurisdiction covers public, private, and community lands as well as all contracts granting enforceable interests in land, such as breach of contract and easements. The same pecuniary jurisdiction granted under Sect. 7 extends to the determination of employment and labor disputes. Claims of a civil nature

[46] The Environment and Land Court is a creation of the Constitution, whose foundations lay on land issues and land governance in Kenya. A historical read of land clashes in Kenya is recommended.

[47] See Section 13 of the Environment and Land Court Act.

[48] Cap 10 Laws of Kenya

[49] See Section 7 of the Land Registration Act.

[50] See Section 9 of the Land Registration Act.

exceeding such jurisdiction should be filed in the court with appropriate jurisdiction to avoid dismissal of suits.

6.8 *Strategic Environmental Assessment (SEA)*

The Environmental Management and Coordination Act (EMCA), of 1999, which was amended in 2015 is the substantive law governing Integrated Environmental Impact Assessment (IEIA).[51] The Act aims to protect the environment through environmental impact assessment provisions, environmental auditing, and monitoring environmental restoration orders, conservation orders, and easements.[52] The Act establishes the National Environmental Management Authority (NEMA), the Public Complaints Committee, the National Environment Tribunal,[53] the National Environmental Action Plan, and County Environment Committees.[54] In its definition section, EMCA defines several terms that are at the center of ESG. The Act calls for a Strategic Environmental Assessment in which formal and systemic processes analyze and address the environmental effects of policies, plans, programs, and other strategic initiatives.[55]

The Authority is tasked with coordinating environmental management activities; taking stock of Kenya's natural resources and their utilization, reviews, and examination of land use practices; carrying out surveys on proper use and management of environmental resources; advising the government on regional treaties and conventions, research and investigations, mobilization, and monitoring of financial and human resources; identifying projects and auditing them, safeguarding the environment by initiating procedures; monitoring and assessing activities to avoid degradation of the environment; enhancing environmental education and public awareness; publishing manuals, codes, and guidelines; giving advice and support; and preparing annual reports on the state of the environment in Kenya and other functions as may be necessary concerning the environment.[56]

Written approval is required for SEA in Kenya. The Act forbids the erection, construction, extension, removal, or demolishing of structures under a river, lake, and wetlands; the excavation, drilling, and disturbing of rivers lakes and wetlands; the introduction of animals and plants; the deposition of environmental-altering substances; and blockage, redirection, and drainage of such water bodies.[57]

---

[51] See the Environment and Management and Coordination Act (EMCA) 1999 as amended by Act No 5 of 2015.

[52] National Environment Management Authority established by EMCA.

[53] This is a quasi-judicial body established under Section 125 of EMCA.

[54] Section 125 of EMCA above.

[55] This provision was made through the amendment of EMCA in 2015.

[56] See Section 8 of EMCA.

[57] See Section 42(1) of EMCA.

6.8.1 Processes of Strategic Environmental Assessments

All policies, plans, and programs for implementation are subject to the Strategic Environmental Assessment (SEA), and all entities seeking SEAs do so at their own expense by writing to NEMA.[58] An IEIA report is in writing, and proponents of projects undertake a full EIA in the form of a study report to NEMA, which thereafter issues a license. NEMA approves and maintains a public register of these experts. Responses by the Director-General of NEMA to SEA reports take place within 6 months of application. If no response is forthcoming, the entity seeking SEA approval can ask for a response 9 months after requesting it. The SEA is published in the *Kenya Gazette*, newspapers circulating in the area of the proposed project, and radio citing the summary of the project, a place where the project will be carried out, a place where the SEA can be inspected, and a time limit of up to 90 days to receive comments on the SEA.[59] A summary of reports is to be published on NEMA's website.[60]

6.8.2 When Is an Environmental Impact Assessment Study Report Required?

The Second Schedule of EMCA provides instances where an EIA study report is required. The projects are listed as major changes in land use including large-scale settlement schemes such as construction of houses for staff, urban development which may include industrial estates, new housing units exceeding 30 units, construction of tunnels and paved roads, any project near a water body such as a river or lake where most flower farms are situated, water storage in dams and barrages, river diversions, flood control at large-scale levels, drilling for underground water resources, aerial spraying which is possible in large flower farms, clearance, reforestation, and afforestation of forests, construction of floricultural projects near forest reserves, introduction of pesticides, pest control, fertilizers, and irrigated agriculture which exceeds 50 hectares, introduction of GMOs, pumped storage systems, and water disposal, commercial exploitation of flora and fauna, actions that may endanger local flora and fauna, wetland reclamation, and actions affecting indigenous forests and projects in environmentally sensitive areas.[61]

---

[58] Section 57 A of EMCA.

[59] For further provisions on further evaluations, fresh EIAs, offences, and transfer, see sections 57A to 68 of Supra 15.

[60] EMCA at Section 59(1).

[61] See Second Schedule of EMCA.

6.8.3 Environmental Monitoring, Auditing, and Quality Standards

NEMA has a legal obligation to audit activities that may affect the environment by an environment inspector in compliance with the terms of the Integrated Environmental Impact Assessments (IEIA). Owners of establishments such as flower farms have legal obligations too to keep records of the projects within the IEIA and to mitigate any unforeseen and undesirable effects that were not covered by the EIA.[62] NEMA recommendations empower the Cabinet Secretary in charge of the environment to establish criteria and procedures for the measurement of water quality, minimum water quantity standards recommendations, analysis of conditions regarding the discharge of effluents, regulation on the preservation of fishing areas, treatment of effluents, and monitoring and control of water pollution. The advice ranges from the discharge of effluents into water bodies, preparation and recommendations on preservation of fishing areas, recommendations on research of the effects of water pollution, advice on investigation of actual or suspected water pollution, and advice on preventing or abating water pollution.

On air quality, NEMA advises on the criteria and procedures of measuring air, emissions, and occupational standards and air pollution control by mobile and stationary sources requiring re-designation of plants or installation of new technology.[63] It also advises on how to reduce greenhouse gases and the application of technology in air quality standards.[64] It also regulates the usage of pesticides which are prevalent in the floricultural industry. Under Section 94, the Cabinet Secretary, upon recommendation of NEMA, determines the standards of pesticides in agricultural products and establishes pesticide control measures, including imports, exports, transportation, and disposal, among others, registration of pesticides, labeling, establishment of laboratories, and enforcement of such regulations.

As noted previously, Kenya's governance structure is divided between the national government and devolved governance in 47 counties. The National Parliament enacts national statutes concerning the environment, while county assemblies enact laws governing environmental matters in the counties. Section 30 of EMCA creates the County Environment Committees whose mandates are to responsibly manage the environment of the county, develop the county's strategic environmental 5-year action plan, and perform other duties prescribed under EMCA or assigned by the governor of the county by way of a Gazette Notice in the *Kenya Gazette*.[65] Under Section 40, the County Environmental Committees are required to undertake public participation[66] exercises and take into account other existing county environmental action plans. The county's strategic environmental plans are thereafter submitted to the Cabinet Secretary in charge of the environment for incor-

[62] EMCA at Section 68.

[63] See Section 78 of EMCA.

[64] Further reading of Section 78 of EMCA.

[65] The *Kenya Gazette* is published and printed by the Government Printer in Nairobi.

[66] Public participation is entrenched in the Kenya legal system.

poration into the national environmental plan.[67] Floricultural companies are therefore granted opportunities to develop these environmental plans by giving their inputs during the public participation exercises.

6.8.4 The National Environmental Complaints Committee

The National Environmental Complaints Committee (NECC) is established under Section 31 of EMCA. The Committee's functions include investigating complaints and allegations against persons and entities about Kenya's environment, preparing and submitting periodic reports of its activities, and other duties assigned by the Cabinet Secretary in charge of the environment. NECC also facilitates access to environmental justice for the public by providing a forum for environmental conflict resolution and the development of environmental policies. It conducts onsite visits to establish and ascertain facts, where it can observe, collect scientific samples, and conduct interviews. It also conducts public hearings and holds consultative meetings with stakeholders.[68] NECC has investigated complaints of water, air, and noise pollution, sand harvesting in rivers, deforestation, EIA and EIA licensing, and solid waste management and proposed ways in which the government and its agencies can use such reports to combat environmental degradation.

6.8.5 The National Environment Tribunal

This Tribunal is established under Section 125 of EMCA. The chairperson of the Tribunal is appointed by the Judicial Service Commission (JSC) and holds the qualifications of a judge of the High Court. The Tribunal comprises other members, i.e., two advocates of the High Court of Kenya and two persons with exemplary knowledge on environmental matters, including, but not limited to, land, energy, maritime affairs, water, forestry, energy, mining, and wildlife. The Tribunal is headed by a chairperson who is deputized by a vice chairperson.[69] The quorum requirements are met when at least three members are present.[70] The Tribunal is empowered to hear grievances related to the refusal, limitation, revocation, and suspension of various licenses prescribed in EMCA. It is also mandated to determine disputes related to fee charges and imposition orders by NEMA. Appeals from the Tribunal are lodged in the Environment and Land Court, which is situated in various counties in Kenya.

---

[67] See Section 40 of EMCA.

[68] Recommended further reading of the functions and procedures of NECC.

[69] See Section 125(7) of EMCA on the qualifications of appointment and composition of the Tribunal.

[70] See Section 128 of EMCA on quorum.

6.9 Waste Management

The Parliament of Kenya enacted the Sustainable Waste Management Act[71] to provide for a legal and institutional framework for the sustainable management of waste[72] and to comply with the constitutional right to a clean and healthy environment. The compliance and enforcement of waste management have been devolved to the county governments, which are responsible for establishing the financial and operational functions to actualize waste management. In the definition section, the Act provides for extended producer responsibility, which provides for an environmental management approach where a producer's responsibility for a product is extended to the most consumer stage of a product's life cycle. This provision provides for multiple legal interpretations in terms of sustainable waste management including a responsibility to ensure that flowers do not inhibit the growth of other plants in the area, use of fertilizers, and disposal of rotten or discarded flowers.

This Act places the responsibility of monitoring and compliance on NEMA. NEMA is obligated to monitor and review the performance of private entities and county governments by ensuring that they comply with the Act. The Act bestows NEMA with the power to enter and investigate whether entities comply with the Act. It is an offense for a person, including legal persons such as companies, to hinder or refuse to give information or give false misleading information to NEMA.[73] The Act provides for a fine not exceeding KSh 1 million or imprisonment not exceeding 5 years or both. In addition, the Act has made provisions for the establishment of the National Environment Complaints Committee to receive and provide redress mechanisms. Redress mechanisms include cleanup and restoration, refusal to grant licenses, impositions of restrictions, conditions, and limitations on the license, and payment of fees. Aggrieved parties can appeal to the National Environment Tribunal.[74]

County governments are expected, under the Sustainable Waste Management Act, to ensure the disposal of waste generated within the particular county where a multinational flower company is situated, provide centralized collection centers, establish waste management infrastructure, maintain data on waste management, plan and budget for waste management, designate disposal sites and landfills, and provide lists of waste providers that multinational companies can become. On this note, multinational companies need to familiarize themselves with national county and county bylaws of the areas they are situated in.

---

[71] See the Kenya Law Reports for comprehensive bills, laws, notices, and amendments made by the Parliament.

[72] This is defined in the Act as the use of material resources efficiently by prioritizing waste hierarchy, circular economy, and clean production. It seeks to reduce the amount of waste generated, deposited, or discarded.

[73] See Section 27 (10) of the *Sustainable Waste Management* Act.

[74] Recommended further reading on the functions and jurisdiction of the Environment Tribunal.

7 Climate Change

The Climate Change Act is a law providing a regulatory framework for enhanced responses to climate change and mechanisms and measures to actualize low-carbon climate developments in Kenya.[75] The Act is applied by the national and county governments in mainstreaming climate change responses, enhancing adaptive capacities, enhancing resilience and disaster risk reduction, ensuring intergenerational and gender equity, incentivizing the private sector to contribute to reducing climate change, enhancing financial transparency, research and development, and sustainable development, and enhancing climate change governance.[76] Floricultural companies can join the Climate Change Council[77] as representatives of the private sector.[78] Climate change obligations can be imposed on a private entity by the Climate Change Council, which monitors and evaluates compliance and may require a private entity to prepare reports of its performance of climate change duties within a prescribed timeline and, if there is failure to comply with the climate change obligations, mandate the private entity to prepare a report on actions taken or to be taken to ensure compliance.[79] Monitoring of compliance is done by NEMA and includes monitoring, investigating, and reporting, ascertaining adherence with instructions prescribed and regulations and enforcement, and monitoring of levels of greenhouse gas emissions levels set by the Climate Change Council.[80] Floricultural companies can incorporate climate change governance in their structures by engaging with the national and county governments on mainstreaming climate change, integrating climate change reports in their reporting, and participating in public consultations on climate change as envisioned by the law.[81]

8 Employment and Labor Services

The Constitution guarantees the rights against slavery, servitude, and the performance of forced labor.[82] It also protects freedom of conscience, religion, belief, and opinion and allows for expressions of these. An employer cannot deny employment because of belief and religion and cannot compel an employee to act against their

[75] Cap 387 A, Laws of Kenya.

[76] See Section 3(2) of Cap 387A.

[77] Established under Section 5 of the Climate Change Act.

[78] The Council is headed by the President, and other members include cabinet secretaries, chairperson of the council of governors, civil society, marginalized communities, and academia.

[79] Section 16 of the Climate Change Act.

[80] Section 17 of the Climate Change Act.

[81] Section 24 of the Climate Change Act.

[82] See Article 30 of the Constitution of Kenya.

religion. The Constitution grants freedom of association[83] such as forming groups of employees and the right to demonstrate.[84] Labor practices rights and freedoms are constitutional provisions under Article 41. It guarantees the right of every person to fair labor practices, such as the right to fair remuneration, reasonable working conditions, the right to form, join, and participate in the activities of a trade union, and the right to go on strike. It also recognizes employers' freedom to join a federation and participate in its activities.

8.1 The Employment Act

This statute declares the rights of employees, provides the basic conditions of employment of employees, and regulates the employment of children.[85] The statute prohibits the recruitment, trafficking, and use of forced labor.[86] It also encourages the elimination of discrimination based on race, color, sex, language, religion, political and other opinions, nationality, ethnicity and social origin, disability, pregnancy, and marital and HIV status.[87]

In addition, this statute states that a contract of employment shall contain the name, address, age, and sex of the employee, name of employer, job description, date of commencement of employment, form and duration of the contract, place of work, hours of work, remuneration, payment intervals, and the date when continuous employment began in instances of a previous employer which counts toward such period such as mergers and name changes in companies. An employee is entitled to the right to annual leave, the right to maternity leave, pre-adoptive leave when adopting a child, sick leave, and adequate housing, water, food, and medical attention. In addition, employers rely on casual labor during various phases of horticultural farming. They should be aware of the operations of employment law, especially Section 2 of the Employment Act that converts casual labour to regular employment. A casual worker has been defined as a person whose terms of engagement provide for payment at the end of each day and who is not engaged for a longer period than 24 hours at a time.[88]

Employers ought to follow the provisions of the Employment Act, specifically Sections 41, 43, 44, 45, and 47 of the Act with regard to termination of employee services. Under Section 41, an employer should explain to an employee, in a language the employee understands, that they are considering termination of their services and that the employee is entitled to have another employee or a shop union

[83] See Article 36 of the Constitution of Kenya.

[84] Article 37 of the Constitution of Kenya.

[85] See the Employment Act, Cap 226, Laws of Kenya.

[86] See Section 4 of the Employment Act.

[87] Read Section 5 of the Employment Act.

[88] See Nyeri Cause No 252 of 2017 Francis Ndirangu Wachira—Betty Wairimu Maina.

official present during this explanation. In claims arising out of the termination of contracts, the reason for the termination should be proved, and failure to do so makes the termination unfair. Section 44 provides for instances when summary dismissal from a contract of service may occur. No employer has the right to terminate the contract of service without notice or with less notice than what an employee is entitled to.

Summary dismissal can occur when an employee, by their conduct, has indicated that they have fundamentally breached their obligations arising out of the contract of service. Lawful grounds for summary dismissal are provided for under Section 44(4) as absence without leave or lawful cause, intoxication during work hours, rendering them unable to work properly, willful neglect of work performance and careless performance of work under their duty, using abusive and insulting language and behaving in an insulting manner toward an employer or someone working under the authority of an employer, knowingly failing to or refusing to obey a lawful command which is within his scope of the duty to obey, in the lawful execution of the power of arrest for an offense punishable by imprisonment, as well as committing a crime or suspected of committing a crime detrimental to their employer or their employer's property. Under Section 45, no employer shall terminate the employment of an employee unlawfully. A termination is unlawful if the employer fails to prove that the termination is valid for reasons of fairness, such as related to conduct, capacity, compatibility, requirements, and fair procedures. Section 47 provides that the burden of proof to prove that an unfair termination of employment or wrongful dismissal has occurred rests on an employee, while the burden of proof of justifying the grounds for the termination of employment or wrongful dismissal shall rest on an employer. Employers should ensure that employment and termination procedures are clear from the beginning and that such processes are fair and transparent by engaging legal and human resources professionals.

8.2 The Employment and Labor Relations Courts

The Constitution mandates the establishment of the Employment and Labor Relations Court (ELRC) to hear and determine matters related to employment and labor.[89] The jurisdiction of the ELRC covers disputes arising out of employment between employer and employee, employer and trade unions, employers' organizations and trade unions, trade union disputes, employer organizations disputes, employer organization and member, registration, and elections of trade unions, and the registration and enforcement of collective agreements. The ELRC has powers to make orders and issue interim preservation orders, injunctions, prohibitory orders, specific performance, declaratory orders, ward compensation, and damages and order the reinstatement of an employee within 3 years of dismissal on conditions the

[89] See Employment and Labour Relations Act, Cap 8 E, Laws of Kenya.

Court deems just and fair. The Court can also call for alternative dispute resolution to disputes before it such as internal methods, conciliation, mediation, and traditional dispute mechanisms. The Court is also an appellate court from decisions made in the magistrates' courts. The magistrates' courts have statutory powers to determine labor disputes within limited pecuniary and territorial jurisdiction under Sect. 7.[90] Appeals from the decisions of the ELRC are heard by the Court of Appeal.[91]

8.3 Legal Provisions on Sexual Harassment at the Workplace

The Employment Act defines sexual harassment as occurring when sexual relations are expressed or implied in the form of promises of preferential statements, threats of detrimental treatment, and threats about the future of employment at the workplace, the use of sexual language, both spoken or written, visual material of sexual nature, and offensive behavior that affects employment, job performance, or job satisfaction.[92] Every company that employs more than 20 employees has a statutory obligation to issue a "Policy Statement on Sexual Harassment." The policy shall contain information that an employee is entitled to employment free of sexual harassment, the employer shall take steps to ensure that employees are not sexually harassed, the employer shall take measures against any person under the employer's direction who subjects an employee to sexual harassment, explain how to bring to the attention of the employer a complaint of sexual harassment, and state that the complaint's and the complainant identity shall be treated confidentially.[93]

The Sexual Offences Act[94] lists various offenses that may occur and/or affect the workplace. Induced indecent acts[95] and the commission of an indecent act with an adult[96] without consent are sexual crimes in the workplace. The law defines sexual harassment in the workspace as the use of a position of authority, persistent sexual advances, and making unwelcome advances at the workplace and imposes a sentence of imprisonment of not less than 3 years or a fine of not less than 100,000 Kenya shillings or both.[97] The burden of proof to be satisfied in a sexual harassment trial includes making sexual requests as a basis for employment, career advancement, or an offer of service.[98] In addition, harassment occurs when such acts interfere with the work environment and lead to a denial of service. Intentional and

[90] See Section 7 of Cap 8 E Laws of Kenya.

[91] See Section 17 on the appellate processes and procedures.

[92] Section 6(1) is recommended for reading and understanding all employers and employees.

[93] See Section 6(3) of the Employment Act.

[94] Act No 3 of 2006.

[95] Section 6 of the Sexual Offences Act.

[96] Section 11A of the Sexual Offences Act.

[97] Section 23(1) of the Sexual Offences Act.

[98] Section 23(2) of the Sexual Offences Act.

unlawful acts that use force, threats of harm, and abuse of power and authority that inhibit the victim from indicating resistance or unwillingness to participate in sexual acts are criminalized in law.[99] Companies and multinationals must draft anti-sexual harassment policies founded on the above sections of the law and ensure that their employees are aware of them. The existence of such policies should be clear from the onset including their posting on websites and job adverts on the premises.

On the other hand, a person convicted of a sexual offense should reveal such information while seeking employment when such employment places him in a position of authority, such as taking care of children and other vulnerable persons in the workplace.[100] Thus companies should carry out due diligence on their workforce by requiring, for example, the submission of a police clearance certificate issued by the Directorate of Criminal Investigations and rightly asking such questions in the interview.

Furthermore, should a sexual offense happen on the premises, it is an offense to interfere with the scene of a crime or the evidence.[101] Interference includes the tampering, interference, and intimidation of witnesses, acts that hinder or obstruct investigations, and material misrepresentation of evidence.[102] The act also criminalizes the making of false allegations under Section 38, and such information should be in any sexual harassment policy drafted and approved in companies. The policy on sexual harassment should also be brought to the attention of employees.[103]

9 Equity, Diversity, and Inclusion

Article 27 of the Constitution grants the right to equality and freedom from discrimination by providing that every person is equal and is entitled to equal protection and benefits of the law and full enjoyment of fundamental rights and freedoms. In addition, men and women have the right to equal treatment in political, social, economic, and cultural aspects of life. The state and other persons, such as companies and individuals, are prohibited from discrimination based on race, sex, pregnancy, marital and health status, ethnicity or social origin, color, age, disability, religion, conscience, belief, culture, dress, language, or birth.[104]

[99] Section 43 of the Sexual Offences Act.

[100] Section 30 of the Sexual Offences Act.

[101] Section 37 of the Sexual Offences Act.

[102] See Section 37(2) of the Sexual Offences Act.

[103] It is recommended to draft policies in line with the Employment and Sexual Offences Act to address sexual harassment in the workplace.

[104] See Article 27(4) and (5) of the Constitution.

10 The Right to Privacy

The right to privacy is a constitutional provision stating that the right to privacy includes the right not to have their person, home, or property searched and the right to have information relating to their family or private affairs unnecessarily revealed.[105] This right is actualized by the Data Protection Act.[106] This law regulates the processing of personal data and provides for the rights of data subjects and the obligations of data processors. It also means that as a data controller and processor, a company ought to be aware not to release employees' details while executing its environmental and social governance procedures. The law interprets data processing as any operation that collects, records, organizes, structures, stores, adapts, alters, retrieves, consults, uses, discloses through transmission, disseminates, makes available, aligns, restricts, erases, and destroys personal information. This right means that every employer should ensure that data regarding employees is protected from the moment they apply for jobs or positions in such companies. This right extends to the termination of employment.[107]

11 Bribery

The Bribery Act[108] makes statutory provisions for the prevention, investigations, and punishment of bribery. In its definition section, it defines advantage as bribery-fueled influences in offices, employment, and contracts. It also defines a private entity as any business incorporated in Kenya under private ownership. The giving and receiving of bribes are criminalized under Sects. 5 and 6. Activities and functions where bribery can occur include businesses, employment, and activities performed by or on behalf of persons including corporates even if such activities are performed outside Kenya.[109] Section 9 requires public and private entities to follow certain laid-down procedures to prevent bribery. The requirements obligate companies to take into account their size and structure and scale to prevent bribery and corruption, ensure that there is no top-level management failure to put up such measures, and seek the assistance of the Ethics and Anti-Corruption Commission (EACC) to develop and put in place such procedures. A private entity commits an offense when it fails to prevent bribery commission or omission. This occurs when bribing another person intending to obtain or retain business for the private entity or advantage in the conduct of business for the private entity.[110] Persons outside private

[105] See Article 31 of the Constitution.

[106] Cap 411 C of the Laws of Kenya.

[107] See Section 2 of the Data Protection Act.

[108] Cap 79 B, Laws of Kenya.

[109] See Section 7 of the Bribery Act.

[110] Section 9 of the Bribery Act.

entities who obtain property to use in bribery, use, have, or transfer property obtained in connection with bribery, and acquire accounting recordings of a private entity through bribery commit offenses under the law.[111] Floricultural companies should familiarize themselves with guidelines and regulations such as those envisaged under Sect. 12. These guidelines are to be developed by the Cabinet Secretary in charge of matters related to justice to assist in the implementation of procedures to prevent bribery.

12 Right to Health and Breastfeeding Areas in Workplaces

Every person has the right to the highest attainable standard of health, including access to the provision of a workplace that promotes good health and preventive, curative, palliative, and rehabilitative health services.[112] This right extends to the right to be treated with dignity and respect and to the right to have healthcare privacy respected.[113] The law also provides for free and compulsory vaccinations of children under the age of 5 as well as free maternal care in public hospitals funded by the state. It is therefore important for companies to allow their staff access to such services when the need arises. The Act also provides for the promotion and upholding of public and environmental health by managing the national government to ensure that food and water are safe for human consumption by empowering state officials to enter institutions to ensure safe sanitation practices are attained. In addition, this statute provides that an employer shall establish lactation stations that are equipped with the necessary equipment such as hand washes, refrigerators, cooling machines, electrical plugs for breast pumps, and comfortable sitting arrangements. Such stations shall not be located in bathroom areas. Employers should also ensure that there is no direct or indirect promotional, marketing, or selling of infant formulas in such areas.[114] Furthermore, they are obligated to ensure that there are regular nursing breaks that are compensable, not lasting for more than 1 hour every 8-hour working period. It is worth noting that private entities are permitted to operate hospitals, clinics, and laboratories when granted licenses[115] and should strictly adhere to all laws regarding healthcare, data protection, and safety in compliance with other laws.

---

[111] Section 13 of the Bribery Act.

[112] See Section 5 of the Health Act, Cap 241, Laws of Kenya.

[113] Section 5 of the Health Act.

[114] See Section 71of the Health Act.

[115] See Section 89 of EMCA.

13 Community Engagements and Corporate Social Responsibilities

The Constitution recognizes community land as land held, managed, or used by specific communities as forests, grazing land, or shrines, land used as ancestral land, and land used by hunter/gatherer communities.[116] When being established, floricultural companies ought to be aware of the customs and traditions of the surrounding communities so as not to interfere with culture and ways of life. The EMCA Act provides for the application of traditional knowledge of sources, components, capabilities, practices, and processes of preparation, usage, and storage of plant and animal species and their genetic resources. Thus, multinational companies should have in their ranks personnel who are aware of the culture and customs of communities around the farms that could be socially or culturally acquired. In addition, the Act encourages the Principle of Voluntary Environmental Management in which landowners are encouraged to grant easements on their land and encourage environmental conservation.[117]

14 International Law

International conventions and treaties that Kenya has ratified are part of the environmental governance system in line with Articles 2(5) and (6) of the Constitution of Kenya.[118] NEMA is also empowered to assist in the negotiations of treaties, agreements, and conventions and to keep a record of all that Kenya is party to. Some of the treaties Kenya has ratified include the International Convention on Economic, Social, and Cultural Rights and the Convention on Biological Diversity. This treaty calls on nations to allocate their maximum available resources to achieve economic, social, and cultural rights. Article 7 obligates states to ensure that the right to work and fair remuneration is upheld, whereas Article 8 recognizes the right of workers to form and join trade unions. In addition, Article 9 recognizes the rights of workers to benefit from social security and social insurance and fair remuneration. The right to family and adequate standards of living (food, clothes, housing, and improved living conditions) is provided for under Articles 10 and 11. Right 12 provides that states must ensure the right to the physical and mental health of their citizens.

Much of Kenya's population lives in rural and semi-urban areas. It is in these areas that many flower farms have been established, thus creating an economic and social link with the surrounding communities. There is an unwritten and

[116] Article 63 of the Constitution of Kenya.

[117] See Section 112 of EMCA.

[118] See constitutional provisions on the application of international law under Article 2 of the Constitution.

unenforceable agreement that such farms should employ locals. However, they attract employees from all parts of Kenya, becoming social and multicultural hotspots.

15 Conclusion and Recommendations

The importation of the Global North's rules and directives of doing business presents a challenge in an area of the world where a majority of the people are reliant on employment or have no jobs at all. The implementation of the CSRD and CSDDD presents what I call an economic implementation challenge where self-preservation through earning an income supersedes the attention that may be given to the implementation of these directives. Secondly is what I call the legal oversight challenge. The Kenyan legal system is yet to be tested in this aspect, i.e., a case directly related to the implementation of CSRD and CSDDD. This could be due to costs, interpretation of the directives, and lack of interest or timing. However, this may change noting that tech giants have been successfully sued in Kenyan courts recently. The final challenge is what I call the social awareness challenge. These directives are meant to be understood and accepted in societies where raw materials and factories are situated. There is no social anthropological research yet in specific locations that can provide clear data on the awareness and understanding of CSRD and CSDDD in Kenya. This, however, presents an opportunity to research on this and fill this gap.

It is in rural areas that many flower farms have been established, thus creating an economic and social link with the surrounding communities. There is an unwritten and unenforceable agreement that such farms should employ locals. However, they attract employees from all parts of Kenya, becoming social and multicultural hotspots. In applying CSRD and CSDDD, multinational entities in the horticultural business ought to center the "human." This human could be individual or a community. Further, a social anthropological study of the area is a necessity.

Floricultural companies should carry out feasibility studies of the geographical areas they will be located in, including the culture and the history of the land, and familiarize themselves with the laws of Kenya to ensure effective environmental and social governance practices. They should hire licensed and experienced in-house legal counsel who has complied with the requirements of the Advocates Act and holds a valid practicing license, establish libraries containing books of laws for reference, and respect the environment by ensuring waste management, sustainable use of resources, and community development. They should ensure that mandatory licenses are up to date and renewed ahead of time and hire qualified personnel in the office, such as human resources managers, accountants, and investments and financial analysts. They should also ensure that signages on legal requirements and regulations such as those on compliance with CSRD and CSDDD and those against bribery and sexual harassment are prominently displayed. In addition, notices on data protection and health and safety should be visible. Finally, they should participate in local community activities, practice corporate social responsibility, and join employers' organizations.

References

Amayi K (2021) Flower growing firms' contribution to community water use management in Naivasha Sub County, Kenya. Environ Challenges 5:100330

E.U. (2024) Directive (EU) 2022/2464 of the European Parliament and of the Council of 14 December 2022 amending Regulation (EU) No 537/2014, Directive 2004/109/EC, Directive 2006/43/EC and Directive 2013/34/EU, as regards corporate sustainability reporting, https://eur-lex.europa.eu/eli/dir/2022/2464/oj/eng Accessed 13 July 2026

Donohoe M (2008) Flowers, diamonds and gold: the destructive public health, human rights and environmental consequences of symbols of love. Hum Rights Q 30:164–182

Kenya Flower Council (2024) https://kenyaflowercouncil.org/ Accessed 13 July 2026

Macchi C (2022) Business, human rights and the environment: the evolving agenda. T.M.C Asser Press, Berlin

Rao Madhura and Bernaz Nadia (2020) Corporate responsibility for human rights in Assam tea plantations: a business and human rights approach. Sustainability 12(18):7409

Too Emmanuel (2020) Uhuru : Stop Social Media Nonsense, The Standard Newspaper, May 1st 2020, https://www.standardmedia.co.ke/nairobi/article/2001369844

Muriuki Sharon is a Kenyan lawyer. She is a member of the Law Society of Kenya and the East Africa Law Society. She holds masters degrees in Colonial and Postcolonial Studies from Linnaeus University, Sweden, where she was a Swedish Institute Scholar and a Master of Laws in Animal Law from Lewis and Clark Law School, Portland, Oregon. Sharon is the founder and Executive Director at The Biodiversity Circle. Her work focuses on climate governance, industrial farming, legal history of agriculture and animal welfare, and economic and social rights.

Taking Seriously the Right of Local Communities to Participate in Environmental Decisions in the Context of Damages Caused by Mining

Rodrigo Alejandro Ramos Gómez and Alfonso Enrique Ramos Gómez

Abstract Grupo Mexico is one of the leading companies in the mining industry in Mexico. On 6 August 2014, one mine of this company spilled thousands of litres of toxic mining acid into the Bacanuchi and Sonora Rivers in Mexico's northern Sonora state, causing a major environmental disaster and affecting the health and lifestyle of the inhabitants of the region. The company and the government, without the participation of the affected communities or the individual victims, agreed on what reparation measures were needed to restore the environment and the sums the company should pay in compensation to the victims. Since then, local communities have complained that the proposed remedies were insufficient. However, it was until 2021 when the Supreme Court ruled that the communities had a right to participate in the environmental decisions related to the restoration of the rivers and bound the government authorities to reopen the case and to consider the views and opinions of the affected groups. Thanks to their involvement, the outcome of the monitoring activities was completely different. After 9 years of struggle, in October 2023, the government finally recognized that Grupo Mexico did not fulfil its obligations to remedy the environmental harm it caused and decided to take further legal action. The Sonora and Bacanuchi Rivers case is an extraordinary opportunity to explore some of the biggest problems local communities face obtaining proper remedies for environmental harms, the weakness of the country's enforcement system when relevant economic actors are involved, and above all the importance of the communities' participation in the environmental decision-making process. Their involvement has proven a cornerstone in the strive for environmental justice in this case.

R. A. Ramos Gómez (✉)
Mexican Federal Judiciary, Mexico City, Mexico

A. E. Ramos Gómez
Alianza Juvenil por la Sostenibilidad, AC, Mexico City, Mexico

S. Talukdar (ed.), *Law, Accountability, and Corporate Conduct*, New Approaches to Business, Human Rights and the Environment 1,
https://doi.org/10.1007/978-3-032-28714-4_4

1 Introduction

Mining activities, all around the world, leave a trail of environmental damage and human rights abuses in every region they take place. Mining, inherently hazardous, ordinarily produces several environmental impacts. This activity entails the discharge of water used in mineral processing, laden with metals and other toxic elements, into surrounding water bodies. Even under controlled conditions, this activity seriously affects the local wildlife.[1] Mining generates noise, vibration, and dust, creating air pollution and a nuisance for nearby residents. The mines also require big portions of land; they alter the landscape and destroy the natural ecosystem in which they are located.[2] Moreover, a failure in the operation of the mines or not having the proper security measures can lead to even major ecological disasters due to the amount and toxicity of the substances used in the mining process.

In addition to the ecological issues, this extractive activity often generates social problems as well. Indigenous and non-indigenous communities residing near mining sites are generally neglected and mistreated by the companies, as well as being provided with low-paid jobs, an increase in addictions, poverty, crime, and criminalization when there is opposition to projects. In almost every country of the Global South, these communities have experienced forced displacement, water scarcity, changes in the landscape, and loss of their land. They are rarely truly consulted before the commencement of mining operations. Furthermore, local population bear the brunt of the consequences of water and air pollution, which naturally impacts their health, and in cases of major disasters, such as dam collapses, they are the first to suffer the losses of their houses, jobs, farming lands, health, and even their lives.

Despite the universally acknowledged risks this industry poses, governments around the world are not always willing or able to take action to prevent damage to the environment or to hold those responsible truly accountable. When major disasters occur, the public authorities generally impose fines on the mining companies but often do not take any further sanctioning action. The individuals directly affected are not even consulted about their needs before deciding on the remediation and compensation measures to be adopted, even though they are the most suitable group to provide insight into the extent of the damage. However, when the relevant population is involved, the remediation of the environment and the reparation to the human rights occur in a much more transparent and efficient manner.

To explore this issue, we chose to analyse a specific case, considered the worst environmental mining disaster in Mexico's history: the 2014 spill of over 40 million litres of toxic mining acid into the Bacanuchi and Sonora Rivers by one subsidiary of the country's largest mining company, Grupo Mexico (the mining company).[3] We believe this case is emblematic, as the affected residents have been fighting for over

[1] Keita et al. (2018, pp. 621–629).

[2] Tambol et al. (2023, pp. 263–275).

[3] Wilton (2015), in New Internationalist.

a decade to defend their right to participate along with the government and the mining company in the decisions related to the adequate and sufficient environmental remediation and compensation measures. Moreover, there has been a completely different outcome in relation to the transparency of the information and to the actions taken in the remediation process before and after the communities' involvement.[4]

This case also shows the importance of giving voice and listening to the affected communities. Before the case was brought before the judicial system, both authorities and the mining company assured that they had finished cleaning the rivers, that there was no more pollution, and that the affected individuals have been fully compensated. However, the Mexican Supreme Court of Justice (Supreme Court) in 2020 ruled that local communities have not been consulted nor allowed to participate in the remediation process.[5] The Supreme Court ordered the authorities to involve the residents of the affected areas in the decision-making process of information gathering and defining a proper strategy to remediate the damage. Finally, in 2023, after several months of collaboration between the communities and the authorities, it was proven that the pollution persisted and that Grupo Mexico had not fulfilled their obligations to clean the rivers nor compensated all the damage made to the health of the population.[6]

Public participation of the affected communities was the key element to reopen the case and to show that Grupo Mexico had not implemented adequate environmental mitigation and reparation measures.[7]

To address this problem, in the first chapter we will provide the historical and factual background of the 2014 environmental disaster. From the beginning of the mining activities in the *Buena Vista del Cobre* mine to the spill of toxic materials into the Bacanuchi and Sonora Rivers and the damages to the affected people and ecosystems. We also include a brief account of the actions taken by the mining company and the authorities in response to the damage it caused by the spill to remedy the environmental harm and to compensate the victims of the toxic spill, the agreement the federal government entered with the mining company, and the administrative resolutions in which the environmental authorities closed the case in 2017 as if the environment was fully restored.

---

[4] Mexico Federal Government (November 2021). Plan of Justice for Cananea. at Plan de Justicia para Cananea | Secretaría del Trabajo y Previsión Social | Gobierno | gob.mx (www.gob.mx).

[5] Comités de Cuenca Ríos Sonora, 4 August 2017 Press Release: Affected by the spill in the Sonora river win amparo lawsuit for water contamination and sue government agencies for failing to attend to their health, available at Afectados por derrame en el río Sonora ganan amparo por contaminación del agua | PODER (poderlatam.org).

[6] Ministry of Environment and Natural Resources. Environmental diagnostic opinion. Sonora River. (2023) at Dictamen Diagnóstico Ambiental Río Sonora | Secretaría de Medio Ambiente y Recursos Naturales | Gobierno | gob.mx (www.gob.mx).

[7] Comités de Cuenca Ríos Sonora and PODER (August 2022). The Road to Truth After 8 Years of Impunity in the Sonora River, at RioSonora8_En.pdf (poderlatam.org).

In Sect. 2, we present the legal basis for the local communities' right to participate in the decision-making process of environmental harm reparation. For such a purpose, we elaborate on the human right to a healthy environment and the right to participate in environmental matters as defined by the Supreme Court. Furthermore, we present a summary of the judicial process the residents of the affected areas filed to defend their right to participate in the discussion of the actions needed to repair the environment and compensate the damages suffered due to the spill of toxic waste. In this section, we also highlight the reasoning of the Supreme Court decision issued in 2020, which held the government responsible for the violation of the petitioners' right to public participation in environmental matters.

Then, Sect. 3 presents an evaluation of the progress made after the public authorities, in compliance with the Supreme Court's resolution, started involving the communities in the remediation process. We explain how the affected communities have effectively participated in the public policies for evaluating and reporting the environmental damage caused by the mining spill of toxic elements. We note that, because of this involvement in the monitoring of the pollution in the river and the health of the residents, the outcome was completely different and showed that the mining company had not taken the necessary steps to remediate the environmental damage it caused. This new information shows the deficiencies of the domestic system to protect the environment, since more than 9 years after the toxic spill, the rivers are still polluted nowadays, and the inhabitants continue facing several adverse consequences in their health and lifestyle.

We consider this case exposes the deficiencies of the domestic system and the challenges local communities face to even be listened to by authorities and economic powers in the context of environmental damage. At the same time, it is a great example of the importance their participation in environmental affairs has and of the major benefits it poses for boosting a more transparent and efficient reparation process. Moreover, the Supreme Court ruling constitutes a relevant precedent for the development of constitutional doctrine on the scope of the right to participate in environmental matters and of the government's obligation to give voice to the victims of major mining disasters in the reparation decision-making process.

2 Buena Vista del Cobre Mine Background, 2014 Spill Consequences, and the Company and the Government's Response to the Environmental Damage

The first records of mineral extraction in the region date back to the time of the Spanish colony at the end of the seventeenth century, when the presence of copper was discovered in the soil of the region in a practically superficial way. Mining activity continued to develop intermittently due to conflict with the Apache tribe (an indigenous people native to the United States) until approximately 1865, when

General Ignacio Pesqueira achieved a certain stability accompanied by the urban development of what is now the municipality of Cananea, in the State of Sonora. Later, with advances in infrastructure in some deposits, in 1899, the American businessman William Cornell founded the Cananea Consolidated Copper Company, which greatly promoted large-scale mining. The mine was owned by foreigners until 1971, when it was nationalized by the Mexican government and renamed *Compañía Minera de Cananea*.[8] Due to political and economic issues, in 1989 it was declared bankrupt and acquired by Grupo México (the mining company), one of the largest corporate groups in the country, which contributed to its continued exploitation with modern technologies and processes. However, in 2007, a new labour conflict began between the miners' union and the company, which lasted 3 years, during which its operation was stopped, until 2010, when the federal police had to take over the facilities, after a complex legal process, whereupon the mine was reopened, adopting its current name, *Buenavista del Cobre* mine.[9]

In this context, at 10 am on 6 August 2014, *Buenavista del Cobre* mine spilled 40 million litres of acidulated copper sulphate into the Sonora and Bacanuchi Rivers. The toxic elements travelled along 254 kilometres of the rivers' waters, reaching the *El Molinito* dam, which supplies water to Hermosillo, the capital city of the state. According to the mining company, the spill occurred due to extraordinary rains that occurred in the area, in addition to the fact that during the event the pumping system was being repaired, which was a direct cause of the spill.[10] The mining company did not report the spill to the authorities that day. It was until the next morning, when residents of the surrounding municipalities noticed an orange colour in the waters of said water bodies and denounced the situation to the state authorities.

Due to this report, as an emergency measure, the National Waters Commission (by its acronym in Spanish, CONAGUA), ordered a restriction on the use of water from the river and from the 322 wells located within 500 metres from each bank of the river.[11] It also initiated various studies to determine its status, reporting shortly thereafter that there was indeed the presence of arsenic, cadmium, copper, chromium, and mercury, well above the limits established in the Official Mexican Standard.[12]

On 8 August 2014, the Federal Attorney for Environmental Protection (the environmental authority or, by its acronym in Spanish, PROFEPA) conducted an inspection of the mine and opened an administrative procedure to investigate the

[8] Moreno Martínez Gustavo (2019) Blog entry at Cananea Chronics.

[9] Grupo México (2020). Mina Buenavista del Cobre at https://minedocs.com/22/Buenavista-CP-2020.pdf

[10] Environmental diagnostic opinion, op cit. note 6.

[11] Comités de Cuenca Río Sonora y PODER (2020). Chronology of Impunity. at https://poderlatam.org/wp-content/uploads/2020/08/Cronologia_delaImpunidad.pdf

[12] Conagua, Semarnat, Profepa (August 2014). Copper sulphate spill in the in the Bacanuchi River, official slides at Presentación de PowerPoint (profepa.gob.mx).

event.[13] However, the mining company formally informed the authorities of the toxic spill on 12 August 2014, 6 days after the event. But it was until 28 August of that year (more than 20 days after the spill) that the environmental authority temporarily and partially closed the mine (which remained closed only until March 2015).[14] Shortly after that, the mining company filed a request to negotiate with the environmental authority to decide the measures that will be taken to remediate, repair, and compensate for the environmental damage caused by the spill.[15]

On 15 September 2014, the federal government and the mining company entered into an agreement in which the latter assumed the obligation to adopt several measures to restore the environment and repair the damage caused by the spill.[16] This agreement resulted in two instruments, the remediation programme approved by the environmental authority and a trust fund to compensate the affected inhabitants and to finance environmental remediation works.[17] The mining company agreed to implement the remediation programme, which included removing contaminated soils and its proper disposal treatment at an authorized site, carrying out regular sampling, cleaning sediments, connecting new wells, and constructing dams. Moreover, it also accepted to create a trust fund of 2 billion pesos ($148 million USD) to address the damage, to build 37 water treatment plants, and to finance the creation of the Epidemiological and Environmental Surveillance Unit of Sonora (by its acronym in Spanish, UVEAS) for medical care, among other actions.[18]

Nevertheless, none of those actions were carried out in a satisfactory manner. By 2017 only 1 of the 37 water treatment plants had been installed, which stopped working due to lack of maintenance soon after. In relation to the UVEAS, its construction was postponed for various reasons that prevented it from functioning. It was established as a temporary measure while the construction was finished, the creation of a space in a residential house for the care of a few affected people. Later, the land that was under construction was occupied by the National Guard for security purposes, and finally a specific area was set up in the Ures general hospital. By December 2019, it was still not operating, with the respective implications for the healthcare of the people affected by the spill. Moreover,

[13] National Commission of Human Rights (2024), Recommendation 50/2024, on the persistence of violations of the human right to a healthy environment, access to drinking water and health of the population living in the municipalities located in the Sonora River Basin, attributed to the spill of 40,000 m^3 of acidified copper sulphate on august 6, 2014. At Recomendación 50/2024 | Comisión Nacional de los Derechos Humanos - México (cndh.org.mx), [44].

[14] Federal Attorney for Environmental Protection. Resolution PFPA/32.5/2C.27.1/0001-17.

[15] Ibid.

[16] Agreement 06-ORD-02022017-A04, adopted by the Technical Committee of the Río Sonora Trust, in which it determined that the trustors accredited that the competent authorities considered that the remediation programme objectives and that repairs were paid.

[17] Recommendation 50/2024, op cit. note 13, [47].

[18] Chronology of Impunity, op cit. note 11.

as it will be more detailed explained below, the waters of the rivers were not clean at all.[19]

Since the occurrence of the incident, the affected communities were actively trying to influence the decisions adopted in relation to the environmental restoration. They report several illegalities and irregularities, challenge decisions by the authorities, promote and coordinate defence necessary to guarantee their human rights, and achieve reparation for the damage. In that sense, the local communities formed a collective called *Comités de Cuenca del Río Sonora* to demand the reparation of the damages generated by the spill.[20]

Notwithstanding, on 1 December 2017, the environmental authority issued a resolution declaring full compliance with the objectives set forth in the remediation programme. It concluded that the proposed remediation actions were achieved, and the levels of contaminants were acceptable; consequently, on 27 January 2017, PROFEPA determined compliance with the measures arisen from the administrative procedure initiated against the mining company.[21] For that reason, the federal government and the mining company entered into a new agreement to terminate the trust fund.[22] Consequentially Grupo Mexico stopped paying the compensatory sums to the affected people.[23]

Despite all the involvement of local communities, these resolutions in which the environmental authority declared that the mining company had duly complied with all the reparation and compensation measures were taken without prior public participation. In other words, neither the environmental authorities nor the mining company informed the affected people that they were going to close the case, therefore without giving them the opportunity to share their opinions before the final decisions were adopted. They were not even consulted before the termination of the trust fund, in spite of there being still around $800 million pesos ($43 million USD) pending to be paid to the victims as compensation.[24]

Local communities did not stay silent. They actively denounced the negligence and omissions of the relevant actors, reported the human rights violations and the damage to the environment in national and international forums and human rights forums, published reports and opinions, and coordinated protests and public demonstrations, among other things.[25] The activity of civil society has been key to expos-

[19] Blust Kendal. The Impact of Mexico's Worst Mining Disaster, 5 Years Later. Published at KJZZ on 2 August 2019, at The Impact Of Mexico's Worst Mining Disaster, 5 Years Later (kjzz.org).

[20] Chronology of Impunity, op cit. note 11.

[21] Federal Attorney for Environmental Protection. Resolution DGGIMAR.710/010733 of 1 December 2016.

[22] Undersecretary and Chairman of the Technical Committee of the Trust-Fund Río Sonora. Communication SPPA/0086/2017 of 26 January 2017.

[23] Chronology of Impunity, op cit. note 11.

[24] Comités de Cuenca Ríos Sonora and PODER (July 2022). Sonora River, six years of unfulfilled promises, at RioSonora6_VocesCCRS_FIN.pdf (poderlatam.org).

[25] See, for example, the participation of Miguel Soto, Director of Strategic Liaison and Campaigns of PODER, in the framework of the Business and Human Rights Forum held in Geneva, 25–28

ing the continuity of the damage despite the position of Grupo México and the authorities. However, as will be discussed in more detail in the following section, one of the most relevant actions they took was bringing the case before the courts to demand their voice to be heard, in other words, to demand respect for their right to participate in the environmental decision related to the rivers upon which their health and lifestyle depended.

3 The Right to Participate in Environmental Reparation Decision-Making Process

This section outlines, in broad terms, the scope of the human right to a healthy environment and the right to participate in environmental matters. It also presents a summary of the amparo petition filed by several individuals of the affected communities of the environmental disaster in Bacanuchi and Sonora Rivers seeking to be considered by the relevant authorities in all the environmental restoration processes. Lastly, this section presents the key arguments upheld by the country's Supreme Court when it decided the government was responsible for not complying with the petitioner's right to participate in the decision-making process for remedying the environmental harm caused by the mining disaster.

3.1 The Right to Participate in the Environmental Decision-Making Process

The human right to a healthy environment is enshrined in Article 4 of Mexico's Constitution[26] and in Article 11 of San Salvador Additional Protocol to the American Convention on Human Rights.[27] The Inter-American Court of Human Rights (ICHR) has interpreted the right to a healthy environment as a two-dimensional

November 2019, at "Los derechos humanos no son negociables" | PODER (poderlatam.org).

[26] Constitutional Article 4 establishes: "Every person has the right to a healthy environment for his development and well-being. The State shall guarantee respect for this right. Environmental damage and deterioration shall generate responsibility for whomever causes as establish by the secondary law".

[27] Additional Protocol to the American Convention on Human Rights in the Area of Economic, Social and Cultural Rights (Protocol of San Salvador) (entered into force 16 November 1999) OAS Treaty Series No 69 (1988) printed in the Oficial Newspaper of the Federation 1998, in force to the Mexican State since 16 November 1999. It establishes:

"Article 11 Right to a healthy environment

1. Everyone shall have the right to live in a healthy environment and to have access to basic public services.

The States Parties shall promote the protection, preservation, and improvement of the environment".

right, encompassing both collective and individual aspects. In relation to the collective aspect, in the renowned Advisory Opinion OC 23–17, the ICHR explained the right to a healthy environment is a universal value owed to both present and future generations. Meanwhile, the individual aspect of this right implies that environmental harm can have direct and indirect impacts on an individual due to its connection to other rights, such as health, personal integrity, and life.[28]

The ICHR acknowledged a link between environmental protection and the realization of other human rights. It also recognized the right to a healthy environment as an autonomous right, independent and not derived from any other right, even though it has significant implications for rights to life, personal integrity, privacy, health, water, and others.[29] On the other hand, the Supreme Court also has affirmed it as an autonomous right, which extends its protective sphere to all ecosystem components, including forests, rivers, and seas.[30] The Supreme Court further emphasized that this right aims to safeguard "Nature" not only for its utility to humans or the potential harm its degradation could cause to other rights but also for its intrinsic value to other living organisms sharing the planet.[31] In sum, both authorities and individuals must strive to implement necessary measures to conserve natural resources and restore ecological balance when conducting any economic activity or making decisions that could impact the environment.[32]

---

[28] Inter-American Court of Human Rights, Advisory Opinion OC-23/17, Environment and Human Rights (State obligations in relation to the environment in the context of the protection and guarantee of the rights to life and to personal integrity—interpretation and scope of Articles 4(1) and 5(1) of the American Convention on Human Rights), Series A No. 23 (15 November 2017), [59].

[29] Ibidem [60–63 and 66]. Despite the adverse opinion of judges Vio Grossi and Sierra, the Court founded that Articles 11 of the San Salvador Protocol and 26 of the American Convention established an autonomous right different from the environmental implications of other rights.

[30] First Chamber of the Supreme Court of Justice (2018). Judgement on the Amparo Review 307/2016. The public version of the ruling (only in Spanish) can be found in the following official website: https://www2.scjn.gob.mx/ConsultaTematica/PaginasPub/TematicaPub.aspx

[31] Jurisprudence thesis 1a. CCLXXXVIII/2018 (10a.), First Chamber of the Supreme Court of Justice, GSJF 61, I, 308. The text if the thesis is the following (translated by the author): "HUMAN RIGHT TO A HEALTHY ENVIRONMENT. THE VIOLATION OF EITHER OF ITS TWO DIMENSIONS CONSTITUTES A VIOLATION OF THAT RIGHT. The human right to a healthy environment has a double dimension, the first one called objective or ecological, which preserves the environment as a legal value in itself, notwithstanding its interdependence with multiple other human rights. This dimension protects nature and the environment not only because of their usefulness for human beings or because of the effects that their degradation could have on other human rights, such as health, life or personal integrity, but also because of their importance for the other living organisms with which the planet is shared, also deserving of protection in themselves. The second dimension, the subjective or anthropocentric, is that according to which the protection of the right to a healthy environment constitutes a guarantee for the realization and validity of the other rights recognized in favor of the individual, so that the violation of any of these two dimensions constitutes a violation of the human right to the environment, without it being necessary to affect another fundamental right."

[32] First Chamber of the Supreme Court of Justice (2022). Judgement on the Amparo Review 54/2021, [173–194]. The public version of the ruling (only in Spanish) can be found in the following official website: https://www2.scjn.gob.mx/ConsultaTematica/PaginasPub/TematicaPub.aspx

Now, as the IACH stated in Advisory Opinion OC-23/17, one of the instrumental pillars of the right to a healthy environment is public participation. Participation of the population in the environmental policies and decisions enables individuals to exercise democratic control over state actions. Consequently, through this process, the public is enabled to scrutinize, assess, and amend when appropriate the execution of public policies. Moreover, the IACH held that public participation is the tool that empowers individuals to be integral to the decision-making process in environmental matters and ensures their voices are heard. It allows holding public authorities accountable for their decisions. Simultaneously, it enhances the efficiency and credibility of governmental procedures. In that line, the human right to a healthy environment entails the state's obligation to ensure effective public participation.[33]

Two different types of environmental decision-making processes require public participation. Firstly, the specific projects, activities, and other processes for granting environmental permits to companies and individuals that have or may have a significant impact on the environment. On the other hand, there are other decision-making processes relating to matters of public interest, which include strategies, policies, programmes, rules, and regulations on environmental issues, for example, the actions to be taken for the restoration of an impacted ecosystem. This right guarantees that relevant groups, such as affected communities, specialized NGOs, and experts, can participate in every decision with severe environmental impacts.[34]

Mexico's Supreme Court has stated that the right to public participation in environmental matters is reflected in various international instruments.[35] These include the Rio Declaration on Environment and Development; the North American Agreement on Environmental Cooperation; the Convention on Access to Information, Public Participation in Decision-making, and Access to Justice in Environmental Matters (Aarhus Convention); and the Guidelines for the Development of National Legislation on Access to Information, Public Participation, and Access to Justice in Environmental Matters (Bali Guidelines). Even when not all these international instruments are binding, the Supreme Court has considered guiding criteria to be taken into consideration by national judges to fully realize the human rights to a healthy environment, access to information, and citizen participation, as protected by constitutional Articles 4, 6, and 35.[36]

It is of particular importance for the region, the Regional Agreement on Access to Information, Public Participation, and Access to Justice in Environmental Matters

[33] Advisory Opinion OC-23/17, op cit. note 28.

[34] ECLAC. Regional Agreement on Access to Information, Public Participation and Justice in Environmental Matters in Latin America and the Caribbean. Implementation guide (6 April 2022) LC/TS.2021/221.

[35] Judgment on the Amparo Review 54/2021, op cit. note 32.

[36] Second Chamber of the Supreme Court of Justice (2020). Judgement on the Amparo Review 640/2019, [173–194]. The public version of the ruling (only in Spanish) can be found in the following official website: https://www2.scjn.gob.mx/ConsultaTematica/PaginasPub/TematicaPub.aspx

in Latin America and the Caribbean, better known as the "Escazú Agreement".[37] Article 7.1 stipulates that states shall ensure the right of public participation. To fulfil this, they commit to implementing open and inclusive participation in environmental decision-making processes.[38] Guided by the Escazú Agreement, public participation in environmental decision-making should follow a three-stage process, in which different obligations take place:[39]

1. Before the process: The state authorities must notify the public and proactively disseminate the necessary information, make efforts to identify persons or groups in vulnerable situations or the public directly affected, and provide minimum information to them.
2. During the process: Public authorities must ensure the population can participate from early stages; provide reasonable time frames; give the opportunity to present observations through appropriate means; support persons in vulnerable situations; and give due consideration to the outcome of the participation process.
3. After the participation process: The state shall proactively inform the public of the decision made in a timely manner; provide grounds and reasons for the decision, including an explanation on how the observations have been considered; and provide information on and allow relevant administrative and judicial actions.

The involvement of the public and, in particular, of the affected individuals or groups, in our point of view, enables a comprehensive analysis of the potential environmental impacts or risks relevant decisions could produce on the environment. Then, it is crucial to take this right seriously if we want to protect the nature more efficiently.

3.2 *The Writ of Amparo Was Filed by Affected Communities of the Sonora and Bacanuchi Rivers Disaster and the Decision of the Supreme Court*

Firstly, it is necessary to mention that the writ of amparo is a judicial process crafted to safeguard the fundamental rights of all individuals within the state's jurisdiction against actions and omissions of official authorities. Through this judicial

---

[37] Economic Commission for Latin America and the Caribbean (ECLAC), Regional Agreement on Access to Information, Public Participation and Access to Justice in Environmental Matters in Latin America and the Caribbean (LC/PUB. 2018/8/Rev. 1), Santiago, 2022.

[38] Even though the Regional Agreement on Access to Information, Public Participation, and Access to Justice in Environmental Matters in Latin America and the Caribbean was not in force at the time of the natural disaster discussed in this chapter, it is still convenient to mention that it came into force in the Mexican legal system on 22 April 2021, and the Supreme Court has acknowledged its relevance in recent cases concerning public participation and access to information in environmental matters, for example, in the judgement of the Amparo Review 679/2023-PS

[39] Implementation guide, op cit. note 34.

procedure, any person (individuals and companies) affected by the state can challenge laws, administrative acts, material actions, or even omissions that might produce a violation of human rights before a federal court.[40] The amparo petition allows federal courts to examine the constitutional regularity of the challenged act and, if it is inconsistent with constitutional law, to override it and implement appropriate measures to rectify the harm caused to the petitioner.[41]

Now, as outlined in Sect. 1, following the toxic spill, the mining company and the federal government agreed to implement a remediation plan. This plan included several actions to clean the Sonora and Bacanuchi Rivers and the establishment of a trust fund to finance these actions and compensate the affected inhabitants for the damages they suffered. In 2017, the environmental authorities declared that the remediation plan had been fulfilled and that the pollutant levels in the rivers were either adequate or acceptable. They also determined that the individual claims for compensation had been satisfactorily resolved, and thus, the trust fund had fulfilled its purpose.

Notwithstanding, the inhabitants of the affected region filed a writ of amparo petition, claiming these administrative resolutions violated their rights to a healthy environment and to public participation. They argued that responsible authorities failed to (a) involve them in various acts of the administrative proceedings initiated against the company responsible for the spill and (b) conduct a prior consultation before considering that the objectives of the remediation programmes had been met and the purposes of the trust fulfilled without listening to their claims.[42]

In the first instance, the District Court dismissed the petition partially due to lack of standing and because it held that there was no violation of the petitioners' rights. In synthesis, the District Court held that the legal norms governing the challenged acts did not provide for the participation of the victims in the decisions related to the reparation measures that should be adopted by the mining company. It stated that the intervention of interested social groups must be made through the established channels, without mentioning which were the proper ways to participate.[43]

The petitioners appealed this decision (recourse of revision), and due to the importance of the case, it was taken up by the Supreme Court. After several years of procedure, the Supreme Court issued its ruling on 15 January 2020, reversing the first instance judgement. It recognized the standing of the inhabitants to challenge the resolutions in which (i) the federal government decided the actions to be taken to remediate the environmental harm, (ii) the environmental authority declared that the damage caused to the environment had been duly restored, and (iii) this same authority decided the affected individuals were fully compensated. Moreover, in the merits of the case, the Supreme Court held that the inhabitants should have been

[40] Fix Zamudio (1979, p. 9).

[41] Franco Gonzalez Salas (2012).

[42] Fourth District Court in Administrative Matters of the First Circuit (2018). Judgement on the writ of amparo 1121/2017.

[43] Ibid.

consulted or given the opportunity to participate before the federal government closed the case against the mining company.[44]

The Supreme Court held the government responsible for not ensuring opportunities for effective public participation early in the environmental decision-making process. All the involved authorities should have made efforts to engage the public in a transparent consultation, granting adequate opportunities to express their views. The petitioners should have been consulted and given the opportunity to participate in the decisions related to the reparation and compensation measures for the damages caused to the environment and human rights by the toxic spill of the *Buena Vista del Cobre* mine prior to the approval of the remediation programmes, since their views could provide a different perspective or lead to a more thorough analysis of the information.

In summary, the Supreme Court held the authorities should have involved the plaintiffs in the process to decide which measures would be the best options to repair the environmental damages, the public health, and to compensate the material damages to the people affected by the toxic spill. Also, they should have guaranteed the opinion and concerns of the affected individuals were duly considered before deciding the damage was fully repaired. The omission to involve the local communities prevented them from being able to influence the decision-making process.

For these reasons, the Supreme Court granted constitutional protection to the petitioners, vacated the challenged acts, and ordered the environmental authorities of the federal government to organize public meetings to inform the public, and particularly the affected communities, about the toxic spill. It also ordered them to explain the actions that were already taken with the purpose of remedying, repairing, and compensating for the environmental damages to public health, as well as repairing the material damages to persons derived from the spill and what the following actions should be, among other things. It also established that in the referred meeting, the petitioners should be given the opportunity to express their concerns and possible suggestions so that the complainants' opinions are heard and considered by the authorities.[45]

---

[44] Judgement on the Amparo Review 640/2019, op cit. note 36.

[45] In the cited Judgement on the Amparo Review 640/2019, the Court phrased such obligation in the following manner:

- *When explaining to them what the environmental measures carried out as a result of the Remediation Programs consist of and what they are, the complainants should be allowed to propose any other measure that may be necessary to eliminate or reduce the pollutants to a safe level for health and the environment or prevent their dispersion in the environment without modifying them.*
- *Before the authority concludes that the remediation levels proposed and authorized for Zone 1 were reached, that the contamination levels in Zones 2 through 5 were identified as acceptable, and that the corrective measures specified in the administrative resolution of March 2, 2005 were complied with, the complainants should be heard. They should be allowed to express their conformity or disagreement in this regard and if, in their opinion, there is any other measure that should be taken in this regard.*
- *Before the authority concludes the remediation plan has been complied with and that the purposes of the trust have been fulfilled, it should hear the plaintiffs so that they may state what is in their best interest.*

4 The Effects of Local Communities' Participation

In this section, we review the actions taken after the Supreme Court ordered the authorities to hold meetings with the local communities and to consider their views in relation to the environmental restoration of Bacanuchi and Sonora Rivers. We highlight the enormous progress in the gathering of relevant information thanks to the involvement of the local communities. However, we also acknowledge that even with the active participation of these affected groups, the boost to the remediation process has not been enough. The authorities have not taken concrete measures to clean the rivers. After more than 10 years, several toxic elements are still present in the waters.

4.1 New Information Regarding the Environmental Harm Produced to the Rivers Was Achieved through the Active Participation of Local Communities

In compliance with the Supreme Court's decision, federal authorities met with the communities collective *Comités de Cuenca Rio Sonora*, to discuss the best way of action to solve the problem of the pollution present in the rivers since 2014. From September 2021 to July 2022, they held at least 21 working meetings, in which the Secretaries of Health and Environment and Natural Resources agreed to implement a new process for monitoring and diagnosing the environmental consequences of the toxic spill. After 9 months of gathering and processing samples of surface water, groundwater, and residential pipelines, and assessing the effectiveness of purification plants, they got new findings that proved that the pollution persisted in the rivers. These findings also refute the results previously presented by the mining company and approved by the federal authorities.[46]

In 2022, the collective *Comités de Cuenca Rio Sonora* issued a report based on the new findings, which showed the presence of massive amounts of metals like lead, arsenic, and cadmium in the water at different points of the basin, decreasing insect populations, and economic losses totalling 10.2 billion pesos ($558 million USD). In particular, the communities' collectively reported the following:

- Residents of the basin presented an evident exposure to metals like lead, arsenic, manganese, and cadmium, the bioaccumulation of which exacerbates their medium- and long-term health impact.[47]
- The mine activity in general negatively affects the structure and functionality of arthropods in the Sonora River Basin; the toxic spill produced an even greater

---

[46] Cananea Justice Plan, op cit. note 4.

[47] The Road to Truth After 8 Years of Impunity in the Sonora River, op cit. note 7, [7]. Also see Ministry of Health (2022), slides 12, 13, and 14 at https://share.mayfirst.org/s/JrNgDetgtFRByEZ?dir=undefined&path=%2F&op-enfile=13022633

impact on this kind of fauna, affecting the ecosystem services they provide, such as pollination, pest control, recycling of nutrients, and the biodiversity of the region. Insect populations of bugs, hornets, flies, mosquitos, and beetles have fallen drastically, reducing the capacity for resilience in agriculture.[48]
- Eight years after the spill, the real cost of damages amounts to 10.2 billion pesos ($558 million USD), more than triple the initial estimate by the government ($164 million USD) in 2014 and five times the value of the Sonora River Trust, which disbursed only 1.2 billion pesos ($65 million USD). "Neither the amount of the fine paid nor the compensations delivered by the Sonora River Trust, under any scenario, covered the direct, indirect, and cumulative impacts on the population, ecosystems, and the economy".[49]
- Pollution by heavy metals persists in different sources of water supply for human consumption and in river water. It was necessary that the water drawn from the wells, where aluminium mercury, iron, and manganese have been found more than once, be subject to a purification process.[50]
- In the report, the communities also highlighted that the installation of purification systems to separate metals and the relocation of wells in each community never took place. Five of the six purification plants were not operating; the other one operated only sporadically. On the other hand, none of the four mobile plants were operational. The commitment assumed previously by the defunct Sonora River Trust was to build 36.[51]

In May 2023, the Ministry of the Environment and Natural Resources also issued a new report with the diagnosis of the current environmental situation in the affected rivers.[52] This report revealed that the mining company monopolized 57% of the concessioned volume of groundwater and that the increase in copper production at the mine produced a severe overexploitation in the aquifers of this region. Moreover, this official diagnosis confirmed that the surface water quality indicated that remediation in this body of water was not satisfactorily performed after the 2014 toxic spill. Heavy metal contamination was persistent all along the river.

On 12 October 2023, the Ministry of the Environment and Natural Resources, in a press release, informed that the General Directorate of Integral Management and Hazardous Activities issued a new resolution concluding that the mining company did not comply with the original remediation programmes and that it requested Grupo Mexico to prepare a new remedial plan after it was proven that the first one

[48] Ibidem [11]. Also see Government of Mexico. 8 April 2022. Cananea Comprehensive Plan for Justice. Roundtable on Environmental Health. Component on soil, air, and biota. Slide 13. Available at https://share.mayfirst.org/s/JrNgDetgtFRByEZ?dir=undefined&path=%2F&openfile=13022622

[49] Ibidem [12].

[50] Semarnat/Conagua (2021). Results of the Analysis of Monitoring of Quality of Surface and Ground Water in the Bacanuchi and Sonora Rivers. August 2021, Slides 11 to 16. Available at: https://share.mayfirst.org/s/KbitRXkQiXPnWPy

[51] The Road to Truth After 8 Years of Impunity in the Sonora River, op cit. note 7, [18].

[52] Environmental diagnostic opinion, op cit. note 6.

was never implemented. The Ministry also presented a criminal complaint before the country's General Prosecutor for not remedying the environmental damage it caused in 2014.[53]

All these new findings demonstrate the importance of involving the communities from the beginning of the environmental remediation process. They usually deliver insights of the region and pushed the authorities to be stricter in the gathering and analysis of the necessary information. In this specific case, the authorities and the mining company had already declared that the environmental reparation and compensation were duly made, since the rivers were sufficiently and satisfactorily cleaned. It was the subsequent participation of the communities (in compliance with the Supreme Court decision) that made it possible to open a proper monitoring process, which at the same time provided information that proved the environment was still affected by toxic substances spilled since 2014. Furthermore, it led to other actions to hold the mining company accountable for the damages it caused.

4.2 *Lack of a New Remedial Plan or Additional Reparation Measures*

However, not everything is smooth sailing; the pressure put on the communities has not been enough to force the responsible parties to act and put in place additional environmental reparation measures. Grupo México keeps denying its responsibility for the persistent environmental pollution in the Sonora River, despite all the findings that evidence to the contrary.[54] In March 2024, Mexico's National Human Rights Commission issued a nonbinding recommendation 50/2024, which documented the persistent violations of the human right to a healthy environment, access to drinking water, and the health of people in the Bacanuchi and Sonora River basins following the toxic spill of 2014. It confirmed what the communities have been denouncing for almost 10 years: neither the authorities nor the mining company has implemented adequate reparation measures for anyone in the region.[55]

The National Human Rights Commission noted several actions were needed to repair and guarantee the human right to a healthy environment of the local population:

---

[53] Ministry of Environment and Natural Resources, 12 October 2023 press reléase, avilable at La Semarnat reitera que el derrame ocurrido en el río Sonora fue por negligencia de Grupo México | Secretaría de Medio Ambiente y Recursos Naturales | Gobierno | gob.mx (www.gob.mx).

[54] Grupo Mexico, 4 October 2023 press reléase, available at "La remediación del Río Sonora fue exitosa, plenamente apegada a la legalidad y avalada por estudios científicos y autoridades (gmexico.com)".

[55] Recommendation 50/2024, op cit. Note 13.

- It recommended federal and local authorities implement a mechanism to guarantee specialized medical attention, access to drinking water, and achieve remediation and full restitution according to national and international environmental standards, which has been postponed for these almost 10 years, and establish a punctual route of the actions implemented in the short, medium, and long term.
- Specifically, environmental authorities should adopt all the necessary measures to ensure compliance with the new remediation programme that the company has to submit, which, it is worth noting, must provide for the remediation and total restitution until reaching an acceptable compliance based on national and international environmental criteria and standards of the persistent environmental impacts caused by the spill that occurred in 2014.
- It exhorted the environmental prosecutor to immediately file an environmental liability judicial proceeding demanding compliance with the obligations, payments, and benefits resulting from the attribution of environmental liability against the mining company.
- It urged the environmental authorities to implement a permanent mechanism with the direct participation of the affected population to inform the communities periodically of the progress in the remediation process until reaching an optimal state of remediation based on the provisions of a remediation programme for the rivers, based on applicable national and international environmental criteria and standards.
- It recommended to the Ministry of Environment and Natural Resources to design and initiate the process of implementing an air quality monitoring programme for emissions from the extraction, handling, and processing of minerals of the mine, following and in accordance with the criteria of the National Air Quality Information System.
- It urged the National Waters Commission to take immediate actions to prevent water pollution and for the conservation of water resources, particularly the Bacanuchi and Sonora Rivers, as well as groundwater in the Sonora River Basin, in order to prevent the continued discharge of contaminating substances and/or wastewater into these bodies of water, and to initiate verification procedures focused on corroborating that the points of wastewater discharges into bodies of water within the Sonora River Basin are covered by discharge permits or current concession titles, as well as verifying that the necessary infrastructure for wastewater treatment is in place in compliance with applicable regulations.

All those pending actions show that negligence and denial of the problem by a sector of the authorities and the company keep residents across the river basin at risk for nearly a decade. In May of 2024, the collective *Comités de Cuenca Rio Sonora* informed that after 2 years of the beginning of their meetings with the authorities, the rivers continue with alarming levels of heavy metals, according to recent results. The water treatment plants have not been built yet, and despite a judge's order, the

Sonora Ministry of Health has still not provided specialized medical attention in toxicology to people affected by heavy metals.[56]

Although progress has been made, much remains to be done, and there continues to be several shortcomings and difficulties in achieving full environmental justice. After 10 years of struggle, there still is no reparation of the damage nor compensation for the victims. However, there are other means the communities might hold the state accountable for its incapacity to protect and restore the environment.

4.3 *Could the Omissions of the State Amount to International Responsibility?*

In the case *Habitantes de la Oroya* vs. *Perú*,[57] the Interamerican Court of Human Rights held the state responsible for the violation of human rights of a non-indigenous community caused by contamination of the environment derived from the constant pollution emitted by a mine. The Court also found a violation of their right to judicial protection enshrined in Article 25 of the American Convention on Human Rights, since the Peruvian Hight Court had already ordered several measures to clean the environment, which were not properly complied with.

From Article 25 arise two specific obligations of the state. The first is to enshrine in law and ensure the due application of effective remedies before the competent authorities to protect all persons under its jurisdiction against acts that violate their fundamental rights or that lead to the determination of their rights and obligations. The second is to guarantee the means to enforce the respective decisions and final judgements issued by such competent authorities so that the rights declared or recognized are effectively protected.

In relation to compliance with judgements, state responsibility does not end when the competent authorities issue a decision or judgement but also requires that the state guarantee effective means and mechanisms to execute the final decisions so that the rights declared are effectively protected. Likewise, this Court has established that the effectiveness of the sentences depends on their execution, whose process must tend to the materialization of the protection of the right recognized in the judicial pronouncement by means of the suitable application of said pronouncement. The Inter-American Court also pointed out that in order to fully achieve the

---

[56] *Comités de Cuenca Ríos Sonora*, 13 March 2024 Press Release: Two years after the announcement of the Cananea-Río Sonora Justice Plan, there is no real plan or justice, available at A dos años de anunciado el Plan de Justicia Cananea – Río Sonora, no hay verdadero plan ni justicia | PODER (poderlatam.org).

[57] Inter-American Court of Human Rights, Case of Inhabitants of La Oroya v. Peru. Preliminary Objections, Merits, Reparations and Costs. Judgment of November 27, 2023. Series C No. 511.

effectiveness of the judgement, the execution must be complete, integral, and without delay.[58]

The *Habitantes de la Oroya* vs. *Perú* case bears great resemblance to the Sonora and Bacanuchi Rivers case. In both, hight courts of the countries ordered the government to consider the local communities in the decision-making process on the environmental restoration, and in both cases, the state's efforts were insufficient to restore the right to a healthy environment of the affected communities. Thus, since there is no new remediation programme, local communities could bring the Mexican State to the Interamerican System to demand the fulfilment of its obligations. Their involvement in the environmental remediation process of the rivers might prove to be the one motor to move the relevant actors into taking the proper measures to remediate the environmental damage caused by the spill.

5 Conclusion

In several regions of the Global South, mining activity generates severe environmental and social problems ranging from the emission of pollutants into the atmosphere and bodies of water to forced displacements of the inhabitants of the regions where the mine is located. State authorities generally do not provide adequate solutions nor carry out the necessary actions to guarantee respect for the rights of the inhabitants and to repair the environmental damage caused by this industry. Often, due to the economic and political influence that mining companies have, they are allowed to operate without adequate measures to prevent the risk of environmental damage. Furthermore, when they cause serious damage to the ecosystems where the mines are located, authorities rarely take measures to hold the companies accountable or to enforce the laws requiring them to repair the harm they caused to the environment and to the inhabitants of the region.

Community participation in decision-making related to the environmental remediation of damage caused by mining activity is an institution that allows reversing the political and economic influence these companies have, through which they usually manage to evade their environmental responsibility. Particularly in cases where severe environmental damage has already been caused, the local population is the main affected and, therefore, the main interested to demand and promote the restoration of damaged ecosystems. The participation of local communities contributes to the process of gathering information and monitoring the implementation of the measures agreed upon by the relevant parties. It also allows the decision-maker to give due consideration to any observation or representation made at a point when it is easier to make appropriate changes, including in the process itself. By engaging

[58] Inter-American Court of Human Rights, Case of Inhabitants of La Oroya v. Peru. Preliminary Objections, Merits, Reparations and Costs. Judgement of November 27, 2023. Series C No. 511

the public, the decision-maker should also be in a better position to anticipate, prevent, and resolve any possible conflict.[59]

Despite the importance of having the participation of the affected population in order to achieve true environmental justice, authorities rarely incorporate the interested communities in an effective participation exercise in environmental decision-making. For this reason, the Latin American experience is particularly important, since in this region of the world an international treaty is in force whose essential content is precisely access to information and public participation in environmental decisions. The Escazú Agreement recognizes the right to public participation as one of the essential pillars of the right to a healthy environment. It even includes some provisions that specifically target the public that is "directly affected" regarding activities and projects and that specific attention be given due to their proximity to the decision or activity and the likely or foreseen impacts.

The case under analysis is another example of the contributions on the right to public participation in environmental matters that have emerged from the region. This case arose from a spill of toxic substances from amine in two rivers in the north of Mexico. To repair the environment, the mining company and the country's environmental authorities signed an agreement establishing the mitigation and remediation actions to be carried out by the company to restore the environment, as well as to compensate the affected individuals. However, the terms of this agreement were not communicated to the affected population nor were they given the opportunity to express their point of view regarding the adequacy of the proposed actions. Then, in 2017, the authorities considered that the company had fulfilled its obligations and, in a few words, declared the case closed, based on the information provided by the mining company itself, again without even considering the opinions of the local communities.

After several years of litigation, the Mexican Supreme Court ruled that local communities have a right to participate in environmental decisions, which derives both from the human right to a healthy environment and the right to participate in the conduct of the country's public policies. Consequently, the Supreme Court ordered the authorities to reopen the investigation and to involve the local inhabitants to monitor whether the rivers were still contaminated and, if so, to define whether the remediation programme was adequate or whether additional actions were required. Following this decision, the members and representatives of the affected communities met with the authorities in order to provide their point of view on the remediation actions necessary to repair the environment affected by the spill.

The participation of the communities in the monitoring and reporting on the rivers' pollution showed that more than 8 years after the spill occurred, the waters still had a very high concentration of toxic metals and that the local inhabitants were suffering various health problems due to the lack of remediation of the environmental damage. This has led to a renewed focus on the environmental responsibility of the mining company and an attempt to define a new path to restore the

[59] Implementation guide, op cit. note 34.

environmental balance of the area. As mentioned in Sect. 3, the new outcomes of the monitoring process on the Bacanuchi and Sonora Rivers demonstrate the importance of involving the communities from the beginning of the environmental remediation process. In this specific case, they have pushed the authorities to be stricter in the gathering and analysis of the necessary information. It was the subsequent participation of the communities (in compliance with the Supreme Court decision) that made it possible to reopen the legal procedures to hold the mining company accountable for the environment.

However, we acknowledge that participation of the communities has not been enough for achieving the full restoration of the environment until this moment. There is still much to be done, as mentioned by the collective *Comités de Cuenca del Rio Sonora*; competent authorities still have to take additional measures, build what they have to build, and hire the specialists needed in the areas of health and water, with the company that caused the spill assuming the resulting costs. But their constant involvement is the best hope that the bureaucratic mechanisms are going to be pushed whenever it is needed until the company repairs the damage caused to the environment and compensates the victims for more than 10 years of affectations to their lives at different levels.

Cases like the Sonora and Bacanuchi Rivers evidence that even when the domestic legal means are slow and extremely cumbersome, the participation of local communities might change this trend and boost the ability of public authorities to take actions to protect and restore the environment. Thus, it is of great importance to keep advancing in the development of the right to public participation in the environmental decision-making process at the domestic and international levels. It has proven to be a cornerstone of the struggle to protect and restore the environment and to reverse the current status quo in which impunity for human-made natural disasters is the rule for big companies.

References

Fix Zamudio H (1979) A brief introduction to the Mexican Writ of Amparo. CWILJ 9:2. https://scholarlycommons.law.cwsl.edu/cwilj/vol9/iss2/2

Franco Gonzalez Salas JF (2012) The writ of amparo versus general norms. In: Tafoya G (ed) Elements for the study of the writ of amparo. SCJN

Keita MM, Ogendi GM, Owuor O, Nyamao WN (2018) Impacts of artisanal gold mining on water quality: a case study of tangandougou commune in Sikasso region, Mali. J Environ Health Sustain Dev 3(4):621–629. https://doi.org/10.18502/jehsd.v3i4.228

Moreno Martínez G, (2019) Cananea: Real de Minas. Blog entry at Crónicas de Cananea. https://cronicasdecananea.blogspot.com/2019/08/cananea-real-deminas-gustavo-a.html

Tambol T, Vodounou GMB, Moussa S (2023) Impacts of mining on the environment in west African Sahel: a review. Environ Prot Res 3(2). https://doi.org/10.37256/epr.3220232723

Wilton J (2015) Mexico's 'Worst environmental disaster in modern times.' In: New Internationalist, consulted at Mexico's 'worst environmental disaster in modern times' | New Internationalist

Rodrigo Alejandro Ramos Gómez is a Mexican lawyer, specialized in constitutional and international law. He was a judicial law clerk in the Mexican Federal Judiciary, with over a decade of experience. He served in several first- and second-instance courts and the Supreme Court of Justice of Mexico. He has contributed to judgements on environmental protection and human rights. Now he is the founding partner of the law firm Legalith in Mexico. He holds an LL.M. in Public International Law from Leiden University and a master's degree in criminal policy from the University of Salamanca.

Alfonso Enrique Ramos Gómez is an environmental and energy law specialist with over 9 years of professional experience. He has worked at institutions such as the Academia Mexicana de Derecho Ambiental and Deloitte Servicios Legales, advising individuals and companies on regulatory compliance of hydrocarbons, electricity and renewable energy projects. He is the founder and current president of Ajuves, a non-governmental organization established in 2017, through which he has led legal actions against environmental violations, including illegal logging, industrial pollution and legal amendments.

ESG Standards and Sector Specific Governance

The Siege Closes on Self-Regulation, Public Rules, and Judicial Precedents to Implement ESG Standards in Brazil

Luciana Bauer and Rafaela Santos Martins da Rosa

Abstract This chapter explores how Environmental, Social and Economic (ESG) standards are maturing and being applied in Brazil. Initially, the text summarizes key developments involving the application of ESG requirements in the Brazilian self-regulation environment. Next, it analyzes recently approved Brazilian laws that reinforce legal duties aligned with the ESG agenda. The chapter then details the role of Brazilian courts, emphasizing how judges applying the Constitution and Brazilian laws, while also ensuring the control of conventionality, act as driving forces in enforcing and penalizing actions that violate ESG standards. Important challenges for the operations of companies in Brazil are highlighted in the following section, and final considerations are discussed in closing.

1 What Are ESG Standards and Why Do They Matter to Brazil?

The acronym ESG embodies a number of commitments. The application of ESG principles leads to the emergence of practices that seek responsible and sustainable development and are seen as economically valuable as they promote a corporate conduct that prioritizes the respect for human rights over a strictly profit-driven approach that disregards fundamental rights such as a healthy environment and a stable climate. In its PR 2030 regulation, published in 2022, the Brazilian Association of Technical Standards (ABNT) established a definition of ESG that is considered

L. Bauer (✉)
University of Vale do Itajaí – UNIVALI, Porto Alegre, Brazil

R. S. Martins da Rosa
12th Federal Court of Porto Alegre/RS, Porto Alegre, Brazil
e-mail: rafaela.rosa@trf4.jus.br

S. Talukdar (ed.), *Law, Accountability, and Corporate Conduct*, New Approaches to Business, Human Rights and the Environment 1,
https://doi.org/10.1007/978-3-032-28714-4_5

valid as a national reference.[1] According to item 3.14 of that regulation, ESG refers to a set of environmental, social, and governance criteria to be taken into account in the assessment of risks, opportunities, and impacts, serving as a guideline for sustainable activities, businesses, and investments.

While self-regulation remains prevalent in ESG standards, Brazil shows a growing trend of mandating previously voluntary standards. This is achieved both by enacting laws that reflect ESG premises and by judicial interpretations of the content of voluntary rules and the legal framework, reinforcing the mandatory nature of compliance as a guarantee of the rights and duties laid down in the Brazilian Constitution, which includes a wealth of provisions aligned with the ESG agenda.

Understanding this ongoing process is relevant both because some Brazilian corporations are important players in the world economy[2] and because many corporations from different countries operate in Brazil as part of their value chain. Brazil also plays a crucial role in committing to preserving its forests and biodiversity, controlling deforestation and forest degradation, and protecting the variety of species, all of which are recognized as essential if efforts to halt the accelerating climate crisis are to succeed. Should Brazil fail to contain the pace of deforestation within its borders, the world will find itself increasingly unable to stay below critical tipping points for the climate system (Flores et al. 2024). The regulatory context and the enforcement of the law by the courts have fortunately never been as favorable to the ESG agenda as they are at present.

Although direct references to ESG terminology are more prominent in regulations with no direct enforceability, such as the standards recently issued by ABNT, and also the sustainable development goals of the United Nations' 2030 Agenda, they nevertheless complement Brazil's approval of new laws that tighten the requirements for alignment with social, environmental, and governance sustainability standards, marking a cohesive and transversal effort to address the lack of mechanisms to hold businesses accountable for adhering to ESG principles in Brazil. In addition to new norms, robust judicial decisions that affirm the normative force of rules for public and private conduct have been issued by Brazilian courts, as well as by judicial courts that directly influence the Brazilian Judiciary, such as the Inter-American Court. These recent advances pave the way for a legal interpretation in Brazil that leverages the premises of the ESG agenda and prepares the country for the challenges ahead, such as the expected clashes concerning the expansion of export monocultures, an energy transition seemingly dominated by

---

[1] The content of the ABNT PR 2030 regulation can be consulted at: https://www.abntcatalogo.com.br/. Accessed on: 10 April 2026.

[2] The largest iron mining company in the world and second largest in nickel production is Brazilian, with exports to many countries: https://www.weforum.org/organizations/vale/; also see https://www.mining.com/web/vale-grows-iron-ore-production-by-6-in-fourth-quarter/ Accessed on April 10, 2026 d. Brazil is also the second largest world producer of cotton and the largest sugarcane producer, resulting in the production of sugar or ethanol. Brazil is also the leading producer and exporter of coffee and orange juice. Brazilian meat production is also an important segment, making the country the largest exporter of beef and chicken: https://www.embrapa.br/en/busca-de-noticias/-/noticia/62619259/brazil-is-the-worlds-fourth-largest-grain-producer-and-top-beef-exporter-study-shows. Accessed on April 10, 2026.

oppressive monopolies, this time involving renewable energies, as well as neocolonial practices in voluntary carbon market contracts that stifle proper consultation and respect for the communities that inhabit traditional territories and Brazilian forests.

Given this context, this chapter will explore the tension between promoting an ESG agenda of regulatory, normative, and judicial commitments and the key pressures and challenges that prevent its concrete implementation in Brazil. The first section will detail the main Brazilian self-regulatory innovations that increase and validate ESG requirements, imposing a series of new challenges for companies that operate with raw materials, products, and services in the country. The second section will map out a few relevant laws recently approved in Brazil that incorporate standards of conduct and compliance, as well as provisions for accountability that are subject to concrete requirements. The third section will point out significant advances in decisions by Brazilian courts that confirm a progressive and affirmative trend in ESG standards, thereby refocusing established jurisprudence about environmental and human rights issues toward addressing current challenges. The fourth section will examine and analyze current and future challenges that arise from the demand for ESG compliance in Brazil. The final section will present the concluding remarks.

2 Self-Regulation in Brazil Is Endorsing ESG Standards

In 2022, the Brazilian Association of Technical Standards (ABNT) issued a set of recommended practices called PR 2030,[3] incorporating the three ESG thematic axes (environmental, social, and governance). Each axis comprises a series of themes and their respective criteria. The environmental axis explores topics such as climate change, water resources, biodiversity and ecosystem services, circular economy and waste management, environmental management, and pollution prevention. The social axis deals with issues such as social dialogue and territorial development, human rights and diversity, equity and inclusion, labor relations and practices, as well as the promotion of social responsibility within the value chain. And lastly, the governance axis discusses corporate governance, business conduct, management practices and controls, as well as transparency in management.

Furthermore, the standard provides an indicator, based on a model in which it is possible to identify which stage of maturity the organization is at within the ESG agenda. There are five stages, ranging from "elementary" to "integrative," the maximum point of the indicator. The ABNT rule also addresses the requirement of double materiality. It is recommended that materiality analysis be used within the following two perspectives: impacts that the organization's activities generate on

[3] The content of the ABNT PR 2030 regulation can be consulted at https://www.abntcatalogo.com.br/. Accessed on April 10, 2026.

people, the economy, society, and the environment (impact materiality) or impacts related to the risks and opportunities that these agents can generate on the organization, affecting its ability to generate value (financial materiality).

Still within the realm of ABNT regulations, PR 2060 was approved in July 2023 with the aim of regulating Brazilian criteria to assess corporate carbon neutrality plans. The document contains requirements to be met by any company or entity seeking to demonstrate carbon neutrality by quantifying, reducing, and offsetting greenhouse gas (GHG) emissions from a uniquely identified object. The ABNT regulation is aligned, for example, with the proposal approved by the European Commission and the European Parliament on March 27, 2024, Directive (EU) 2024/825,[4] which aims to strengthen the rights of consumers and to empower them in the transition to more sustainable consumption practices. The European proposal also states that products cannot be advertised as carbon neutral if this neutrality is based solely on compensation schemes involving carbon credits. While the ABNT standards do not have the force of law, they are validated in many Brazilian judicial precedents as references for conduct to be adopted in the event of a specific legal gap on the subject, so ultimately they become expected standards of behavior for companies operating in Brazil.

In the field of Brazilian financial institutions, the increase in requirements and standards aligned with the ESG agenda has also been notable over the last few years. The Federation of Brazilian Banks (FEBRABAN) approved a new regulation in March 2023 determining that banks subjected to self-regulation codes of practice will require their meat processing customers in the Legal Amazon to implement a traceability and monitoring system by December 2025, which will allow them to demonstrate that they have not purchased cattle associated with illegal deforestation from either direct or indirect suppliers. The measure provides that companies without comprehensive supply chain traceability will no longer be able to receive credit as of January 2026. Membership in financial institutions is voluntary. In total, 21 banks have adhered to the regulations, including relevant institutions in agribusiness financing, such as Bradesco, Itaú, Banco do Brasil, and Sicredi.[5]

Furthermore, starting in July 2024, the International Sustainability Standards Board (ISSB) will assume responsibility for monitoring the Task Force on Climate-Related Financial Disclosures (TCFD), replacing the role of the Financial Stability Board (FSB). In June 2023, the ISSB issued two standards—IFRS S1 and IFRS S2—that set a new stage for sustainability-related disclosures in capital markets around the world. A standardized reporting language was also created to disclose how climate-related risks and opportunities can impact the financial performance of the companies. On October 20, 2023, the Brazilian Securities Commission (CVM) published CVM Resolution 193, allowing public companies, investment funds, and

[4] The content of directive 2024/825 can be found at https://eur-lex.europa.eu/eli/dir/2024/825/oj. Accessed on April 10, 2026.

[5] Italo Bertão Filho "Meat processing plants begin to disclose animal tracking information in the Amazon" https://capitalreset.uol.com.br/agronegocio/pecuaria/frigorificos-comecam-a-divulgar-rastreio-de-animais-na-amazonia/. Accessed April 10, 2026.

securitization companies—on a voluntary basis—to prepare and disclose reports related to sustainability based on the international standards (IFRS S1 and S2) issued by the ISSB.[6]

In order to contribute to the development of the Sustainable Brazilian Taxonomy, which the Brazilian government has drawn up as part of its proposal to implement the Ecological Transformation Plan, FEBRABAN's current taxonomy is being updated so as to have a greater interface with the federal initiative, incorporating specific demands and needs of the sector, such as supporting the transition plans of the institutions.

Under the Ministry of Economy's Sustainable Finance Taxonomy, the Brazilian federal government also launched parameters in 2024 to mobilize and redirect capital flows toward the investments needed to combat the climate crisis.[7] This document encompasses a classification system that defines activities, assets, and project categories that contribute to climate, environmental, and/or social objectives, providing specific criteria and indicators that make it possible to assess whether an activity contributes to sustainability and/or the transition to a sustainable economy, based on the definitions of the International Capital Markets Association (ICMA). This taxonomy aims not only to indicate which investment is an accelerator of the climate transition but also to ensure that the process of tackling it takes place democratically, generating jobs and other sources of income, promoting competitiveness and productivity, tackling environmental and climate challenges, and reducing inequality in all its dimensions.

In a world where financial markets are essential for financing the energy transition to a low-carbon economy, the main strategic objectives of Brazil's Sustainable Taxonomy are as follows: (1) mobilizing and redirecting public and private investments toward sustainable, inclusive, and regenerative economic activities with positive environmental, social, and climate impacts and (2) fostering technological advancements that promote environmental, social, and economic sustainability while enhancing the productivity and competitiveness of the Brazilian economy in a sustainable manner. These macro- and microeconomic goals also aim to create the basis for producing reliable information on sustainable financial flows by encouraging transparency, integrity, and a long-term perspective for economic and financial activity while serving as a means to monitor and implement the full strategy of transforming Brazil to a carbon-neutral economy.

The taxonomy sets out the following climate objectives: mitigating and adapting to climate change; protecting and restoring biodiversity and ecosystems; promoting the sustainable use and conservation of land; managing and making sustainable use

---

[6] Brazil is the first country in the world to adopt financial information reports related to sustainability issued by the ISSB: Commission of Securities (CVM): https://www.gov.br/cvm/pt-br/assuntos/noticias/brasil-e-1o-pais-no-mundo-a-adotar-relatorio-de-informacoes-financeiras-relacionadas-a-sustentabilidade-emitidas-pelo-issb. Accessed on April 10, 2026.

[7] Information about the Brazilian green finance taxonomy can be found at https://www.gov.br/fazenda/pt-br/orgaos/spe/taxonomia-sustentavel-brasileira/materiais-do-plano-de-acao. Accessed on April 10, 2026.

of forests; ensuring the sustainable use and protection of water and marine resources; transitioning to a truly circular economy; and preventing and controlling the contamination and deterioration of natural resources. In addition, it outlines socioeconomic objectives of great importance in our Federal Constitution: the generation of dignified work and higher incomes; the reduction of socioeconomic inequalities, taking into account racial and gender aspects; the reduction of regional and territorial inequalities; as well as promoting a higher quality of life, guaranteeing rights, and expanding access to basic social services, thus promoting a green economy focused on the balance resulting from sustainable development and the well-being of society.

On June 27, 2022, the Superintendence of Private Insurance (SUSEP) published Circular 666, which sets out the sustainability requirements to be met by insurers, open supplementary pension entities (EAPCs), capitalization companies, and local reinsurers.[8] The SUSEP standard requires supervised entities to implement the following: sustainability risk management (environmental, social, and climate), a sustainability policy, and a sustainability report. The sustainability risk management must be integrated into the risk management structure and operational processes, particularly with regard to risk pricing and underwriting, the selection of investments and service providers, and may establish risk concentration limits and/or restrictions on doing business. Should supervised bodies fail to comply with the provisions of the standard, SUSEP may apply the sanctions provided for in the regulations or, alternatively, call for plans to correct the deficiencies found.

Also among those regulations without the force of law, but which positively impact compliance with ESG standards in Brazil, is the widespread adherence of public[9] and private companies in the country to the sustainable development objectives of the United Nations 2030 Agenda.[10]

The Brazilian Judiciary itself signed an agreement with the United Nations in 2019, aligning itself with its objectives. Since then, a robust movement demanding the implementation of these objectives has gained momentum within all Brazilian judicial bodies.[11] Judicial proceedings in Superior Courts, such as the Supreme Court and the Superior Court of Justice, are classified according to the objectives of

---

[8] Brazilian SUSEP Circular 666 of 2022 can be consulted at https://www.greenfinanceplatform.org/policies-and-regulations/circular-susep-no-666-de-27-de-junho-de-2022-regulation-no-6662022#:~:text=In%20June%202022%2C%20the%20Brazilian,effective%20on%201%20August%202022. Accessed on April 10, 2026.

[9] Many Brazilian cities, such as São Paulo, have action plans to implement the objectives of the 2030 Agenda and use the agenda's goals and indicators as a benchmark for fulfilling their management initiatives: https://www.prefeitura.sp.gov.br/cidade/secretarias/governo/planejamento/agenda_2030/. Accessed on April 10, 2026.

[10] The Brazilian support service for Brazilian micro and small companies (SEBRAE) is one of the many institutions that uses the objectives of the 2030 Agenda as a guideline for conduct: https://sebrae.com.br/sites/PortalSebrae/estudos_pesquisas/saiba-como-o-sebrae-contribui-para-a-agenda-2030,9d71d3cec7310610VgnVCM1000004c00210aRCRD. Accessed on April 10, 2026.

[11] The Brazilian National Council of Justice (CNJ) maintains a dedicated web portal for tracking progress on the Agenda's objectives: https://www.cnj.jus.br/programas-e-acoes/agenda-2030/. Accessed on April 10, 2026.

the 2030 Agenda that they are debating in every case.[12,13] Among the national goals of the Judiciary since 2020 is Goal 9, which calls on the Judiciary's network of innovation laboratories to develop innovative projects that can result in improved delivery of justice and achievement of sustainable development objectives.[14]

In addition to voluntary regulations and initiatives that rely on optional adherence, laws have been passed in Brazil that has advanced the conversion of ESG standards into legally binding obligations. The next section will focus on these.

3 The Scenario of New Brazilian Laws and Their Adherence to ESG Standards

The past decade has seen a growing movement in Brazil to enact laws that endorse ESG standards. This is key in giving the ESG agenda the normative force it needs to be enforced by administrative authorities or judicial bodies. Some relevant laws that have been introduced and that fulfill exactly this objective of making the ESG agenda mandatory in the country will be discussed below.

In the wake of demands from the corporate sector, as well as in reaction to street demonstrations demanding an "end to corruption," the Brazilian Congress enacted Law No. 12,864/2013, a landmark bill meant to improve practices in the corporate environment.[15] Known as the "Anti-Corruption Law," it provides not only sanctions for companies involved in corruption but also the possibility of reducing the penalties if companies adopt compliance programs as a risk management principle. The law assists companies in preventing fraud, regulating internal company processes, and monitoring the behavior of suppliers. More recently, companies have been required to address yet another aspect of compliance and governance, which is the protection of digital data. Since 2018, the General Data Protection Law (LGPD, Federal Law number 13.709/2018[16]) has been in force, establishing a series of

[12] The Brazilian Supreme Court maintains an area on its website dedicated to the objectives of the 2030 Agenda and classifies all actions being judged by the Court according to the objectives: https://www.researchgate.net/publication/375471870_Automated_Labelling_of_Judicial_Controversies_Before_the_Brazilian_Supreme_Court_According_to_the_Sustainable_Development_Goals. Accessed on April 10, 2026.

[13] The Superior Court of Justice (STJ) also maintains an area on its website dedicated to the objectives of the 2030 Agenda and classifies all actions being judged by the Court according to the objectives: https://www.stj.jus.br/sites/portalp/Paginas/Comunicacao/Noticias/29062021-Hotsite-traz-evolucao-das-iniciativas-do-STJ-em-prol-da-Agenda-2030-da-ONU.aspx. Accessed on April 10, 2026.

[14] Information about Goal 9 of the Brazilian Judiciary can be consulted at https://www.athensjournals.gr/law/2022-1-X-Y-Dias.pdf. Accessed on April 10, 2026.

[15] Law 12,864/2013 can be consulted at https://www.legiscompliance.com.br/legislacao/norma/29. Accessed on April 10, 2026.

[16] Law 13,709/2018 can be consulted at https://www.gov.br/anpd/pt-br/centrais-de-conteudo/outros-documentos-e-publicacoes-institucionais/lgpd-en-lei-no-13-709-capa.pdf. Accessed on April

requirements for the proper processing of personal data. In 2022, Constitutional Amendment 115 was enacted, which inserted section LXXIX into the list of fundamental rights and guarantees in Article 5 of the Federal Constitution: "The right to the protection of personal data, including in digital media, is guaranteed, under the terms of the law."

A Deloitte survey shows a significant increase in Brazilian companies prioritizing ethical conduct. Between 2016 and 2018, 40% adopted internal compliance policies and dedicated departments for achieving integrity goals. This number jumped to 70% by 2022.[17] Companies that adopt strong ESG practices benefit from a system that prevents wrongdoing, potentially reduces fines, and attracts investors, particularly international ones. These benefits for senior management and shareholders explain why a recent survey conducted by Transparency International Brazil and Quaest, involving 100 of the 250 largest Brazilian companies, revealed that 95% of respondents support the Anti-Corruption Law.[18]

In the field of gender equality, Brazil's Federal Constitution and Consolidation of Labor Laws (CLT) guarantee equal pay for women and men. Federal Law 14,611/2023 strengthens these rights by promoting equal pay for equivalent work, combating salary discrimination, and ensuring women receive fair wages equal to men's for the same job.[19]

Furthermore, the Brazilian Congress has historically responded to traumatic national events that inflict disproportionate hardship on specific communities and regions. Two recent catastrophic mining dam collapses, in Brumadinho and Mariana, both located in the state of Minas Gerais, prompted the enactment of a new law aimed at preventing such tragedies. While not the primary intention of lawmakers, such regulations, a reactive response to concrete events, ultimately reinforce the ESG agenda.

This was the case with the December 2023 reform to the National Civil Defense Policy (Law 12,608/2012), which marks a significant step toward environmental and social responsibility for corporations that cause disasters. The new section of the law is called the Management of Accidents and Disasters Induced by Human Action[20] and establishes a series of duties for the public or private sector, based on

10, 2026.

[17] The survey carried out by Deloitte in 2022 can be consulted at https://www2.deloitte.com/br/pt/pages/risk/articles/integridade-corporativa-evolucao-do-compliance.html. Accessed on April 10, 2026.

[18] The survey carried out by Transparência Internacional Brazil and Quaest can be consulted at https://transparenciainternacional.org.br/posts/lei-anticorrupcao-e-aprovada-pelas-maiores-empresas-brasileiras-mas-sistemas-de-integridade-ainda-sao-considerados-imaturos/. Accessed on April 10, 2026.

[19] Law 14,611 of 2023 can be consulted at https://www.ibanet.org/brazil-new-equal-pay-law#:~:text=In%20July%202023%2C%20the%20Brazilian%20government%20approved,big%20step%20towards%20gender%20parity%20in%20Brazil. Accessed on April 10, 2026.

[20] Law 12,608/2012 can be consulted at https://www.planalto.gov.br/ccivil_03/_ato2011-2014/2012/lei/l12608.htm. Accessed on April 10, 2026.

their project's risk of accident or disaster, as defined by authorities. These duties include adopting measures to prevent accidents or disasters, which includes conducting risk analyses prior to the implementation of the project or activity, as well as any modification or expansion of the project during its operation. Additionally, a contingency plan or another related document must be prepared and implemented for activities and undertakings involving high risks of accidents or disasters. Finally, the law requires companies to allocate resources for project safety and to compensate for any damage to human life, the environment, and public property in case of accidents or disasters.

The law further clarifies the responsibilities of those responsible for a given business or activity in the event of an imminent accident or disaster, which includes (a) issuing advance warnings to the population for immediate evacuation of potentially affected areas; (b) monitoring the situation and providing technical advice to public authorities in all disaster response actions and, specifically, guaranteeing relief and assistance to those affected; (c) providing temporary residence to affected people and promoting the reconstruction of residences destroyed or damaged by the disaster or, as the case may be, paying for public authorities to promote the resettlement and ensure permanent housing in a suitable location for people who were forced to permanently abandon their homes due to the disaster; (d) offering specialized care to those affected, with a view to full social reintegration; (e) recovering the degraded area and making full reparation for civil and environmental damage; (f) paying compensation or providing priority and continued assistance to the physical and mental health of those affected by disasters, in addition to that provided by public authorities; and (g) paying for independent technical advice, of a multidisciplinary nature, chosen by the affected communities and without interference from the company, with the aim of guiding them and promoting their informed participation in the entire process of full reparation for the damages sustained. The resettlement of the displaced people will be carried out by the public authorities and will be monitored by an independent, multidisciplinary consultancy, paid for by the company, through negotiation with the affected community.

Consolidating many principles set out in international standards on human rights and corporate activities, Federal Decree 9571/2018 internalizes in Brazil the principles of corporate responsibility in the area of human rights.[21] The Decree confirmed the existence of effective legal standards to hold corporate executives accountable for their actions along the entire production chain. It provides guidelines on human rights to be adopted by large and small, national and multinational companies operating in Brazil and requires assertive action to be taken across their chain of operations.

[21] The content of Decree 9571/2018 can be consulted at https://climate-laws.org/document/decree-9-571-2018-establishing-national-guidelines-on-business-and-human-rights_ce6b, and the content of Decree 11,772/2023 which establishes the Interministerial Working Group to prepare a proposal for the National Human Rights and Business Policy can be consulted at https://www.planalto.gov.br/ccivil_03/_Ato2023-2026/2023/Decreto/D11772.htm#art10. Accessed on April 10, 2026.

In November 2023, Decree 9.578 was revoked by the federal government. However, it should be mentioned that this was prompted by the creation of an inter-ministerial task force that will develop a new standard to create a National Policy on Human Rights in the Business Sector. The guidelines for drafting this policy will be (I) improving the effectiveness of current sectoral programs and public policies related to the defense and promotion of human rights in the corporate sector; (II) encouraging the implementation of corporate mechanisms to prevent human rights violations; (III) monitoring business activities to ensure compliance with human rights obligations; and (IV) aligning with the United Nations Sustainable Development Goals.

In the next section, we will analyze how Brazilian courts, guided by rulings and norms issued mainly by the National Council of Justice, are playing a crucial role in promoting the implementation of ESG standards.

4 The Support of ESG Standards by Brazilian Courts

A fundamental step to ensure that regulatory and legal advances in ESG standard requirements can be applied in Brazil is the support provided by the decisions handed down by the courts. On this point, it is essential to understand that the Brazilian Judiciary, in addition to its legal tradition of civil law, is strongly influenced by the precedents of international and regional courts, as well as by its own judicial decisions classified as having "general repercussion," that is, the principle whereby a prior decision establishes precedent for subsequent claims. Therefore, recent decisions such as those handed down by the European Court of Human Rights in the case *KlimaSeniorinnen v. Switzerland*,[22] recognizing that a state must have an executable climate ambition plan under penalty of violating human rights, as well as the decision by the International Tribunal for the Law of the Sea in the opinion consultancy on the duties to combat climate change based on the Convention of the Law of the Sea,[23] will certainly influence Brazilian courts in future judgments.

For context, the decision of the International Tribunal for the Law of the Sea reinforced the duty of due diligence that states must demand from those whose conduct may cause significant damage to the marine environment, recognizing that GHG emissions are pollutants. This decision bears a relevant parallel with the recent decision of the Inter-American Court of Human Rights in the Peruvian case

[22] Information about the case can be found at https://climatecasechart.com/non-us-case/union-of-swiss-senior-women-for-climate-protection-v-swiss-federal-council-and-others/. Accessed on April 10, 2026.

[23] ITLOS. Commission of Small Islands States on Climate Change and International Law. Request for advisory opinion submitted by the Commission of Small Island States on Climate Change and International Law: https://www.itlos.org/en/main/cases/list-of-cases/request-for-an-advisory-opinion-submitted-by-the-commission-of-small-island-states-on-climate-change-and-international-law-request-for-advisory-opinion-submitted-to-the-tribunal/. Accessed on April 10, 2026.

Habitantes de La Oroya v. Peru,[24] where due diligence duties were also detailed and required.

In this sense, the Brazilian Judiciary has at least two norms published by its National Council of Justice that order Brazilian courts to control conventionality and respect the precedents of the Inter-American Court of Human Rights: Recommendation 123,[25] from 2022, and the most recent one, Resolution 544, from January 2024.[26] These decisions foresee that the courts will create Monitoring and Inspection Units for decisions of the local Inter-American Human Rights System (local FMUs) with a view to strengthening the exchange of information and ensuring the implementation of rulings from the Inter-American Court. Indeed, Brazil recently hosted public hearings of the Inter-American Court within the scope of the advisory opinion on the duties of states in response to the climate emergency, and this decision by the IACtHR is also bound to directly influence judges in Brazil.[27]

Even before that decision from the Inter-American Court in the advisory opinion on the climate emergency, or the decision awaited by the International Court of Justice due to the consensual adoption of Resolution A/77/L.58 in the United Nations General Assembly,[28] the Brazilian Supreme Court had already handed down landmark decisions on the topic of climate change. In ADPF 708, the so-called Climate Fund case, the Supreme Court recognized that the Paris Agreement is a human rights treaty and that it has supralegal force in the country.[29] The decision recognized that Brazil must fulfill its share of the mitigation effort to achieve the goal set out in the agreement. This decision implies that the entire Brazilian legal regime, as well as the actions of public and private entities, is subject to judicial scrutiny from the perspective of whether or not they comply with the mitigation agenda that has legal force in Brazil.

This judgment adds to other recent Supreme Court decisions[30] that interpret the constitutional text (mainly Article 225) and state that Brazil is conceived as an eco-

---

[24] The statement of the Inter-American Court's decision in the case *Habitantes de La Oroya v. Peru* can be consulted at https://www.corteidh.or.cr/docs/comunicados/cp_17_2024.pdf. Accessed on April 10, 2026.

[25] Recommendation 123 of the National Council of Justice can be consulted at https://atos.cnj.jus.br/atos/detalhar/4305. Accessed on April 10, 2026.

[26] Resolution 544 of the National Council of Justice can be consulted at https://atos.cnj.jus.br/atos/detalhar/5403. Accessed on April 10, 2026.

[27] The request for an advisory opinion on the duties of States in matters of climate emergency was made in January 2023 by Colombia and Chile and can be consulted at https://www.corteidh.or.cr/docs/opiniones/soc_1_2023_es.pdf. Accessed on April 10, 2026.

[28] The progress and judgment of the advisory opinion on the duties of States in response to climate change by the International Court of Justice can be followed at https://www.icj-cij.org/case/187. Accessed on April 10, 2026.

[29] The decision handed down by the Brazilian Supreme Court in the ADPF 708 case (*PSB* et al *v. Brazil*), can be consulted at https://www.climatecasechart.com/document/psb-et-al-v-brazil-on-deforestation-and-human-rights_d678. Accessed on April 10, 2026.

[30] The so-called Green Agenda comprises seven cases related to environmental protection and sustainable development in Brazil. Three of these cases are climate related and concern the federal

logical democracy (May et al. 2024) and that the understanding of environmental protection has evolved to encompass climate change (de Carvalho and da Rosa 2023). The Court also recognizes that Brazil must respect and pursue the transnational goals of decarbonization and energy transition to which it has committed.

Another major decision was the ruling of the Declaratory Action of Unconstitutionality by Inaction (ADO) 59,[31] which had a strong climate focus. In this case, the government's inaction in relation to fulfilling its environmental protection duties in the Amazon Fund case was contested. According to the ruling, the 1988 Federal Constitution determines and obliges the state to protect the climate by preserving its forests. The decision emphasized that these duties are of particular importance as they are social and environmental rights and as such require normative and practical actions for their enforcement. The first paragraph of Article 5 in the Federal Constitution requires the executive branch to create the necessary conditions for the effective implementation of these rights by means of norms and concrete measures.

No less important was the vote cast by Supreme Court Justice Cármen Lucia in the judgment ADPF 760,[32] *PSB* et al. *v. Brazil* (on deforestation and human rights), in which she referred to Brazil as an ecological constitutional state, emphasizing that the protection of the environment is a matter of planetary scope and that it is the duty of the state and society to ensure ecological balance for present and future generations. Environmental dignity is seen as a central element of contemporary constitutionalism and must consider not only the dignity of the human person but also the dignity of the human species and the preservation of the environment as a whole. Environmental ethics is seen as an essential principle to guarantee the respectful coexistence between human beings and nature. With the ruling, the Brazilian Supreme Court adopted parameters that were already national climate commitments under international treaties and incorporated them as central elements of Brazil's constitutional interpretation regarding climate change commitments and the United Nations 2030 Agenda.

Specifically in the field of liability for environmental damage, Brazilian courts have a uniform understanding that this damage has an objective nature and carries a duty of full reparation. In 2023, the National Council of Justice (CNJ) approved

---

government and government actions that allegedly contravene the constitutional right to an ecologically balanced environment. The cases are as follows: the Direct Action for Fundamental Rights (ADPF) 708, the ADPF 760, and the Declaratory Action of Unconstitutionality by Inaction (ADO) 59. In these cases, the initial petition and votes refer to climate impacts, according to the IPCC reports, the Paris Agreement, and the UN Agenda 2030 Sustainable Development Goals.

[31] Brazil. Federal Court of Justice. Declaratory Action of Unconstitutionality by Inaction (ADO) 59/ DF. Justice Rosa Weber. Jurisprudence Research, Judgments. 08/24/2023. Available at https://www.climatecasechart.com/document/psb-et-al-v-brazil-on-amazon-fund_f10a. Accessed on April 10, 2026.

[32] Brazil. Federal Court of Justice. Allegation of Non-compliance with Fundamental Precept (ADPF) 760. Rapporteur: Justice Cármen Lúcia. Jurisprudence Research, Judgments. 04/10/2021. Available at https://scholarlycommons.law.case.edu/cgi/viewcontent.cgi?article=2684&context=jil. Accessed on April 10, 2026.

Recommendation 145, which instructs Brazilian judges to apply a specific protocol when judging environmental actions.[33] Among the relevant measures of the protocol is the validation of the use of satellite images and remote sensing as sufficient evidence to condemn conduct such as deforestation and forest fires. Furthermore, Resolution 433, from 2021, also from the National Council of Justice, mandates Brazilian judges to observe whether, in the cases under consideration, there was respect for free, prior, and informed consultation of indigenous peoples and traditional communities, as provided for in Convention 169 of the International Labor Organization. Article 14 of the Resolution also stipulates that Brazilian courts, in cases involving environmental damage, must consider the impact of the damage on global climate change in their decision, factoring climate damage into the total compensation stipulated.[34,35]

The role of the judiciary in labor disputes is also raising the bar for foreign companies to respect ESG standards. A recent example was the condemnation of the Cargill group by the Judiciary of the State of Bahia, due to proven practices of subjecting workers to conditions analogous to slavery, as well as employing child labor.[36] The action against the multinational was filed in 2021 by a group of prosecutors dedicated to combating child labor and slavery. The lawsuit included reports that revealed cases of slave labor or child labor among Cargill's suppliers. In the ruling, the judge argued that the defendant (Cargill) was not being held directly to account for the labor rights violations observed throughout the cocoa production chain. Rather, the claim and the sentence were made from the perspective that the company, given its power of control and influence, should not omit itself in light of the existing reality (working conditions analogous to slavery and child labor) and which tends to perpetuate itself if effective action is not duly taken.

The court not only ordered Cargill to pay out damages but also to formalize contracts with cocoa producers and suppliers within 30 days, including social clauses against the use of child labor. The multinational was given 60 days to create a control mechanism "within its purchasing departments." The sentence also ordered the company to create a permanent advertising campaign against child and slave labor within 3 years.

In another representative action, the Federal Prosecutor's Office (MPF) investigated Swiss commodities giant Glencore, along with companies Vitol and Trafigura,

[33] Recommendation 145 of 2023 of the National Council of Justice can be consulted at https://atos.cnj.jus.br/atos/detalhar/5278. Accessed on April 11, 2026.

[34] Resolution 433 of 2021 of the National Council of Justice can be consulted at https://atos.cnj.jus.br/atos/detalhar/4214. Accessed on April 11, 2026.

[35] Regarding the concept of climate damage and the premises for its liability, see ROSA, Rafaela Santos Martins da. Dano Climático: conceito, pressupostos e responsabilização. São Paulo: Tirant Lo Blanch Publisher, Second Edition, 2024.

[36] Details about the ruling against the multinational Cargill can be found at https://duediligence.design/cargill-liable-for-child-and-forced-labour-in-cocoa-supply-chain/#:~:text=Cargill%20ruling,for%20%E2%80%9Ccollective%20moral%20damages%E2%80%9D. Accessed on April 10, 2026.

for paying millions in bribes to Petrobras employees during Operation Lava Jato. The kickback scheme involved around 160 transactions related to purchase and sale operations of oil and petroleum derivatives, in addition to rental contracts of fuel storage tanks between 2009 and 2014. At the beginning of 2022, the company signed a leniency agreement with Petrobras to pay the state-owned company US$39.6 million for acts of corruption.[37]

Future cases will likely serve as a testing ground for how these regulatory, legal, and judicial decisions are applied in practice, particularly regarding mandatory ESG compliance.

5 Expected Conflicts in Implementing ESG Standards in Brazil

The implementation of renewable energy projects can have unintended consequences for the biomes in which they are deployed. A central problem involves the transmission lines associated with such projects. For instance, the Annual Deforestation Report (RAD),[38] released by MapBiomas, revealed that in 2022 more than 4000 hectares of the caatinga biome were deforested due to wind and solar energy plants, primarily for the construction of transmission lines. The caatinga biome, the only genuinely Brazilian biome, is the most suitable for the implementation of solar or wind energy. However, it is also a **highly effective carbon sink**, playing a crucial role in mitigating climate change (Mendes et al. 2020). We therefore face a significant contradiction when companies, many of which are international operations, promote their commitment to ESG principles, but their renewable energy projects result in the destruction of unique biomes known for their high carbon sequestration capacity. Not surprisingly, this shift to green energy[39] has raised concerns about the potential for greenwashing in the industry.[40]

Other emerging conflicts in Brazil involve the voluntary carbon market. The Pará State Public Defender's Office is prosecuting national and foreign companies that

[37] For reporting on the leniency agreement signed by the Swiss company Glencore, see https://economia.uol.com.br/noticias/redacao/2022/05/24/acordo-mpf-empresa-paga-us-396-mi-petrobras.htm. Accessed on April 10, 2026.

[38] Mapbiomas Alerta. Autoria de LAMA, Carolina Del et al. *Relatório Anual do Desmatamento no Brasil—RAD 2023*. Available at https://storage.googleapis.com/alerta-public/rad_2023/RAD2023_COMPLETO_FINAL_28-05-24.pdf. Accessed on April 10, 2026.

[39] Costa, Heitor Scalambrini. "Negócios do vento" no Nordeste brasileiro: caso a investigar. *Instituto Humanas Unisinos*; *Adital*. 28 de março 2018. Available at https://www.ihu.unisinos.br/publicacoes/78-noticias/577430-negocios-do-vento-no-nordeste-brasileiro-caso-a-investigar. Accessed on April 10, 2026.

[40] Damasio, Kevin. Expansão da energia eólica e solar no Nordeste promove desmatamento e gera conflitos entre empresas e comunidades. *Instituto Humanas Unisinos; Adital*. 29 de janeiro 2024. Available at https://www.ihu.unisinos.br/categorias/636296-caatinga-vive-o-dilema-da-transicao-energetica-justa. Accessed on April 10, 2026.

operate in that state on suspicion of grabbing public lands and using invalid documents. Four public civil lawsuits were filed at the State Court against the companies and the municipality of Portel, which is accused of authorizing construction projects on public lands traditionally used by local communities. The Public Defender's Office alleges that four companies are operating in protected areas with REDD+ projects overlapping an area of five state agroextractive settlements: RMDLT Property Group Ltda (194,000 hectares), Avoided Deforestation Project Manaus Limited (ADPML) (148,000 hectares), Brazil Agfor, LLC (165,000 hectares), and Amigos dos Ribeirinhos of the Union of Rural Producers of Portel (205,000 hectares).[41] The Public Defender's Office alleges that these projects, operated primarily by foreign companies, generated and sold carbon credits on preserved areas without the settlers' knowledge or consent. The complaint further states that the credits were certified using Rural Environmental Registries (CAR) obtained from the settlers. These settlers were allegedly misled into believing that the document would grant them definitive title to the land.

In June 2024, the Brazilian Federal Police carried out Operation Greenwashing in the state of Rondônia, aiming to dismantle a criminal organization focused on the irregular sale of carbon credits in the voluntary market. The investigation revealed a land fraud scheme that spanned more than a decade and started in Lábrea, state of Amazon, involving the duplication and forgery of property titles. These frauds resulted in the illegal appropriation of around 538,000 hectares of public lands. The criminal organization expanded its illicit activities, reusing property titles, and entering false data into the Land Management System (SIGEF), with the collaboration of public workers and external professionals responsible for signing off the paperwork. The irregularities identified include the issuance of false certificates by an official within the Amazonas State Land Secretariat (SECT/AM), the overlapping of land titles, and the misappropriation of public lands.[42] Among the illegal activities identified are forestry and livestock within protected areas, including "ghost" cattle raised to circumvent environmental restrictions, in addition to the sale of fraudulent timber credits and environmental licenses.

These cases have not yet been judged on their merits but ought to be monitored, as they will signal the position of courts on issues such as the validity of land ownership documents in REDD projects and the requirement to obtain the consent of the communities affected by these voluntary carbon market projects. Foreign companies intending to operate in Brazil with projects such as wind energy and voluntary carbon markets must closely monitor the legal developments in these cases, as they will define the expected level of compliance requirements.

---

[41] These cases have not yet been decided but can be monitored in the database of Brazilian climate disputes maintained by the Rio Grande do Sul Federal Court project, JusClima2030: https://jusclima2030.jfrs.jus.br/litigio/. Accessed on April 10, 2026.

[42] Information about the operation and the companies involved can be found at https://www.gov.br/pf/pt-br/assuntos/noticias/2024/06/pf-deflagra-operacao-greenwashing-para-investigar-venda-irregular-de-creditos-de-carbono. Accessed on April 10, 2026.

6 Final Considerations

Brazil's unique environmental, social, and economic particularities result in a distinct set of challenges and opportunities for ESG adoption. Progress in implementing these standards hinges on a combination of factors: the self-regulatory environment, existing laws, and judicial decision-making. The latter two elements serve to reinforce the normative force of ESG principles, ultimately strengthening their implementation potential.

Below we will discuss some of these particularities in more detail:

6.1 Biodiversity and Environmental Preservation

Boasting the world's greatest biodiversity and unique biomes such as the Amazon and Atlantic Forest, Pantanal, Cerrado, Pampa, and Caatinga, Brazil requires robust policies for forest conservation and the protection of endemic fauna and flora. The country's exceptional biodiversity is crucial not only for its own well-being but also for the global ecological balance. Sustainable exploitation of these resources is essential to maintain healthy ecosystems and prevent environmental degradation.

6.2 Energy and Sustainability Issues

Brazil has high potential for renewable energy, especially hydroelectric, wind, and solar power. However, the transition to a renewable-based energy system and ensuring universal access to clean energy involve other challenges. While Brazil's current energy supply sources are already among the cleanest in the world, further diversification and expansion of renewable sources are crucial for reducing dependence on fossil fuels and minimizing environmental impacts.

6.3 Social Responsibility and Inclusion

Brazil faces significant social disparities, ranking among the most unequal countries in the world, with high rates of poverty and social exclusion. This reality necessitates a strong focus on social and economic inclusion within Brazil's ESG framework. Effective ESG policies must prioritize promoting equity, improving the quality of life for vulnerable communities, and guaranteeing access to essential services, such as education and healthcare.

6.4 Corporate Governance and the Challenge of Endemic Corruption

Brazil has a long history of political corruption and lawfare against those who fight against corruption, a persistent problem that erodes trust in institutions and businesses. This calls for a robust emphasis on transparency and anti-corruption measures within the Brazilian ESG framework. Strong corporate governance practices and a commitment to ethical conduct are essential to ensuring fair and transparent business operations.

6.5 Impact of Climate Change

Approximately 90% of Brazil's territory is susceptible to extreme weather events such as droughts and floods. We must also develop local initiatives to address the need for climate change adaptation and mitigation policies. The direct impact of climate change on economic activities and populations, particularly in rural areas and traditional communities, underscores the urgency of resilience strategies.

6.6 Relationship with Indigenous and Traditional Communities

Brazil is home to a significant population of indigenous and quilombola communities, representing nearly 1% of the national population. Many of these isolated groups require support to ensure their continued survival with dignity. The presence of these communities, with their distinct territorial and cultural rights, in addition to conflicts related to land use and natural resources, demands careful consideration. Developments near indigenous and quilombola territories, particularly those impacting rivers and water resources they rely on, require particular ESG scrutiny. Respecting and including these communities are not only fundamental for social justice and cultural preservation but also recognize them as valuable partners in environmental conservation.

6.7 Sustainable Development and Innovation

Although the country ranks among the world's leading deforesters and pesticide users, Brazil harbors immense potential for innovation in sustainable agriculture, biotechnology, and clean technologies. A central pillar of a genuinely Brazilian approach to ESG is the growing green entrepreneurship sector, where start-ups offer solutions to environmental and social challenges. By fostering innovation in these areas, Brazil can address its environmental and social concerns while promoting sustainable and inclusive economic growth, particularly in rural areas. This growth must prioritize respect for traditional communities and avoid land use practices that lead to agrarian conflict or the illegal use of public lands.

6.8 The Role of the Brazilian Judiciary in ESG Enforcement

Access to justice and the right to take legal action are fundamental rights in Brazil. This translates to the judiciary playing a crucial role in ensuring the implementation of ESG standards. There is a growing trend of Brazilian judges strongly affirming the values of social, environmental, and governance sustainability. This is achieved by applying constitutional norms, adhering to international conventions, observing the decisions from the Inter-American Court of Human Rights, and extending transnational legal duties to all companies operating within the country.

References

Brazil. ABNT PR 2030 regulation can be consulted at. https://www.abntcatalogo.com.br/. Accessed 11 April 2026

Brazil. Law 14,611 of 2023 can be consulted at https://planalto.gov.br/ccivil_03//////_Ato2023-2026/2023/Lei/L14611.htm. Accessed 11 April 2026

Brazil. Law 12,608/2012 can be consulted https://www.planalto.gov.br/ccivil_03/_ato2011-2014/2012/lei/l12608.htm. Accessed 11 April 2026

Brazil. Decreto 9,571/2018 can be consulted at https://www.planalto.gov.br/ccivil_03/_ato2015-2018/2018/decreto/d9571.htm, and the content of Decree 11,772/2023 which establishes the Interministerial Working Group to prepare a proposal for the National Human Rights and Business Policy can be consulted at https://www.planalto.gov.br/ccivil_03/_Ato2023-2026/2023/Decreto/D11772.htm#art10. Accessed 11 April 2026

Brazil. Finance Minister. Green Finance Taxonomy. https://www.gov.br/fazenda/pt-br/orgaos/spe/taxonomia-sustentavel-brasileira/materiais-do-plano-de-acao. Accessed 11 April 2026

Brazil. SUSEP Circular 666 of 2022. https://www.greenfinanceplatform.org/policies-and-regulations/circular-susep-no-666-de-27-de-junho-de-2022-regulation-no-6662022#:~:text=In%20June%202022%2C%20the%20Brazilian,effective%20on%201%20August%202022. Accessed 11 April 2026

Brazil. National Council of Justice. Recommendation 123 can be consulted at https://atos.cnj.jus.br/atos/detalhar/4305. Accessed 11 April 2026

Brazil. National Council of Justice. Recommendation 145/2023 can be consulted at https://atos.cnj.jus.br/atos/detalhar/5278. Accessed 11 April 2026

Brazil. National Council of Justice. Resolution 544 can be consulted at. https://atos.cnj.jus.br/atos/detalhar/5403. Accessed 11 April 2026

Brazil. National Council of Justice. Resolution 433/2021 can be consulted at https://atos.cnj.jus.br/atos/detalhar/4214. Accessed 11 April 2026

Brasil. Brazilian Supreme Court (ADO) 59/DF. Rapporteur: Justice Rosa Weber. Pesquisa de Jurisprudência, Acórdãos. 24/08/2023. https://www.climatecasechart.com/document/psb-et-al-v-brazil-on-amazon-fund_f10. Accessed 11 April 2026

Brazil. Brazilian Suprem Court (ADPF) 708 case (PSB et al v. Brazil), can be consulted at https://www.climatecasechart.com/document/psb-et-al-v-brazil-on-deforestation-and-human-rights_d678. Accessed 11 April 2026

Brazil. Brazilian Supreme Court in the (ADPF) 760. Rapporteur: Justice Cármen Lúcia. Decided 04/10/2021. https://scholarlycommons.law.case.edu/cgi/viewcontent.cgi?article=2684&context=jil. Accessed 11 April 2026

Costa HS. "Negócios do vento" no Nordeste brasileiro: caso a investigar. Instituto Humanas Unisinos; Adital. 28 March 2018. https://www.ihu.unisinos.br/publicacoes/78-noticias/577430-negocios-do-vento-no-nordeste-brasileiro-caso-a-investigar. Accessed 11 April 2026

da Rosa RSM (2024) Dano Climático: conceito, pressupostos e responsabilização, 2ª edn. Tirant lo Blanch, São Paulo

Damasio K. Expansão da energia eólica e solar no Nordeste promove desmatamento e gera conflitos entre empresas e comunidades. Instituto Humanas Unisinos; Adital. 29 January 2024. https://www.ihu.unisinos.br/categorias/636296-caatinga-vive-o-dilema-da-transicao-energetica-justa. Accessed 11 April 2026

de Carvalho DW, da Rosa RSM (2023) Climate constitutionalism as a foundation for climate litigation in Latin America. J Hum Rights Pract 16:–71, 88. https://doi.org/10.1093/jhuman/huad055

Europe Commission. Directive 2024/825 can be found at https://eur-lex.europa.eu/eli/dir/2024/825/oj. Accessed 11 April 2026

European Court of Human Rights. Case KlimaSeniorinnen v. Switzerland. https://climatecasechart.com/non-us-case/union-of-swiss-senior-women-for-climate-protection-v-swiss-federal-council-and-others/. Accessed 11 April 2026

Flores BM, Montoya E, Sakschewski B et al (2024) Critical transitions in the Amazon forest system. Nature 626:555–564. https://doi.org/10.1038/s41586-023-06970-0

Inter-American Court. Case Habitantes de La Oroya v. Peru at https://www.corteidh.or.cr/docs/comunicados/cp_17_2024.pdf. Accessed 11 April 2026

ITLOS. Commission of Small Islands States on Climate Change and International Law. Request for advisory opinion submitted by the Commission of Small Island States on Climate Change and International Law. https://www.itlos.org/en/main/cases/list-of-cases/request-for-an-advisory-opinion-submitted-by-the-commission-of-small-island-states-on-climate-change-and-international-law-request-for-advisory-opinion-submitted-to-the-tribunal/. Accessed 11 April 2026

Mapbiomas Alerta. Autoria de LAMA, Carolina Del et al. Relatório Anual do Desmatamento no Brasil – RAD 2023. https://storage.googleapis.com/alerta-public/rad_2023/RAD2023_COMPLETO_FINAL_28-05-24.pdf. Accessed 11 April 2026

May J, Dantas M, Bauer L (2024) Climate rights in Brazil and the United States: a convergence in contrasts. Case West Res J Int Law 56:439. https://scholarlycommons.law.case.edu/jil/vol56/iss1/19/

Mendes KR et al (2020) Seasonal variation in net ecosystem CO2 exchange of a Brazilian seasonally dry tropical forest. Sci Rep 10:9454. https://doi.org/10.1038/s41598-020-66415-w. Accessed 11 April 2026

Luciana Bauer is an educator and legal scholar specializing in climate change, democracy, and human rights. She is a former federal judge in Brazil and an active member of Judges for Democracy Brazil, where she advocates for environmental and indigenous rights. She is currently pursuing a Ph.D. in Legal Science through a joint program between the University of Vale do Itajaí (Brazil) and Widener University (USA), with research focusing on climate law and governance.

Rafaela Santos Martins da Rosa is a federal judge in the Fourth Circuit of the Brazilian Federal Court. She holds a Ph.D. in Law from Unisinos and has been a visiting researcher at the University of California, Berkeley, and is currently a visiting senior fellow at the Grantham Research Institute for Climate Change at the London School of Economics. She is actively involved in judicial training on climate change law and contributes to national policy initiatives on environmental governance. She is also the author of *Climate Damage: Concept, Assumptions, and Accountability* (2024).

Smart Regulation in Palm Oil Governance: Enhancing the Implementation of ESG Principles in Indonesia

Kenny Cetera and Azam Hawari

Abstract With the rise of the green economy in Indonesia, palm oil industries are adapting their strategies to embrace environmentally sustainable practices. This includes the promotion of ethical and social values since extractive industries are often associated with human rights violations, such as labor exploitation and land grabbing. One of the mechanisms is to implement environmental, social, and governance (ESG) principles on the whole business operations. For private companies, reporting ESG is essential to capture the existing market trend, which is shifting to green products.

Utilizing the "smart regulation" concept, the chapter purports to scrutinize the potential of ESG implementation to help improve human rights and the environment and its interaction with relevant legal instruments. Smart regulation proposes the utilization of "mix" instruments beyond command-and-control instruments, such as economic instruments, voluntary standards, and industrial norms. Our analysis will first map out the existing regulations that govern or pertain to ESG basic tenets and values, especially in land use sectors.

This chapter discussed three categories of mixes, namely, state-based oversights, certification standards, and voluntary action. These mixes represent the interaction of widely accepted industrial norm and domestic laws, which essentially provide certain layers of human rights and environmental protection in palm oil sectors. Several incoherences were found among the instruments, hindering the application of smart regulations. Corporate social responsibility (CSR) as voluntary action has been overlooked and misunderstood as a compliance tool. Further, the recent issuance of the EU Deforestation Regulation (EUDR) can be a great momentum to enable a smart regulation ecosystem, considering its huge influence on producer countries like Indonesia.

K. Cetera (✉) · A. Hawari
Jakarta, Indonesia
e-mail: kenny.cetera@globalinitiative.net

S. Talukdar (ed.), *Law, Accountability, and Corporate Conduct*, New Approaches to Business, Human Rights and the Environment 1,
https://doi.org/10.1007/978-3-032-28714-4_6

1 Introduction

The global palm oil market size was estimated at USD 74.5 billion in 2024 and is projected to reach USD 113.9 billion by 2035.[1] About 85% of global palm oil productions comes from Indonesia and Malaysia, with the rests also coming from several African, South American, and Southeast Asian countries.[2] Palm oil producer countries are mostly dominated by those which belong to "Global South" group, which denotes a mix of political, geopolitical, and economic commonalities between nations.[3] Global South countries are also associated with "developing" countries, which have low or medium per capita income.[4]

With the growing market demand for addressing environmental, social, and governance issues (ESG), Global South countries, as major palm oil producers, are required to meet and enhance their ESG standards. Global consumers are increasingly recognizing the importance of fulfilling these standards and are demanding more socially and environmentally responsible investments. Palm oil industries are often associated with various social and environmental issues, such as land grabbing, human rights violations, deforestation, and more. The sector often faces pressure from nongovernmental organizations, the media, and the international community to adopt more sustainable practices. Transparency and accountability are key to ensuring that companies genuinely uphold their ESG commitments.

As one of the major palm oil producers globally, both the government and the private sector in Indonesia have initiated numerous preventive and compliance measures. For example, the government has implemented various regulations to reduce the negative impacts of the palm oil industry on social and environmental aspects, including a moratorium on new land clearances and business licenses for palm oil.[5] Companies are also beginning to adopt sustainability certifications, such as Roundtable on Sustainable Palm Oil (RSPO), to demonstrate their commitment to sustainable practices.[6]

However, implementation on the ground often encounters challenges. Numerous ESG violations persist among palm oil companies. For instance, many cases of indigenous land grabbing by palm oil companies are still reported in various regions. Just in October 2023, a local dweller died because of a deadly clash between police officers and local communities in Seruyan District, Central Kalimantan, Indonesia.[7] The overlapping land title between a palm oil concession and communities triggered the long-standing land conflict, which culminated in the clash. Hence, a local NGO called *Konsorsium Pembaruan Agraria* (Consortium for Agrarian Reform)

---

[1] See Grand View Research (2025).

[2] See Voora et al. (2023).

[3] See Heine (2023).

[4] See Davis and Pargendler (2025).

[5] See Aji (2019, pp. 187).

[6] See Pirard et al. (2015, pp. 2–3).

[7] See Progress et al. (2023).

documented 108 cases of land conflicts related to palm oil commodities just in 2023.[8] Often, this is driven by weak government oversight, the complexity of licensing and land use regulations, and insufficient human resources, compounded by corruption.

The purpose of this chapter is to analyze how different actors and legal norms interact and shape ESG implementation in the overall palm oil governance in Indonesia. Utilizing the "smart regulation" concept, the chapter purports to scrutinize the coherence among relevant legal instruments to achieve objectives related to ESG. The smart regulations concept, first introduced by Gunningham et al. (1998), proposes the utilization of "mix" instruments beyond command-and-control instruments, such as economic instruments, voluntary standards, and industrial norms.[9] The concept encourages the utilization of complementary instrument mixes over single instrument approaches while avoiding the risk of "smorgasbordism," namely, wrongly assuming that all instruments should be used rather than the minimum number necessary to achieve the desired results.[10] Subsequently, this research aims to answer two questions: (1) How are the interactions among multiple legal instruments in Indonesia that shape the environmental, social, and governance (ESG) principles in the oil palm sector? (2) How should we design the "smart regulation" concept to improve the implementation of ESG principles in the palm oil sector in Indonesia? What are the enabling factors?

Given the complexity of palm oil governance, we agree with the smart regulation idea that relying solely on command-and-control (CAC) instruments, or in simple terms, state-based law, is insufficient. Instead, an integrated approach is required. We will discuss several mixes of instruments representing the interaction of widely accepted industrial norms, domestic laws, and foreign laws, which collectively address various ESG objectives. Currently, our analysis found that those identified legal instruments are scattered and not well integrated, leading to overlapping regulations and standards that hinder the supervision and compliance process. This disharmony must be addressed through efforts to synchronize material aspects and law enforcement governance.

For instance, there is disharmony in forestry regulations regarding free, prior, and informed consent (FPIC) principles and challenges in integrating reporting mechanisms and enforcement. Achieving coherent supervision requires harmonizing these instruments so they complement rather than negate each other. The central argument of "smart regulation" suggests that using multiple policy instruments and involving a broader range of regulatory actors typically result in better regulation.[11] This approach allows for implementing complementary combinations of instruments and participants tailored to address specific issues. In essence, this approach demands a more imaginative, flexible, and pluralistic strategy for ESG regulation

[8] See Fitria (2024).

[9] See Gunningham and Grabosky (1998, pp. 4).

[10] Ibid.

[11] Ibid, pp. 8–9.

than has been adopted in most jurisdictions. The subsequent sections of this chapter will apply this notion to Indonesia's palm oil governance, outlining how existing regimes can be implemented using the smart regulation concept to ensure compliance by palm oil companies operating in Indonesia.

After the introduction, the next section will discuss the notion of ESG and smart regulation, as well as elaborate on the Achilles heel of relying solely on CAC or state-based law on palm oil sectors. Section 3 will then examine three categories of available ESG instruments in Indonesia, namely, state-based oversight, certification standards, and voluntary action. Before conclusion, Sect. 4 will then analyze the coherence among those instruments, with supplementary discussion about harnessing EU Deforestation Regulation as foreign laws to shape a smart regulation ecosystem in palm oil governance.

2 ESG, Smart Regulation, and Problems with Enforcing Traditional Regulations on Palm Oil Sectors in Indonesia

Environmental, social, and governance ("ESG") norms are a set of standards for a company's operations that are being largely noticed by various stakeholders to assess sustainable business practices.[12] It is a review of the social, economic, and environmental impact of the everyday business operations of the company.[13] The concept of ESG emerged in 2004 when the UN Secretary-General Kofi Annan invited CEOs of major global financial institutions under the auspices of the UN Global Compact.[14] ESG helps stakeholders understand how an organization manages risks and opportunities related to environmental, social, and governance criteria.[15]

ESG is a general set of principles that can be implemented in various sectors. Specific quintessential indicators are varying as non-state actors, such as private consulting firms, research institutions, and nongovernment organizations (NGOs) already produced myriad versions of indicators. In forestry sectors, one of the ESG manifestations, for instance, is the No Deforestation, No Peat, and No Exploitation (NDPE) policy for palm oil products. The NDPE policy is made voluntarily by the private sector due to pressure from consumers and NGOs on sustainable products.[16] The policy was produced to demonstrate the company's commitment not to take palm oil products originating from deforestation, peatland conversion, and exploitation of the rights of indigenous peoples, farmers, and workers in the oil palm

[12] See Gupta and Chancal (2022, p. 2).

[13] Ibid., p. 3.

[14] Ibid.

[15] Ibid, p. 4.

[16] See Pirard et al. (2015, p. 4).

plantation sector.[17] Since it is internal and voluntary, NDPE policy standards may vary between companies.

In Indonesia and Malaysia, groups of companies that have declared NDPE policy represent 74% of the total palm oil production capacity in these two countries.[18] That is, the pressure exerted by the market (consumers) can lead companies to improve internal policies to be more sustainable. The NDPE policy can change the company's culture to be more inclusive, including by providing a complaint and grievance handling system so that every stakeholder can submit complaints on company operations that violate NDPE principles.[19] A key challenge in accelerating the implementation of NDPE commitments identified by diverse stakeholders working on sustainability in the palm oil industry is how to monitor, understand, and report on progress in delivering NDPE commitments in a transparent way.[20]

As for relevant NDPE indicators, the Accountability Framework Initiative (AFI) established by conservation NGOs provides 12 sets of principles for companies working in agriculture and forestry sectors to improve their ethical supply chains. AFI's 12 set principles consist of (1) protection of forests and other natural ecosystems, (2) respect for human rights, (3) specification of commitments, (4) a company system to drive effective implementation, (5) supply chain assessment and traceability, (6) managing for supply chain compliance, (7) site establishment, (8) site management and long-term protection, (9) remediation and environmental restoration, (10) collaboration for landscape and sectoral sustainability, (11) monitoring and verification, and (12) reporting disclosure and claims.[21]

Since ESG principles derive mostly from non-state actors and can be classified as voluntary, it is thought-provoking to see how this regime interacts with prevailing laws and regulations and then shapes palm oil governance in Indonesia. This is where smart regulation theory takes the role to assess how the interactions achieve particular objectives in palm oil governance, including environment and human rights protection. Smart regulation was first introduced by Gunningham et al. in 1998. They defined "smart regulation" to expand the interpretation of "regulation" beyond command-and-control regulation or state-based law.[22] The notion includes the consideration to harness other types of environmental policy instruments, e.g., self- and co-regulation, environmental audits, environmental management systems, eco-labeling schemes, liability rules for banks and insurers, environmental reporting, and other policy innovations.[23] Vant Erp et al. (2019) used "smart mix" terminology rather than smart regulation, but the notion is pretty much similar.[24]

---

[17] Ibid.

[18] See Steinweg et al. (2017, p. 1).

[19] Ibid, p. 2.

[20] See Larsen et al. (2018, p. 2).

[21] Ibid.

[22] See Gunningham and Grabosky (1998, p. 4).

[23] Ibid., p. 18.

[24] See Erp et al. (2019, pp. 9–10).

"Regulation" thus can take various forms: international treaties, domestic law, private standards, economic incentives, transparency and information disclosure, and procedural rights. The concept promises improved environmental performance but at a price acceptable to business and community.[25]

Smart regulation aims to promote the utilization of multiple legal instruments rather than a single instrument, which commonly is centralized to the use of CAC instruments. Criticisms on CAC concerns around its reliance to government agencies, which are susceptible to political wills, rigidness, and complexities.[26] In Indonesia, we have one interesting case on the palm oil sector in Aceh, the westernmost province in Indonesia, which envisaged how burdensome and complex it is to enforce strategic enforcement against companies.[27] The case involves land clearing and peatland burning by a palm oil company where all CAC resources, namely, administrative, criminal, and civil suits, were utilized against the company.[28]

The start of legal action against the company was in 2012 and was treated with the multi-door approach initiative for environmental crimes.[29] In simple terms, the multi-door approach was a means for law enforcement authorities to cooperate in combined crime cases that can be prosecuted under various regulations, such as the laws on the environment, forestry, mining, taxation, money laundering, corruption, and plantations.[30] In this case, the company was imposed with an administrative sanction by revoking their interim use permit (IUP), a criminal sanction of Rp 3 billion in fine, and compensation and environmental restoration sanctions of Rp 366 billion. However, along the way, enforcement of these sanctions also encountered several obstacles, particularly in cashing out the compensation.

The use of an administrative suit was the starting point, where, in 2011, an NGO initiated a lawsuit filed at the district administrative court to revoke the plantation business permit (*Izin Usaha Perkebunan/IUP*) of the company. The issuance of a business permit was considered to be in conflict with several laws and regulations, and it would have taken away the livelihoods of local residents and, not to mention, led to a huge ecological impact. Moreover, the company had started the land clearing before all the permit procedures were completed. Initially, the local administrative court rejected the case, claiming they did not have jurisdiction to read the case.[31] However, this decision was annulled by the higher administrative court and subsequently upheld by the Supreme Court's decision; thus, the permit was revoked.[32]

---

[25] Gunningham and Grabosky (1998, p. 10).

[26] See Orts (1995, pp. 1–6).

[27] PT Kallista Alam (KA) is a palm oil company based in Aceh, Indonesia. The court has ruled it is responsible for forest fires back in 2015. All court decisions against the companies can be accessed here: https://putusan3.mahkamahagung.go.id/search.html/?q=pt.kallista

[28] Ibid.

[29] See Abdul Wahid Situmorang (2015, p. 9).

[30] Ibid.

[31] See Banda Aceh State Administrative Court Decision No.19/G/2011/PTUN-BNA.

[32] See Medan State Administrative High Court Decision Number: 89/B/2012/ PT.TUN-MDN jo. Supreme Court Decision Number 455 K/TUN/2012.

Based on the court decision, the governor issued a decree to revoke the business license of the company. However, the company did not remain silent and responded by filing a new lawsuit in the same local administrative court asking for the annulment of this decree. Unfortunately, the court granted the lawsuit and decided to cancel the license revocation decree.[33] This decision was contentious because it annulled the decision of the Supreme Court and envisaged a never-ending legal battle just for revoking a business license.

Hence, criminal and civil suits were also pursued against the company for the land fires in its working area. The burned areas were estimated to be 1000 ha between 2009 and 2012 based on expert calculation. The District Court imposed a criminal fine of Rp 3 billion on the company, which was later upheld by the Banda Aceh High Court decision and the Supreme Court decision.[34] In addition, several key employees were also targeted by the public prosecutor. The estate manager was charged with environmental crimes based on Law No. 32/2009 for the land fires and got sentenced to imprisonment and fines. However, the director and majority shareholder of the company were freed from all the charges.

The civil suit was a spotlight in 2015 due to the gargantuan amount of compensation and restoration costs for IDR 366 billion (around USD 22 million). Despite the enormous amount, it was very challenging to request compensation from the companies. The companies again took a counterattack legal action by filing a lawsuit against the government agencies, arguing that there was an error in the coordinates of the area managed by the company as mentioned in the decision.[35] Moreover, the company found that approximately 300 ha of working area, as mentioned in the court decision, was managed by local communities.[36] This fact showed that the peatland was not damaged because oil palm trees could still thrive on it. Inconsistent with the previous decision, the local District Court controversially granted this lawsuit and stated that the Supreme Court decision was inaccurate.[37] Fortunately, this contentious decision was annulled at the higher courts, so the civil verdict for compensation and restoration costs of IDR 366 billion remains owed by the company.[38] However, this lawsuit certainly hampered the execution process because the District Court, which was supposed to carry out the execution, granted the company request for annulling the execution.

After this counterattack lawsuit, the District Court initiated the administration to organize a public auction to sell the company assets, such as 5769 ha of certified lands, including buildings and plants on it. Based on existing sources, the execution was still hampered until now because the company always rejected and resisted the

---

[33] See Banda Aceh State Administrative Court Decision No. 18/G/2012/PTUN-BA.

[34] See Meulaboh District Court Decision No. 131/Pid.B/2013/PN.MBO, Banda Aceh High Court Decision No. 201/Pid/2014/PT.BNA, and Supreme Court Decision No. 1554 K/Pid.Sus/2015.

[35] See Meulaboh District Court Decision No. 16/Pdt.G/2017/MBO.

[36] Ibid.

[37] Ibid.

[38] See Banda Aceh High Court Decision No. 80/PDT-LH/2018/PT.BNA jo. Supreme Court Decision No. 2906 K/Pdt/2019.

asset valuation by the Public Appraisal Office.[39] The company also took another legal action by filing a lawsuit at another local District Court, requesting the postponement or cancellation of the execution. This case was rejected, arguing that the panel of judges did not have the authority to postpone or cancel the execution order.

The community's activities on the disputed land were also an obstacle to executing the civil decision. Parties claiming to be members of the local community also filed a lawsuit to prevent the execution of the court decision. A cooperative claimed to have control over 300 ha of customary land and filed a lawsuit to annul the execution at the local court.[40] Eighteen members of a local community also filed for an annulment of the execution and claimed that the burned land was individually owned and could be proven with a land certificate.[41] In both cases, the District Court decided that the panel of judges had no authority to annul the execution of the decision and that the authority rested with the first District Court issuing the decision, so the lawsuit was rejected. After almost 10 years, it was reported that the company only paid IDR 57 billion (USD 3.4 million) out of IDR 366 billion, and there was no latest news about the auction of the company's assets.[42]

The process of this case has envisaged several challenges in enforcing CAC measures or sanctions on state-based laws. The first challenge was the resistance by the perpetrators. In this case, companies filed multiple lawsuits to challenge the revocation decree and compensation amounts. For the revocation case, the company's request was even granted, so their business permits are still applicable. Our online search did not find any follow-up actions on the State Administrative Court Decision regarding the annulment of permit revocation. Although the company's efforts to fight back were unsuccessful in the civil suit, the cases were quite time-consuming and resulted in delays in the execution of auctioning the company's asset for the payment of restoring the degraded forests. Lastly, land is a valuable resource. During the delay for liquidating the compensation, local people began to utilize the abandoned yet disputed area for small-scale plantation. They even took legal action to claim their rights in the disputed land because it has been cultivated.

Since the concept criticizes the heavy reliance on CAC, smart regulation also encourages the inclusion of non-state actors to contribute to environmental policy development.[43] Palm oil governance consists of numerous stakeholders involved and legal instruments being implemented; thus it will be a good case study for the application of smart regulatory design principles. The coordination between public and private regulators can strengthen the enforcement of forest protection and its associated rights.[44] In North America, processes have been established for information sharing to enable public regulators to rely on the audits conducted by

---

[39] See Wicaksono (2022).

[40] See Suka Makmue District Court Decision No. 2/Pdt.Bth/2019/PN Skm.

[41] See Suka Makmue District Court Decision No. 1/Pdt.Bth/2019/PN Skm.

[42] See Forests Insights (September 29, 2023).

[43] See Gunningham and Grabosky (1998, p. 18).

[44] See Liu, Chap. 8 in Erp, JV, et al. (2019, pp. 175–181).

certification schemes.[45] This saves the resources of public regulators, which can then be allocated for other purposes.[46] However, one might question the relationship between smart regulations and the social dimension as well as governance, because Gunningham and Grabosky designed this concept for addressing environmentally harmful activities rather than social and governance-focused instruments.

This chapter argues that it is now inevitable to perceive the environment and human rights in coherence instead of as two separate agendas. In international law, the concept of the right to a healthy environment (RHE) has been recognized in many parts of the world in the constitution, including Indonesia. RHE is the simpler term of the right to a safe, clean, healthy, and sustainable environment and is rooted in the principle of the 1972 Stockholm Declaration on Human Environment.[47] Various states have recognized RHE by putting the notions in the constitution. RHE enjoys direct constitutional protection in 100 countries and has received recognition in legally binding instruments from at least 155 countries.[48] As for governance, transparency is a key component. Access to information promises better monitoring of environmental impacts and changes, leading to more effective preventive measures.[49]

Amid various instruments that shape smart regulation, we opine that ESG emerged as self-reflexive law. Orts (1995) defines self-reflexive law as a legal theory and a practical approach to regulation that seeks to encourage self-reflective and self-critical processes within social institutions concerning the effects they have on the natural environment.[50] The idea is to harness law not directly in terms of giving specific orders or commands but indirectly to establish incentives and procedures that encourage institutions to think critically, creatively, and continually about how their activities affect the environment and how they may improve their environmental performance[51] A key challenge of contemporary environmental governance is the identification of mixes, which may serve the purpose of environmental protection[52] or in the context of the present chapter will include human rights and access to transparency aspects under palm oil regimes in Indonesia. In total, this chapter discusses a total of three categories of instruments that intersect with ESG principles.

[45] Ibid.

[46] Ibid.

[47] See Boyd (2018, p. 18).

[48] Ibid.

[49] See Finck and Mueller (2023, p. 111).

[50] See Orts (1995, p. 783).

[51] Ibid.

[52] See Erp et al. (2019, p. 23).

3 The Role of State-Based Oversight, Certification, and Voluntary Action in Implementing ESG

3.1 State-Based Oversight

Palm oil is one of the heavily regulated sectors, and it has many oversight instruments. These instruments encompass laws across various sectors, including plantations, spatial planning, and forestry. In the specific regulations for the palm oil sector, there are three oversight instruments: (1) plantation business assessment (PUP),[53] (2) supervision based on plantation business progress reports,[54] and (3) supervision based on public report.[55] These instruments collectively ensure that the palm oil sector operates within legal and sustainable frameworks.

All plantation companies that have obtained a plantation business license must undergo a plantation business assessment (PUP). This assessment is conducted for companies in both the development and operational stages.[56] The plantation business assessment evaluates various aspects of the company, including legality, management, resolution of land rights issues, realization of plantation development and/or processing units, ownership of facilities and infrastructure, fire prevention and control systems, and management of pests. It also assesses the implementation of environmental impact assessment (EIA) results, the development and empowerment of local communities/cooperatives, and reporting.[57] The assessment is carried out by certified plantation business assessors,[58] typically from regional agencies. Companies are classified into different plantation grades, ranging from A to E (for development stage) and 1 to 5 (for operational stage). Violations of these provisions may result in administrative sanctions, including the revocation of the plantation business license.[59]

Second, plantation business operators are required to submit plantation business progress reports twice a year to the licensing authority.[60] Failure to submit these reports may result in administrative sanctions, including written warnings and revocation of the business license.[61] Plantation companies are required to report this

[53] Ministry of Agriculture Regulation No. 07/Permentan/KU.410/2/2009 on Guidelines for Plantation Business Assessment, Art. 4.

[54] Ministry of Agriculture Regulation No. 98/Permentan/OT.140/9/2013 on Guidelines for Plantation Business Licensing, Art. 44.

[55] Government Regulation No. 28 of 2025 on Implementation of Risk-Based Business Licensing, Art. 251.

[56] Ministry of Agriculture Regulation No. 07/Permentan/KU.410/2/2009, Art. 4.

[57] Ibid, Arts. 5, 6.

[58] Ibid, Art. 11.

[59] Ibid, Arts. 22, 25, 26.

[60] Ministry of Agriculture Regulation No. 98/Permentan/OT.140/9/2013 on Guidelines for Plantation Business Licensing, Art. 44.

[61] Ibid, Arts. 48, 49, 50, 51, 52, 53, 54, 55.

information through the Plantation Licensing Information System (SIPERIBUN), an integrated reporting platform under the Ministry of Agriculture. Components reported include obligations to develop plasma plantations for communities, CSR obligations, and compliance with environmental standards and regulations.[62]

Lastly, the public can report if a company is suspected of violations, including obligations for environmental protection. However, violations of human rights are not specified; rather, the focus is on issues related to plantation business activities, such as the development of community plantations.[63] These reports will be followed by the licensing authority according to their jurisdiction and will result in administrative sanctions ranging from written warnings to revocation of the license.[64]

3.2 Certification Standard

There are two major certification standards for palm oil commodities, namely, Indonesian Sustainable Palm Oil Certification (ISPO) and Roundtable Sustainable Palm Oil (RSPO). To integrate various regulations and sustainable plantation standards at both national and international levels, the Indonesian government issued the ISPO policy in 2011. This mandatory certification system aims to ensure that a palm oil company is economically viable, socially and culturally appropriate, and environmentally friendly based on certain principles and criteria.[65] The Indonesian government initiated the formation of a team to strengthen the Indonesian Sustainable Palm Oil (ISPO) certification in 2016. This initiative arose because ISPO was considered inadequate in addressing challenges related to sustainable palm oil in Indonesia. Firstly, there was a need to bolster the legal foundation of this policy. Palm oil governance involves multiple ministries and agencies, making it impractical to regulate through a single ministerial regulation from the Ministry of Agriculture. Secondly, the independence of ISPO was questioned, preventing it from aligning with nationally and internationally recognized certification standards. The ISPO scheme should be guided by the National Accreditation Committee, which adheres to international committee standards. Consequently, in 2020, the President issued Presidential Regulation No. 44 of 2020 on ISPO (PR No. 44/2020). In 2025, PR No. 44/2020 was repealed and replaced by the Presidential Regulation No. 16 of 2025 on ISPO (PR No.16/2025).

---

[62] Ministry of Agriculture Regulation No. 45 of 2019 on Electronically Integrated Business Licensing Services in the Agricultural Sector, Arts. 25, 148.

[63] Ministry of Agriculture Regulation No. 45 of 2019 on Electronically Integrated Business Licensing Services in the Agricultural Sector, Arts. 25, 148 jo. Government Regulation No. 28 of 2025 on the Implementation of Risk-Based Business Licensing, Art. 251.

[64] Government Regulation No. 28 of 2025 on the Implementation of Risk-Based Business Licensing, Art. 265. Jo. Ministry of Agriculture Regulation No. 98/Permentan/OT.140/9/2013 on Guidelines for Plantation Business Licensing, Arts. 48, 49, 50, 51, 52, 53, 54, 55.

[65] See Down To Earth article (2011).

Based on Article 6 of PR No. 16/2025, the ISPO certificate is issued by certification bodies, which are independent auditors outside the government. This certificate is issued to plantation companies and smallholders. Plantation companies that do not have an ISPO certificate or violate ISPO principles and criteria may face administrative sanctions, including written warnings, fines, temporary suspension, freezing of the ISPO certificate, and/or revocation of the ISPO certificate. According to Article 19 of PR No.16/2025, the ISPO implementation is coordinated by the ISPO Committee, chaired by the Minister of Plantations and consisting of government elements, business association representatives, academics, and independent monitors.

Meanwhile, the RSPO is an international multi-stakeholder organization founded in 2004, incorporating the 3P concept (people, planet, and profit) in its principles and criteria. RSPO emerged from concerns raised by various NGOs regarding the environmental externalities caused by palm oil production.[66] RSPO's membership includes a diverse range of nongovernmental stakeholders, such as palm oil producers, processors or traders of palm oil, consumer goods manufacturers, retailers, banks and investors, environmental or nature conservation NGOs, and social or developmental NGOs.[67] In contrast to ISPO, which is a binding and mandatory government initiative, RSPO is a voluntary initiative by its members who agree to undergo a certification process and comply with specific principles and criteria. Palm oil businesses are expected to adhere to these criteria in line with applicable regulations and laws across various sectors, including environmental protection and sustainability.[68]

3.3 Voluntary Action

Another instrument that can manifest ESG implementation is voluntary action. This chapter highlights the role of corporate social responsibility (CSR) and its legal aspect under Indonesian law. In many parts of the world, CSR is a form of corporate moral ethical responsibility to the social environment and voluntary. In European countries, for instance, CSR is deemed a voluntary business contribution and active corporate engagement that goes beyond legal compliance.[69] Interestingly, the Indonesian legal system encourages the transformation of CSR into a mandatory and binding obligation for private companies. Rather than using CSR terminology, Indonesian law utilizes the definition of corporate social and environmental responsibility (CSER). CSER is defined by Law No. 40 of 2007 on Limited Liability Company (LLC Act) as the commitment from the company to participate in

[66] See Roundtable Sustainable Palm Oil, "Who We are", https://rspo.org/who-we-are/

[67] Ibid.

[68] See ISPO and RSPO Secretariat (2015).

[69] See Andrini (2016, p. 516).

sustainable economic development in order to increase the quality of life and environment, which will be valuable for the company itself, the local community, and society in general.[70] Article 74 of the LLC Act further regulates that companies having business activities pertaining to natural resources are obliged to perform their social and environment responsibility. Article 74(3) even elaborates that companies' failure to perform CSER shall be imposed with sanctions.

Despite transforming CSER into "mandatory" for companies operating in natural resources sectors, and it is irrefutable that palm oil is included, the LLC Act does not elaborate further about the manifestation of CSER, the form of sanctions, and the monitoring mechanism in detail.[71] In 2008, business associations challenged the constitutionality of Article 74 of the LLC Act in the Indonesian Constitutional Court. They argued that the basic tenet of CSR shall be ethical, moral, and voluntary, cut a significant portion from the profit, and instill arbitrary actions from authorities to impose sanctions.[72] The Constitutional Court rejected the argument and maintained that CSER is mandatory for companies having business related to natural resources.[73] In addition, the Constitutional Court also mentioned that sanctions against the violation of CSER have been regulated in sectoral acts related to natural resources management, such as laws and regulations in forestry, water, mining, etc.[74]

4 Designing Smart Regulation into Palm Oil Governance

As we provide illustrations on how ESG infiltrates legal instruments pertaining to palm oil governance in Indonesia, we have to describe the coherence among those instruments in creating a smart regulation ecosystem: whether the instruments are complementary or have negative effects on each other. Once again, the palm oil sector is obviously a heavily regulated sector. Cunningham and Grabosky emphasize the risk of smorgasbordism, an approach that uncritically assumes that the more instruments, the better and is the regulatory equivalent of throwing in everything bar the kitchen sink.[75] Ill-considered mixes can easily cause unintended consequences and be counterproductive (see Fig. 1).[76]

From the six instruments that we discussed, one can assume resemblance among the instruments. For instance, ISPO can also be categorized as state-based oversight because the dominant role of the government is to establish mandatory palm oil

[70] See Art. 1(3) of Indonesian Limited Liability Company (LLC) Act.

[71] See Andrini (2016, p. 517).

[72] See Indonesian Constitutional Court Decision No. 53/PUU-VI/2008.

[73] Ibid.

[74] Ibid.

[75] See Gunningham and Grabosky (1998, pp. 24–25).

[76] Ibid.

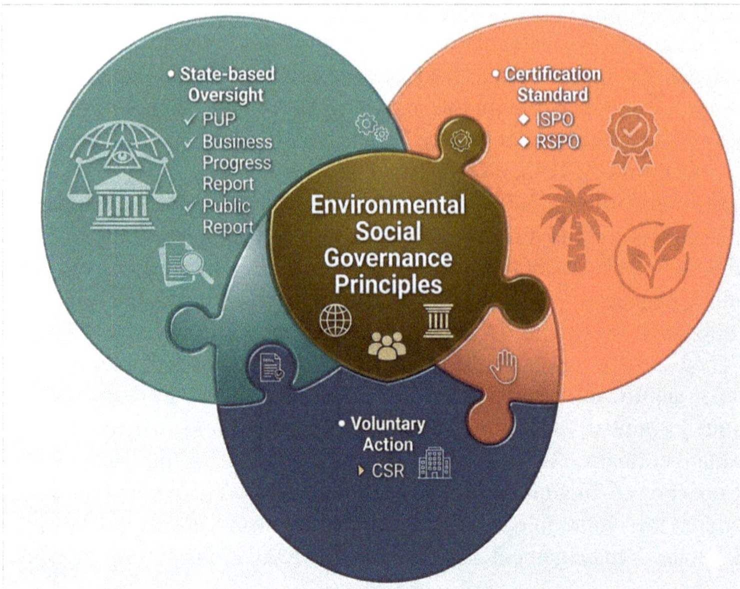

Fig. 1 Visualization of regime interaction in palm oil regulations. Source: processed by authors, 2026

certification. The domestic industries might question whether ISPO was meant to be a competition for RSPO, the more well established yet voluntary certification system. Hence, RSPO can also be considered a voluntary action, the same category as CSR. To answer these ambiguities, this chapter will discuss the coherence and potential conflicts among the instruments.

Certification systems are typically nongovernmental and voluntary because they lack binding legal force. Their implementation relies on market conditions, which drive compliance based on the necessity to sell a product. RSPO, for instance, only binds its members and cannot extend to corporations outside its organization. Voluntary certification can operate alongside CAC instruments due to their distinct legal features. ISPO represents an effort to unify the voluntary certification system into a mandatory one, aligning it with legal obligations under the CAC framework.

This situation can be examined from two angles. First, ISPO can be perceived as integrating sectoral regulations into a cohesive audit system. The consolidation of regulatory frameworks streamlines the supervision process by enabling the obligations imposed by different regulations and ministries/agencies to be managed within a unified system. In contrast, the ISPO certification may be perceived as adding additional administrative complexities without addressing the core issues. From this standpoint, emphasis should be placed on enhancing existing CAC instruments rather than developing a new certification scheme reliant on state-based oversight. The PUP audit system, which is mandated by the government, renders the ISPO certification somewhat redundant as an administrative layer in the pursuit of sustainable palm oil objectives.

The two views are closely related in several contexts. Despite their similarities, ISPO and PUP have fundamental differences. ISPO aims to comply with international standards to gain global market acceptance, whereas PUP is primarily focused on national supervision. Additionally, international and national standards can differ, such as in the case of high conservation value (HCV). National land law does not clearly define HCV, rendering the obligation to protect HCV ineffective. Furthermore, national land regulations state that companies with land titles must develop the land within a specified timeframe. Failure to do so can lead the government to classify the land as abandoned and revoke the company's permit. Often, land title is granted in HCV areas. This contradicts the principles in international standards, such as the RSPO, which clearly opposes this matter. ISPO provides clearer regulations regarding this issue. Nevertheless, these regulations should ideally be governed by higher-level legislation, such as national acts.

Further, there is ambiguity in the application of the FPIC process. According to Constitutional Court Decision No. 138/PUU-XIII/2015 and the Plantation Law, plantation companies must have a business permit and land title to commence operations, including land clearing.[77] This means that to operate, companies must have complete licensing and land that is clean and clear of claims from other parties. Therefore, companies are required to obtain approval from the community landowners and those affected by the plantation development. However, forestry regulations allow companies to clear land without a registered land title as long as they obtained a timber cutting permit referred to as non-forestry timber utilization (PKKNK).[78]

In addition to what has been previously mentioned, we found that various regulatory frameworks between other instruments remain overlapping and lack coherence. For example, in the context of state-based oversights, such as PUP and supervisory instruments based on business progress reports. Our review of nine State Administrative Court rulings on the revocation of palm oil permits that have achieved final legal status shows inconsistent application of administrative sanctions.[79] The government did not revoke company permits following the procedures outlined in the PUP instrument. This is despite the fact that these companies had undergone the PUP process, which is explicitly regulated under Minister of

[77] See Constitutional Court Decision No. 138/PUU-XIII/2015, available at https://www.mkri.id/public/content/persidangan/putusan/138_PUU-XIII_2015.pdf

[78] The Minister of Environment and Forestry Regulation No. 8/2021 does not explicitly require an HGU (Land Use Title) as a basis for issuing IPK (Timber Cutting Permit) or PKKNK (Non-Forestry Timber Utilization).

[79] See (1) Supreme Court Decision No. 189K/TUN/2011, (2) Supreme Court Decision No. 169 PK/TUN/2016, (3) Supreme Court Decision No. 170 PK/TUN/2016, (4) Supreme Court Decision No. 497 K/TUN/2012, (5) Supreme Court Decision No. 334 K/TUN/2017, (6) Supreme Court Decision No. 382 K/TUN/2017, (7) Supreme Court Decision No. 322 K/TUN/2012, (8) Supreme Court Decision No. No. 435 K/TUN/2013, and (9) Supreme Court Decision No. 347 K/TUN/2013, available at https://putusan3.mahkamahagung.go.id/

Agriculture Regulation No. 07/2007. Instead, the government revoked the permits according to procedures applied to business progress reports.

Based on the above discussion, a key takeaway is the essential need for regulatory coherence. The various supervisory instruments available can be viewed as different channels for enforcing the law. Nonetheless, these channels will not operate effectively without clear regulations. The overlapping regulations need to be harmonized. This can be achieved in two ways: first, by aligning local regulations with international standards, and second, by ensuring that domestic regulations do not conflict with one another. These adjustments must be made comprehensively rather than piecemeal, as the effectiveness of law enforcement through various instruments relies on the clarity and consistency of the regulations.

Hence, certification can provide additional monitoring and assurance to the public enforcement capacity. For instance, multiple indicators under ISPO and RSPO are designed to see compliance from the companies with prevailing public regulations. Certification does not, however, automatically improve monitoring and oversight. Certifiers may be captured by their customers in order to secure income.[80] ISPO and RSPO attempt to tackle this issue by establishing a multi-stakeholders committee to oversee the overall implementation of the certification system. Through this multi-stakeholder forum, ISPO and RSPO also brought improvements on independent monitoring. Reporting is an essential part of ESG monitoring. According to Indonesian law, publicly listed companies and financial institutions under the supervision of the Financial Service Authority are obliged to produce a report highlighting their ESG performance.[81] For years, the NGOs have again played a crucial role in monitoring any leaks in the ESG claims made by the companies and providing curated and credible information to the end consumers who wish to consume sustainable products.

In some countries, false sustainable claims by the private sector are punishable under "greenwashing" crimes. This is where we think there is a vacuum of CAC measures under Indonesian law. It seems that indications of crimes or other punishable incompliances found during certification and state-based oversight are not automatically followed up with the exertion of CAC instruments. Obviously, there are several bottlenecks for creating this ideal enforcement ecosystem. For instance, certification bodies are bound by the service contract to not disclose information about the companies due to the confidentiality clause. By regulating greenwashing, enforcement agencies can target recalcitrant companies and even the certification bodies that contribute to the dissemination of false ESG claims.

We also think of CSR as an underutilized instrument which can be an important piece in manifesting smart regulation for ESG implementation. As discussed before, CSR, which is in principle voluntary, was deviated as a mandatory obligation for

[80] See Liu, Chap. 8 in Erp et al. (2019, p. 182). For example, in Sweden, objections brought by NGOs to certification have seldom led to the withdrawal of certificates.

[81] See OJK Regulation No. 51/POJK.03/2017 TAHUN 2017 regarding the Implementation of Sustainable Finance for Financial Service Institutions, Issuers (Emiten), and Public Companies. Apparently, there are 26 palm oil companies listed in Indonesia Stock Exchange.

companies having their business operations pertain to natural resources in Indonesia. However, it is unclear what sanctions and which authorities can enforce the failure of implementing CSR or, in Indonesia's legal term, CSER obligations. Regarding sanctions, the Constitutional Court opined that sanctions for CSER are embedded in several sectoral laws and regulations on natural resources, such as the Forestry Act, Water Act, Mining Act, etc.[82] These sectoral laws have concluded several obligations and sanctions for companies that failed to comply with provisions related to the environment and social aspects of the business.[83] For palm oil sectoral laws, Act No. 39 of 2014 on Plantation does not mention anything with CSER, but the normative obligation for plantation companies to conduct CSER is regulated under lower regulation, namely, Ministry of Agriculture Regulation, but this once again does not elaborate further on sanctions and enforcement procedures about CSER.

Andrini (2016) disagreed with the opinion of the Constitutional Court that sanctions for CSER are embedded in sectoral laws and its imposition shall be executed based on the company's incompliances.[84] Fulfilling of the legal obligations under sectoral natural resources law, such as obtaining business permits and conducting environmental impact assessments for activities that potentially affect the environment, shall be interpreted solely as legal obligations instead of completing CSER.[85] The authors shared a similar opinion with this argument. CSER is not an instrument to verify compliance of the private sector but rather a supplementary instrument for companies to do what is right or morally appropriate beyond the obligations that have been stipulated by the laws. The focus shall be defining the sanctions for CSER to fill the vacuum of laws as left by the LLC Act.

Indonesia is a republic country that divides the government system into three layers: national, provincial, and municipal. Though laws and regulations at the national level, such as the LLC Act, Plantation Act, and Ministry of Agriculture Regulation, do not define the sanctions, some local regulations at the provincial and municipal level have formulated sanctions for the absence of CSER. Interestingly, some local regulations also provide incentives for companies that have already completed CSER. We selected four local regulations from regions with vast palm oil plantations and made the comparison as follows (see Table 1).

Though CSER is mandated by national law, in practice, the implementation of CSER is dependent on the political will of regional governments. All aforementioned regulations also stipulate that funding for CSER monitoring can be derived from the regional state budget. Some regulations were already mentioned about the imposition of administrative sanctions for failure to implement CSER. Interestingly, all the local regulations also regulate the "reward" mechanism for companies that actually implement CSER programs in their regions. Ease for doing business, such

---

[82] See Indonesian Constitutional Court Decision No. 53/PUU-VI/2008.

[83] Ibid.

[84] See Andrini (2016, p. 524).

[85] Ibid.

Table 1 Comparative analysis of local regulations pertaining to CSR in palm oil-producing regions

	Local regulation of Bengkalis No. 9 of 2019 on corporate social responsibility	Local regulation of East Kalimantan Province No. 17 of 2017 on corporate social and environment responsibility of limited liability company as well as partnership program and environment development	Local regulation of Central Kalimantan Province No. 11 of 2012 on the implementation of corporate social and environment responsibility	Local regulation of Musi Banyuasin Regency No. 22 of 2016 on corporate social responsibility
Level of regulation	Municipal	Provincial	Provincial	Municipal
Monitoring mechanism	Municipal government will coordinate CSER forum to oversee the implementation. The forum comprises of members from government, companies, and public elements	Provincial government will coordinate implementing coordination team. The team comprises of members from government, companies, public, and academician elements	Provincial government will coordinate CSER implementing forum	Municipal government will coordinate CSR forum
Sanction for not implementing CSER	1. Written warning 2. Limitation of business activities	1. Written warning 2. Limitation of business activities 3. License suspension 4. License revocation	1. Written warning 2. License revocation	None
Reward/incentive for companies	Ease for managing permit and taxation	Governor is allowed to provide reward, but the form of rewards is not stipulated further	Governor is allowed to provide reward, but the form of rewards is not stipulated further	Regent is allowed to provide reward, but the form of rewards is not stipulated further

Source: processed by authors, 2026

as for permits and taxation, will entice the companies to seriously formulate their program.

It is essential to reemphasize that CSR as a concept shall go "beyond compliance" and not be confused with compliance with the provisions of laws.[86] The

[86] See Pollman (2021, p. 4).

confusion might be found because commonly there are several provisions in state-based laws that serve the social and environmental cause. The phenomenon is normal because notions of CSR and obligations under the law vary widely around the world so that activity that would be considered CSR in some countries is mere compliance in others.[87] For instance, plantation companies are required to allocate 20% from their working area to be developed as a plasma plantation for surrounding communities and partner with communities to manage this area.[88] Thus, a company shall not claim the managed area as part of either CSR or ESG commitment since, in essence, CSR or ESG implementation shall be treated as voluntary and self-regulatory instead of CAC instruments.

4.1 Foreign Policy as a Complementary Instrument to Smart Regulation in Palm Oil Governance

Though the smart regulation concept as originally discussed by Cunningham and Grabosky only covers domestic policies as case studies, we believe it is also important for this chapter to expand the discussion on foreign policies that can influence palm oil governance in Indonesia. Demand-side policies have emerged in the past two decades to address the sustainability issues of deforestation-driven commodities, such as timber and oil palm. Demand-side policies from consumer countries are essential to tackle "imported" deforestation, namely, deforestation in producer countries, which was driven by growing agricultural import.[89] The EU is one of the Indonesia's main buyers of agricultural products, which influences the way Indonesia governs its forest.

In the timber sector, the EU and Indonesia have entered into a Voluntary Partnership Agreement (VPA), which brought improvements to the Indonesian Timber Legality Assurance System. Until now, Indonesia is the only implementing Forest Law Enforcement Governance and Trade (FLEGT) license country, meaning that Indonesian timber products enjoys a "green lane" to enter the EU market without the need to pass due diligence. Apparently, the creation of the EU Deforestation Regulation (EUDR), which entered into force on June 29, 2023, creates significant influences for Indonesia to adapt to new requirements as producer countries.[90] EUDR applies to seven commodities that are associated with deforestation and its derivative products, namely, cattle, cocoa, coffee, oil palm, rubber, soya, and wood.[91]

---

[87] Ibid, p. 5.

[88] See Article 12 of Government Regulation No. 26 of 2021 on Agriculture Management.

[89] See Karsenty and Picard (2021).

[90] See Regulation (EU) 2023/1115 of the European Parliament and of the Council of May 31, 2023, on the making available on the Union market and the export from the Union of certain commodities and products associated with deforestation and forest degradation and repealing Regulation (EU) No 995/2010 (EUDR) [2023] L 150/206.

[91] Ibid, Art. 1(1).

In principle, EUDR requires that these seven commodities be "deforestation-free" to be exported to the EU market, meaning that the relevant products contain, have been fed with, or have been made using relevant commodities that were produced on land that has not been subject to deforestation after December 31, 2020, and in the case of relevant products that contain or have been made using wood, that the wood has been harvested from the forest without inducing forest degradation after December 31, 2020.[92] It also requires the commodities to be produced "in accordance with the relevant legislation of the country of production" and "covered by a due diligence statement."[93]

The EU importer of those seven commodities has to establish a three-step due diligence process when bringing the goods into the EU, namely, (1) collect detailed information that demonstrates the products comply with the EUDR, (2) carry out a risk assessment in relation to each product to ascertain the risk of noncompliance with the EUDR, and (3) mitigate risks by carrying out independent surveys/audits, gathering additional documentation, or working with suppliers (particularly SMEs) through capacity building and investments.[94]

Hence, the EUDR recognizes the social dimension of forests and mentions the role of Environmental Human Rights Defenders (EHRD), indigenous people, smallholders, and small medium enterprises in its preamble. It defines EHRD as those ".. who strive to protect and promote human rights relating to the environment, including access to clean water, air, and land..." as well as acknowledges the alarming rate of the attacks targeting EHRD and indigenous people.[95] EUDR also encourages the EU member states to partner with producer countries for supporting "...the role and rights of indigenous peoples, local communities, smallholders, and micro, small and medium-sized enterprises (SMEs), improving governance and land tenure, increasing law enforcement and promoting sustainable forest management...."[96] Under international law, the content of the preamble of an agreement is an integral part of the agreement itself and should be taken into consideration when interpreting any other provision.[97] The EUDR interprets human rights protection as relevant issues triggering member state obligations in the context of deforestation. By clarifying that actions to address deforestation should take human rights into account, the agreement helps to mainstream human rights norms into the ongoing implementation and evolution of agricultural trade between the EU and producer countries.

Further, the EUDR also attempts to internalize the social cost as part of the sustainable and legal verification system. The main control feature to prevent the entry of illegal commodities into the EU market is putting a "due diligence" obligation on EU operators and traders. In a nutshell, the operators/traders must declare that they

[92] Ibid, Art. 2(13).

[93] Ibid, Art. 3.

[94] Ibid, Art. 8. See also Forwood (2023).

[95] Ibid, Para. 7 of the preamble.

[96] Ibid., Para. 29 of the preamble.

[97] See Knox (2020, p. 327).

have exercised an adequate control system to ensure that the commodities are produced according to the national laws of producer countries and are "deforestation-free."[98] Human rights aspects shall be considered during the risk assessment, which is the subset of the overall due diligence obligation. Risk assessments must include a broad view of whether the goods were produced in accordance with relevant local laws, including the principle of free prior and informed consent (FPIC) of indigenous peoples.[99] There are 14 criteria on the risk assessment, some of which are relevant to human rights protection: (1) the presence of **indigenous peoples** in producer countries; (2) the consultation and cooperation in good faith with **indigenous peoples** in the production; (3) the existence of duly reasoned claims by **indigenous peoples** based on objective and verifiable information regarding the use or ownership of the area used for the purpose of producing the relevant commodity; and (4) concerns in relation to the country of production and origin or parts thereof, such as level of corruption, prevalence of document and data falsification, lack of law enforcement, **violations of international human rights**, armed conflict, or presence of sanctions imposed by the UN Security Council or the Council of the European Union.[100]

The EUDR also introduced a new feature as risk classification for producer countries or country benchmarking. The European Commission divides countries and/or regions into three tiers: high risk, low risk, and standard risk.[101] The categorization of risk implicates to due diligence obligations of operators and traders: the obligations are simplified for products originating from low-risk countries and enhanced for products originating from high-risk countries.[102] In addition, operators and traders of products from low-risk countries are not required to undertake risk assessments and mitigation measures when they have ascertained that their supply chain is not too complex and that there is at most a negligible risk of circumvention of the EUDR and of their products mixing with products of unknown origin or origin in high-risk/standard-risk countries.[103] As for indicators to determine the risk profile, the Commission refers to primary assessment criteria: (1) rate of deforestation and forest degradation; (2) rate of expansion of agricultural land for relevant commodities; and (3) production trends of relevant commodities and relevant products.[104] Interestingly, the producer country's commitments on transparency and human rights are also subsidiary criteria that shall be considered.[105] In addition, information submitted by NGOs, local communities, indigenous people, and CSOs on the effective covering of emissions and removals from agriculture, forestry, and

[98] See Regulation (EU) 2023/1115., Art. 3.

[99] See Forwood (2023).

[100] See Regulation (EU) 2023/1115., Art. 10(2).

[101] Ibid, Art. 29(1).

[102] Ibid, Art. 13.

[103] Ibid, Art. 13(1).

[104] Ibid, Art. 29(3).

[105] Ibid, Art. 29(4).

land use in the nationally determined contribution is also considered, leading to more transparency and multi-stakeholder engagement.[106]

We believe all the aforementioned provisions and features under the EUDR represent ESG principles that can improve palm oil governance in Indonesia. Article 30 of the EUDR also requires intensive engagement with producer countries to facilitate compliance with the EUDR, paying particular attention to the needs of indigenous people, local communities, and smallholders. Some features, such as due diligence and country benchmarking, require adequate supply information from the producer countries; thus, the EU Commissions operators and traders can make informed decisions to import legal and "deforestation-free" products to the EU market.

In a recent joint press release, the European Union and Indonesia have announced their ongoing efforts to harmonize EU legal standards with Indonesian national laws. This initiative, formalized during the second meeting of the Ad-Hoc Joint Task Force, underscores a mutual commitment to aligning regulatory frameworks to facilitate smoother cooperation and trade between the two regions.[107] The recent meeting focused on five main workstreams aimed at aligning regulatory standards between the EU, Indonesia, and Malaysia.

1. Workstream 1: addressed the inclusion of smallholders in supply chains. The EU recognized the challenges posed by the EUDR deadlines and agreed to assist Indonesia and Malaysia in creating and accelerating smallholder registration systems to ensure their integration into legal, deforestation-free supply chains.
2. Workstream 2: involved analyzing gaps in Indonesian Sustainable Palm Oil (ISPO) and Malaysian Sustainable Palm Oil (MSPO) certifications. The EU, Indonesia, and Malaysia agreed to finalize assessments and collaborate on addressing these gaps to meet EUDR requirements.
3. Workstream 3: highlighted Malaysia's national tool systems and Indonesia's National Dashboard for Commodities. The EU will support these traceability initiatives and facilitate regional dialogue on key commodities while also aiding in legality assessments for timber, rubber, cocoa, and coffee.
4. Workstream 4: reviewed scientific data on deforestation, focusing on the EU's Observatory and exploring joint efforts with Indonesia and Malaysia on geospatial mapping.
5. Workstream 5: discussed privacy concerns related to geolocation data. The EU clarified that such data is not linked to personal information and agreed to address any additional concerns.[108]

---

[106] Ibid.

[107] See the press release of Ministry of Agriculture, Indonesia, available at https://ditjenbun.pertanian.go.id/pemerintah-indonesia-dorong-dashboard-komoditas-sebagai-alat-ketertelusuran-yang-terintegrasi/

[108] See Joint Press Release: the 2nd meeting of the Ad Hoc Joint Task Force on the EUDR, available at https://www.eeas.europa.eu/delegations/indonesia/joint-press-release-2nd-meeting-ad-hoc-joint-task-force-eudr_en?s=168

Given the context, the harmonization of EUDR with national policies represents a key element in reinforcing monitoring mechanisms. The partnership between the European Union and Indonesia illustrates how foreign policy instruments can serve as complementary measures to existing regulations in the palm oil sector. Such foreign policy tools can significantly enhance governance and regulatory frameworks concerning palm oil at the national level.

5 Conclusion

Global South countries are facing challenges to meet the increasing demand for legal and sustainable palm oil products. Major reform on laws is often crucial to ensure environmental and social principles are enforced in every stage of supply chain. ESG as a self-reflexive law can be a complementary instrument to existing CAC instruments for achieving environmental and social objectives from palm oil industries. In this chapter, we use Indonesia as a case study in Global South, to discuss three categories of legal instruments that represent ESG norms, namely, state-based oversights, certification standards, and voluntary action. Conflicts of laws still exist and prevent the creation of smart regulation systems. For instance, CSR, as a voluntary instrument, has not been used to its maximum potential and can be misunderstood as a compliance tool under Indonesian law. We also discussed how foreign policy from "Global North" can influence legal reform in Global South palm oil producer countries. The EUDR, which will be implemented soon, can be an alternative avenue for improving CAC and non-CAC instruments. The law contains principles covering anti-deforestation, forest governance, as well as human rights protection that shall be met by the EU's supplier countries, including Indonesia.

References

Aji SB (2019) Moratorium Sawit Jokowi dalam Perspektif Kebijakan Pembangunan Berkelanjutan ala Politik Hijau. JHLI 5(2):186–207

Andrini L (2016) Mandatory corporate social responsibility in Indonesia. MH 28(3):513–523

Boyd DR (2018) Catalyst for change: evaluating forty years of experience in implementing the right to a healthy environment. In: Knox JH, Pejan R (eds) The human right to a healthy environment. CUP, Cambridge

Davis KE, Pargendler M (2025) Legal heterodoxy in the global south. CUP, Cambridge

Down To Earth (2011) Indonesian sustainable palm oil scheme speed palm oil development. https://www.downtoearth-indonesia.org/story/indonesian-sustainable-palm-oil-scheme-speed-palm--oil-development#_edn3

Erp JV et al (2019) Smart mixes for transboundary environmental harm. CUP, Cambridge

Finck S, Mueller SM (2023) Access to data for environmental purposes: setting the scene and evaluating recent changes in EU data law. JoEL 35:109–131

Fitria N (2024) 241 Konflik Agraria pada 2023, mayoritas di perkebunan sawit. https://jikalahari.or.id/kabar/klipingberita/241-konflik-agraria-pada-2023-mayoritas-di-perkebunan-sawit/

Forest Insights (2023) Perkebunan PT Kallista Alam Cicil Rp 57,1 Miliar Pembayaran Ganti Rugi Lingkungan Karhutla, Total 114,3 Miliar. https://forestinsights.id/perkebunan-pt-kallista-alam-cicil-rp571-miliar-pembayaran-ganti-rugi-lingkungan-karhutla-total-rp1143-miliar/

Forwood G et al. (2023) EU adopts new rules for deforestation-free products. https://www.whitecase.com/insight-alert/eu-adopts-new-rules-deforestation-free-products

Grand View Research. Palm Oil Market (2025–2035). https://www.grandviewresearch.com/industry-analysis/palm-oil-market

Gunningham N, Grabosky P, Sinclair D (1998) Smart regulation: designing environmental policy. OUP, Oxford

Gupta N, Chancal A (2022) Mainstreaming ESG and role of the board. JoG 5(1):1–30

Heine J (2023) The global south is on the rise—but what exactly is the global south?. The Conversation. 3 July 2023. https://theconversation.com/the-global-south-is-on-the-rise-but-what-exactly-is-the-global-south-207959

ISPO and RSPO Secretariat (2015) Joint study on the similarities and differences of ISPO and RSPO certification system. https://rspo.org/wp-content/uploads/ispo-rspo-studi-bersama-ispo-rspo-joint-study-english.pdf

Karsenty A, Picard B (2021) Imported deforestation: how Europe contributes to tree loss worldwide and what we can do about it. https://theconversation.com/imported-deforestation-how-europe-contributes-to-tree-loss-worldwide-and-what-we-can-do-about-it-169708

Knox JH (2020) The Paris agreement as a human right treaty. In: Akande D et al (eds) Human rights and 21st century challenges: poverty, conflict and the environment. Oxford Academic, Oxford

Larsen RK et al (2018) Hybrid governance in agricultural commodity chains: insights from implementation of "no deforestation, no peat, no exploitation" (NDPE) policies in the oil palm industry. JoCP 183:544–554

Liu J (2019) Smart mixes in forest governance. In: Erp JV et al (eds) Smart mixes for transboundary environmental harm. CUP, Cambridge

Orts EW (1995) A reflexive model of environmental law. BEQ 5(4):779–794

Pirard R et al (2015) Zero deforestation commitments in Indonesia: governance challenges. CIFOR, Bogor

Pollman E (2021) Corporate social responsibility, ESG and compliance. University of Pennsylvania Carey Law School, Philadelphia

Progress, JPIC & Yayasan Masyarakat Kehutanan Lestari (2023) Community Massive Actions That Leads to The Shooting Tragedy on PT Hamparan Massawit Bangun Persada (HMBP) Amid The Implementation of Jurisdictional Approach on Sustainable Palm Oil in Seruyan District, Press Conference. https://www.forestpeoples.org/sites/default/files/documents/Press%20Conference%20Seruyan%0HMBP.pdf

Situmorang AW (2015) Road to improving Forest governance in Indonesia: Initial assessment on the implementation of joint regulation on the multi-door approach to address natural resources and environment-related crimes in Forest areas and Peatlands. UN-REDD Programme

Steinweg T et al (2017) Unsustainable palm oil faces increasing market access risks: NDPE sourcing policies cover 74 Percent of Southeast Asia's refining capacity (updated version). Chain Reaction Research, Washington DC

Voora V et al (2023) Global market: palm oil prices and sustainability. IISD and SSI. https://www.iisd.org/system/files/2023-06/2023-global-market-report-palm-oil.pdf

Wicaksono RA (2022) PN Suka Makmue harus dampingi penilaian aset PT Kallista Alam. https://betahita.id/news/detail/6982/pn-suka-makmue-harus-dampingi-penilaian-aset-pt-kallista-alam.html?v=1641787832

Kenny Cetera is a legal consultant specializing in environmental law and forestry crimes. He holds both bachelor's and master's degrees in law from Universitas Gadjah Mada. His work focuses on forest governance, illegal wildlife trade, and illegal timber trade. He was a Young Southeast Asian Leaders Initiative (YSEALI) Professional Fellow awarded by the US Department of State. During his fellowship, he did research on the influence of deforestation policies from demand-side countries, like the United States and European countries, on forest product supplier countries like Indonesia.

Azam Hawari is an environmental lawyer at ClientEarth, specializing in international environmental law, forestry, land use, and sustainable commodity supply chains. He has experience at a government mission to the United Nations and with international organizations/think tanks. He holds an LL.M. in International Environmental Law from the Elisabeth Haub School of Law at Pace University as a Fulbright scholar.

Ethical Issues and the Applicability of Environmental, Social and Governance (ESG) Standards in the Moroccan Tourism Industry: The Case of the Seaside Resort Taghazout Bay (Agadir)

Rachid El Bazzim and Hassan Edman

Abstract This study examines whether the Taghazout resort in the Agadir region is on track to implement environmental, social and governance (ESG) standards, addressing the gap left by previous research on the noneconomic factors linked to ESG risks in Morocco's tourism demand.

Using a longitudinal case study approach grounded in semi-structured interviews and document analysis, the research explores ESG implementation in the Taghazout Bay Station. The findings indicate that, contrary to official statements, the implementation of ESG standards is behind schedule, facing significant delays and challenges. The study highlights that the lower-than-expected integration of environmental concerns and local communities exposes weaknesses in the Taghazout project. The research emphasises the need for stakeholders in the Agadir region to focus on successfully implementing ESG standards to enhance future tourism demand by safeguarding the environment and preserving local community values.

1 Introduction

The tourism sector, key to in Morocco's economy, is currently being called upon to comply with new requirements in terms of sustainability. The observation of the multi-stakeholder governance of Moroccan tourism projects highlights the role of the adoption and implementation of environmental, social and governance (ESG) standards as management tools enabling this governance.

ESG standards can address issues considered important by various organisational stakeholders (e.g. consumers, employees, suppliers, non-governmental organisations) that are not addressed by organisational financial performance

R. El Bazzim (✉) · H. Edman
Faculty of Juridical, Economic and Social Sciences, Ibn Zohr University, Agadir, Morocco
e-mail: r.elbazzim@uiz.ac.ma; h.edman@uiz.ac.ma

S. Talukdar (ed.), *Law, Accountability, and Corporate Conduct*, New Approaches to Business, Human Rights and the Environment 1,
https://doi.org/10.1007/978-3-032-28714-4_7

measures.[1] As such, an organisation's ESG practices aim to address particular issues related to the environment, the society and their governance to improve the overall performance of the organisation.[2]

This study aims to explore how the Taghazout Bay tourist resort can effectively implement ESG standards while respecting ethical principles and ensuring alignment between discourse and practice. It seeks to understand the main challenges and opportunities in applying ESG frameworks within the Moroccan tourism sector. Specifically, the research addresses how governance structures, stakeholder engagement and local environmental and social dynamics influence the success or failure of ESG integration.

Given initiatives to combat climate change and the increased emphasis on preserving natural resources, ESG practices have become increasingly critical. Additionally, tourism business stakeholders are demanding the adoption of ESG as a necessity of business operations. For example, ESG practices have been used by companies as effective tools to achieve the United Nation's Sustainable Development Goals (SDGs). Thus, executives of hotel facilities and boards of directors of tourism companies disseminate their ESG objectives and results linked to specific SDGs. In addition, the COVID-19 pandemic has caused shifts in the behaviour of players in the tourism sector, who now favour the search for long-term stability to mitigate risk.

This study is based on the case study of the Taghazout Bay resort. The Taghazout Bay resort, opening onto one of the bays of the Kingdom of Morocco, stands out in terms of its natural assets—with 4.5 km of beaches—hinterland and climate. The eco-responsible commitment deployed at all stages and all levels of this project requires the involvement of stakeholders in the development of the seaside resort in the Souss-Massa region. The implementation of this station aims to respond to the changing needs of stakeholders rather than focusing solely on financial performance. Additionally, the resort views the current uncertain environment as an opportunity to promote ESG metrics in its strategic planning. The tourism and hospitality industry has many stakeholder groups and expectations and has been hugely impacted by the COVID-19 pandemic.

In general, because the ESG framework is a practical way to anchor corporate responsibility and sustainability commitments, it is believed that its application in the tourism and hospitality sector would be effective in helping companies in the sector improve their performance and resilience.[3] Moreover, as the tourism and hospitality industry's upstream suppliers and downstream consumers are widely distributed across different sectors, the effects of ESG measurement guidelines for tourism companies can spread to other sectors, thus greatly impacting environmental and societal issues and improving the overall efficiency of the sector's management.[4]

---

[1] Çakar and Uzut (2020), p. 5.

[2] Fatemi et al. (2018), p. 1.

[3] Chen et al. (2022), p. 2.

[4] Camilleri (2018), p. 7.

In this contribution, we aim to fill three research gaps to address the aforementioned aspects. Firstly, although general ESG metrics have been disclosed to guide ESG practices and strengthen social responsibility and sustainable development, the development of ESG metrics for the tourism and hospitality sector in Morocco remains in its infancy. Secondly, while previous literature has focused on the link between ESG performance and financial performance, this contribution aims to study the case of the Taghazout Bay station in Morocco, revealing its opportunities and weaknesses. Thirdly, current ESG measures and standards have mostly been designed by developed countries.[5] However, the case of the tourism industry of a developing country such as Morocco can be essential to further improve and promote ESG standards. As such, we pose the following research question: How can the Taghazout Bay tourist resort implement ESG standards while respecting ethical principles and bridging the gap between discourse and practice?

This study examines the measures implemented in the Taghazout Bay seaside resort, with a three-pronged objective: economic, social and environmental. By seeking to preserve natural resources, maintain socio-cultural authenticity and promote the well-being of host communities, the Taghazout Bay seaside resort is part of a sustainable development approach to tourism.

2 Methodology

To explore these questions, this study adopts a longitudinal case study approach, which is particularly suited to understanding how processes evolve over time and which factors influence their dynamics.[6] This method allows for an in-depth understanding of such phenomena, especially the evolution of causal relationships over time, because longitudinal case studies involve examining the changes and impacts of phenomena over an extended period. In the context of this research, the data collection tool selected to examine the various dimensions concerning the experience of the Taghazout seaside resort is the semi-structured interview. Such interviews enable direct contact between the stakeholders and the researcher. Interviews conducted with ten project stakeholders gathered the information needed to understand the meaning of standards in the promotion of sustainable tourism and to approach the subject without prejudice by observing this experience in its singularity. Data from the interviews were supplemented and consolidated by an analysis of documents including sources such as newspapers, legislative texts, annual reports from public bodies and secondary sources. The interviews were the mainstay of the data collection; documents were used primarily to cross-check and clarify the factual data provided by interviewees. Several field visits occurred to directly observe current practices and adopt an immersive approach, thus allowing a more in-depth

[5] Singhania and Saini (2023), p. 10.

[6] George and Bennett (1999), p. 65.

understanding of the local context, primarily in May and June 2024, with a final visit in early July 2024 to verify and refine the results obtained.

3 Literature Review

The Moroccan tourism industry faces complex challenges, including environmental preservation, social responsibility and transparent governance. ESG standards provide an essential framework for assessing the sector's sustainable performance. In this context, examining these standards can help shape a positive future for tourism in Morocco.

3.1 ESG Standards and Sustainable Performance

The tourism industry is increasingly adopting ESG practices to promote sustainability and responsibility.[7] Thus, tourism companies seek to minimise their environmental impact by implementing practices such as waste reduction, water management and the use of renewable energy. In short, the adoption of ESG practices in the tourism sector aims to contribute to the preservation of the environment, well-being of local communities and sustainability of the industry.[8]

In Morocco, many large business groups are now adopting ESG principles. Supported by certain media, this subject is becoming a key focus of consulting firms, which are now organising a series of activities on this subject. In fact, numerous studies have highlighted the significant impact of ESG criteria on company value creation. The overall performance of the three ESG pillars (environmental, social and governance) promotes investment returns,[9] including market valuation, financial performance, operational performance and even stock prices. However, research opportunities to deepen the understanding of ESG adoption in this sector remain. Investors and other stakeholders are increasingly demanding quality ESG information to assess companies' long-term risks and opportunities.[10] However, even if managed sustainably and according to ESG standards, tourism alone cannot constitute a universal solution for development problems. Furthermore, the tourism sector in the Global South struggles to free itself from the influence of multinationals from the Global North, particularly with regard to the dissemination of information and destination marketing.[11]

---

[7] Jørgensen and McKercher (2019), p. 913.

[8] Han et al. (2020), p. 313.

[9] Ionescu et al. (2019), p. 824.

[10] De Grosbois and Fennell (2022), p. 7.

[11] Arib (2005), p. 41.

The COVID-19 pandemic and climate crisis have highlighted the importance of social standards and corporate governance for the sustainability of businesses. The recovery of Morocco's hotel sector, which generates between 6% and 10% of the nation's GDP, albeit reassuring, raises key questions regarding its environmental and ecological impact. Before 2010, Moroccan hotels displayed few, if any, ecological measures related to sustainable tourism. However, this situation has since evolved, with many establishments, in both urban and rural areas, now committing to an eco-responsible approach.[12]

However, critiques have targeted the use of unified measures and concepts[13] proposed from different perspectives. Thus, it was emphasised that the Sustainability Accounting Standards Board (SASB) pays particular attention to shareholders and market valuation when determining matters that may affect the financial position or operational performance of a company.[14] This could explain why the SASB-compliant restaurant list does not contain information on many topics considered important by various stakeholders in the restaurant industry but instead focuses primarily on financial risks linked to ESG factors. However, it may underestimate the long-term benefits of sustainability and social responsibility. In addition, the SASB relies on information provided by the companies themselves (e.g. annual reports, declarations). If a company does not provide accurate or complete data, the rating may be biased.

Moreover, ESG rating mechanisms have been criticised for their lack of standardisation and transparency. Scholars such as Berg et al. (2022) have shown that ESG scores can vary significantly across rating agencies, leading to confusion among investors and stakeholders. This inconsistency opens the door to greenwashing, where companies exaggerate or misrepresent their sustainability efforts to appear more responsible than they are.[15]

This growing ambiguity in ESG assessments raises important questions about how tourism companies, particularly in the hospitality sector, are responding to these challenges in practice. In this context, hotel companies present widely varying levels of transparency regarding issues linked to climate change; some stand out by providing comprehensive reports, detailing their actions and strategies to reduce their carbon footprint and minimise their environmental impact. In contrast, other hotel companies do not publish any reports on these crucial issues.

The theoretical framework underpinning this analysis draws on stakeholder theory and institutional theory. Stakeholder theory emphasises the importance of addressing the expectations of all parties affected by corporate actions, not just shareholders. Institutional theory, on the other hand, explains how organisations

[12] In 2023, the Sol Oasis hotel in Marrakech is committed to sustainability by using solar energy to ensure around 80% of its electricity supply. In addition, the hotel has invested in a wastewater treatment plant, an example to follow for the rest of the hotel industry.

[13] Chen et al. (2022a), p. 12.

[14] Kim and Lee (2020), p. 3.

[15] Berg et al. (2022), p. 1320.

conform to social norms and regulatory pressures, which is particularly relevant in the context of ESG compliance in tourism.

The literature has highlighted the importance of developing specific ESG standards for companies in the tourism and hospitality sector that should consider the particularities of each country and specificities of each company. Indeed, national contexts, local regulations and stakeholder expectations vary considerably between regions.

To better understand how ESG principles are being adapted across different tourism contexts, it is useful to examine regional case studies.

For instance, studies in Southeast Asia (e.g. Baloch et al. 2023) have examined how tourism development can align with environmental sustainability through structured ESG frameworks.[16] Their research highlights the importance of integrating ecotourism principles into national tourism strategies, particularly in regions where natural ecosystems are under pressure from mass tourism. The authors propose a model that balances economic growth with environmental preservation, emphasizing the role of government regulation and stakeholder engagement. This Southeast Asian perspective offers valuable insights for countries like Morocco, where similar tensions exist between tourism expansion and ecological protection.

In Europe, Font et al. (2016) have explored how ESG reporting in the hospitality sector influences consumer behaviour and corporate accountability,[17] while in African countries, Salihi et al. (2025) have examined how environmental sustainability can be advanced through financial inclusion and technological innovation.[18] Their study, covering 54 African countries, highlights the importance of ESG-aligned strategies such as green financing, renewable energy investment and sustainable business practices. These findings underscore the need for context-specific ESG frameworks that reflect the institutional and technological realities of African nations.

In short, the core mission of ESG is to support sustainable development; this should not be pure speech or fashion. These standards aim to promote sustainability, transparency and accountability in the sector while minimising adverse effects on the environment and local communities.[19]

Legal frameworks are also evolving to support ESG integration. The European Union's Corporate Sustainability Reporting Directive (CSRD), for example, mandates detailed ESG disclosures for large companies, aiming to harmonise sustainability reporting and reduce greenwashing (European Commission 2023).[20] In emerging markets, countries such as South Africa have introduced ESG disclosure

[16] Baloch et al. (2023), p. 5920.

[17] Font et al. (2016), p. 180.

[18] Salihi et al. (2025), p. 315.

[19] Su and Chen (2020), p. 1.

[20] Directive (EU) 2022/2464 of the European Parliament and of the Council of 14 December 2022 on corporate sustainability reporting, OJ L 322, 16.12.2022, p. 15–80, available at: https://eur-lex.europa.eu/legal-content/EN/TXT/?uri=CELEX:32022L2464

requirements through the Johannesburg Stock Exchange (JSE 2022).[21] In Asia, India has made Business Responsibility and Sustainability Reporting (BRSR) mandatory for its top 1000 listed firms (SEBI 2023),[22] and the ASEAN region is developing a unified taxonomy for sustainable finance (ASEAN 2023).[23] These legal instruments are crucial in reducing greenwashing and ensuring accountability.

In summary, although many studies have been conducted on the relationship between ESG practices and financial performance in the tourism sector, the literature reveals that the adoption of ESG standards in this sector, particularly from the perspective of developing countries such as Morocco, has not yet been fully dedicated or gained sufficient ground.

3.2 *Building Sustainable Tourism*

Today, tourists place increased importance on safety when traveling. The COVID-19 pandemic prompted people to think more carefully, perhaps for the first time, about potential risks to their health and the environment. They now seek guarantees of sustainability in the design and operation of their destination's hotel establishments, and they want broader commitment from funders to these concerns. In this context, the concept of sustainable tourism (TD) emerged, with the aim of reducing the negative effects of mass tourism, which have accelerated in recent decades. The final document of the Rio+20 conference, crucial in promoting sustainable tourism, states that the correct path for the development of society is to reduce poverty, promote social justice and preserve natural resources.[24] Accordingly, sustainable tourism provides guidelines for tourism planning and management, considering environmental, social, economic and climatic aspects. Tourists question not only the safety and potential well-being in a given hotel but also the long-term environmental consequences of their stay; they wonder about the impact of their travels on the ecosystem and its preservation for future generations. Today, the Internet offers concrete answers to these questions, informing customer decisions with data on environmental impacts. Additionally, the ESG efforts adopted by some tourism establishments are crucial in this awareness.

Tourism is a key component of SDGs 8, 12 and 14, which aim to promote inclusive and sustainable economic growth, ensure sustainable consumption and

[21] Johannesburg Stock Exchange (2022).

[22] Securities and Exchange Board of India (2023), BRSR Core – Framework for Assurance and ESG Disclosures for Value Chain, Circular No. SEBI/HO/CFD/CFD-SEC-2/P/CIR/2023/122, 12 July 2023, available at https://www.sebi.gov.in/legal/circulars/jul-2023/brsr-core-framework-for-assurance-and-esg-disclosures-for-value-chain_73854.html

[23] ASEAN Taxonomy Board (2024).

[24] Resolution 66/288, "The future we want", adopted by the United Nations General Assembly, 123rd plenary session, July 27, 2012, A/RES/66/288. https://sustainabledevelopment.un.org/futurewewant.html

production patterns and conserve oceans, seas and marine resources for sustainable development. In this context, the Moroccan Ministry of Tourism, Crafts and the Social and Solidarity Economy aims to compete with major global destinations and has outlined an ambitious vision: welcoming 26 million tourists by 2030. However, it is essential to consider the environmental consequences of the tourism industry. The construction of tourism facilities can result in an excessive ecological footprint, putting the future of humanity at risk. To improve the future of Moroccan tourism, the government can certainly revolutionise its policies, processes and structures in terms of environmental sustainability and the protection of human rights and the free market. Assessing the impact of ESG risk mitigation measures is crucial in shaping the future of the tourism sector.[25]

In Morocco, the tourism sector occupies a preponderant place in the economy, exerting significant influence on the development of the regions. It promotes cultural and social growth while laying the foundations for new entrepreneurial opportunities. However, this field faces the challenge of harmoniously integrating economic, social and environmental dimensions. In other words, it is imperative to incorporate the concept of sustainable development into tourism policies while rethinking economic models to manage these complex dynamics. Tourism demand in Morocco may depend on non-economic factors such as ESG risk factors, which also raises questions about the importance of such factors for the future of tourism in the country. The link between countries' tourism demand and each facet of their ESG risk performance has been studied in the literature. For example, regarding environmental factors, climate has been a key determinant of tourism demand, with tourists seeking destinations with a relaxed atmosphere.[26]

The World Tourism Organisation (UNWTO 2003), in its Djerba Declaration, recognises a bilateral association between CO_2 emissions and tourism demand, a position reinforced by Hamilton et al. (2005), who argue that extraordinary destinations could attract more tourists than warm destinations due to global warming. The Moroccan tourism industry is working to promote sustainable tourism in response to the growing attention given to this issue globally. In 2017, the UNWTO proclaimed the International Year of Sustainable Tourism for Development, highlighting four essential components of sustainable tourism: raising awareness of and promoting sustainable travel, disseminating information on sustainable travel, developing sustainable travel policies and providing sustainable travel education. These actions encourage the tourism sector to prioritise non-financial performance, emphasising environmental and social contributions rather than focusing solely on financial results. Since tourism depends on human resources, sustainability has become a key issue for the sector. This promotion of sustainable tourism is a step towards a future where tourism contributes positively to the well-being of local communities and preservation of the planet.

[25] Goymen (2000), p. 1040.

[26] Aguilo et al. (2005), p. 229.

Indeed, the non-financial elements of a business encompass efforts aimed at improving governance, contributing to social issues and preserving the environment. ESG issues are truly consistent with sustainability.

4 The Taghazout Bay Seaside Resort

The longitudinal case study of the Taghazout Bay resort in Agadir explores the relationship between the discourse on ESG standards and approaches to sustainable tourism in the Moroccan context. This resort, located 15 km from Agadir, presents itself as an example of eco-responsible tourism.

4.1 Presentation of the Taghazout Bay Seaside Resort

Located on the Atlantic coast of Morocco, 15 km north of the city of Agadir and covering the territories of the communes of Taghazout and Aourir, the Taghazout Bay seaside resort is considered one of the tangible successes of the AZUR plan[27] (2010) and the 2020 Tourism Vision. The project was designed and developed by the Taghazout resort development and promotion company (SAPST, **S**ociété d'**A**ménagement et de **P**romotion de la **S**tation de **T**aghazout) to be truly anchored and integrated into its local environment, hence its name, the "New Integrated Tourist Station of Taghazout". The tourist resort is renowned for its harmonious blend of modern luxury and social and environmental responsibility.

The resort extends over 615 ha along sandy beaches and presents a complete, diversified, attractive and continually developing tourist offering. Its primary components (see Fig. 1) include luxury accommodation offered by hotel and residential units, spaces and infrastructure for water activities including surfing, a holiday village, top-notch wellness and relaxation facilities and varieties of dining and entertainment products. The project also includes world-class golf courses, the first Argan museum in the world and areas of connection with the local environment, including public and private facilities.

The discourse of public actors sees that the development of Taghazout Bay is part of a vision of sustainability, integrating innovative environmental management practices and strong commitments in terms of social responsibility. The project is presented as a model of sustainable tourism in Morocco, following the four paradigms of responsible tourism: natural, experiential, sensory and healthy (see Fig. 2).

---

[27] A development initiative aimed at creating high-quality hostels while respecting the principles of sustainable development. The term "Azur" refers to the blue colour associated with clear skies or the sea, symbolising the region's coastal beauty. The implementation of this plan is intended to drive dynamic growth through an increase in tourism, which will also generate a significant number of jobs.

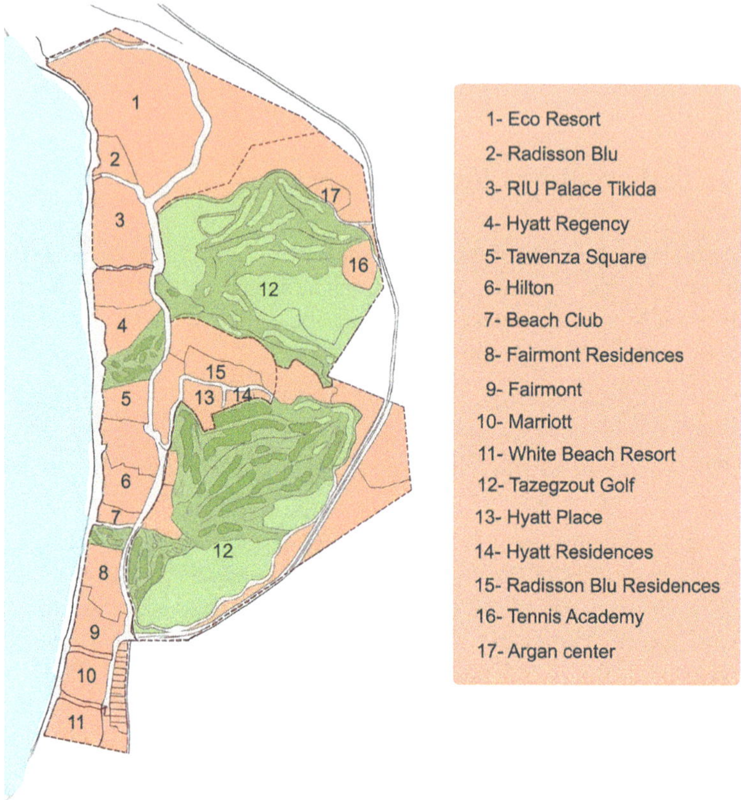

Fig. 1 Ground plan of the Taghazout Bay seaside resort. *Source:* Processed by authors (2026), using SAPS (2022) data

The resort stands out for its commitment to respecting international standards for sustainable development, including the protection of fragile coastal ecosystems and reduction of the carbon footprint through initiatives such as the efficient use of resources and promotion of energy renewable.

To fully and effectively adhere to the social and environmental commitments of the 2020 Tourism Vision, the SAPST (2022) has included the station in an integrated approach:

- Embark on a quality, safety and environment (QSE) approach applied to all project activities and processes
- Engage in an high environmental quality (HEQ) development approach integrating the whole of Taghazout Bay, as well as an HEQ approach for residential and non-residential buildings, applied to the residential and other components of the project

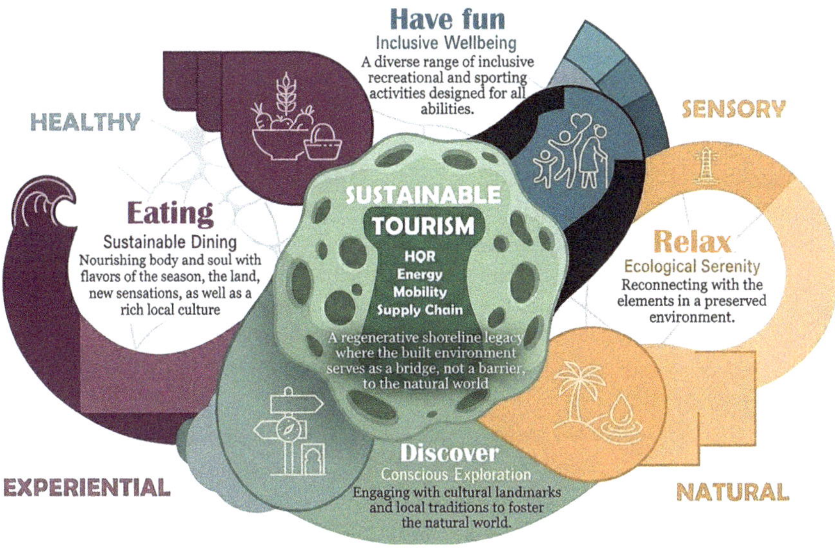

Fig. 2 Sustainable tourism, paradigms and concepts of the Taghazout Bay seaside resort. *Source:* processed by authors (2026)

- Start a Green Globe approach applied to the golf course, the Golf Hotel and the surf village

The QSE and HEQ approaches applied to the entire station encompass four main axes:[28] a sports-focused destination, including mountain biking, trekking, hang gliding and water sports; a cultural and discovery offer highlighting innovative architecture and rich plant diversity; a nature destination offering exceptional sites, such as routes along the wadis, hiking and an environment combining blue and green; and finally, a sustainable commitment including the promotion of local culture, conservation of 100 ha of argan trees and integration of local populations into the project.

Taghazout Bay aims to play a crucial role in local economic development by creating jobs and stimulating commercial activities in the region. It also strives to be an example of successful collaboration between the private sector and public authorities to promote sustainable and responsible tourism.

4.2 Data Collection and Analysis

To collect information on the experience of the Taghazout seaside resort, semi-structured interviews were chosen as the primary data collection tool. This type of interview promotes direct contact between local actors and researchers, making it

[28] Benattou (2023), p. 489.

possible to understand the role of standards in promoting sustainable tourism and explore the resort experience, observing its specific aspects.

Interviews were conducted with local elected officials,[29] local residents, representatives of local associations and station staff (employees and managers). This made it possible to compare rhetoric to practice. We had the opportunity to interact with staff and tourists for several days, which allowed for an in-depth analysis of the Taghazout Bay tourist resort development project. This study was conducted in Agadir, with data collected between March and June 2024.

The data collected during the interviews were enriched and verified by documentary analysis, including newspapers, legislative texts, annual reports of public bodies and secondary sources. While interviews formed the core of the data collection, documents were used primarily to cross-check and clarify the information provided by interviewees.

Data collection occurred in May and June 2024, through face-to-face or telephone interviews with local managers and stakeholders of the Taghazout Bay station. A semi-structured interview guide was used, structured around open-ended questions aimed at exploring the application of ESG standards in the resort. This guide is based on a grid of items relating to ESG standards, adapted to the particularities of the tourism sector.

The questions asked during the interviews covered the following aspects:

- Measures implemented to improve the environmental and social impacts of tourism in Taghazout Bay, especially with regard to the local community
- Actions taken to respect governance standards and ensure the transparency of tourism operations
- Sustainable development strategies applied to maximise benefits for local communities while minimising negative impacts on cultural heritage and the environment
- Long-term plans to ensure the sustainability of the tourism project

In addition to the interviews, we conducted several field visits to directly observe current practices and adopt an immersive approach, thus allowing a more in-depth understanding of the local context. These visits occurred place in May and June 2024, with a final visit in July 2024 to verify and refine the results obtained.

In addition to the field survey, our corpus of data comprised various documents, including notes, charters, reports, descriptions of procedures, press releases, development plans, brochures, websites, catalogues, press releases from associations and petitions from members of civil society. These documents were used to enrich and complete the data collected to identify significant findings and launch a process of reflection on the ethical issues of the applicability of ESG standards to the tourism sector in Morocco, particularly at the resort level.

[29] Elected from the following territorial authorities: Souss Massa region, Agadir Idaoutanane prefecture and the municipality of Taghazout.

5 Findings and Discussion

As part of our qualitative study on ESG standards in Taghazout Bay, we explored how these standards could be integrated into a sustainable tourism approach for this seaside resort. The main objectives was to identify the obstacles linked to ethical issues encountered by local actors and the levers necessary to overcome them. We were able to identify results that fall into two categories: endogenous and exogenous. On the one hand, we identified issues linked to the internal limitations of the resort to adopt a sustainable tourism approach; on the other, we highlighted difficulties associated with relationships and interactions with the project territory.

5.1 Integrating a Sustainable Tourism Approach: Inabilities and Difficulties

Indeed, despite the certifications obtained by Taghazout Bay mentioned above, this research reveals significant shortcomings, particularly with regard to waste collection and wastewater treatment. This highlights a dissonance between the good intentions of official discourse and reality. At this level, this is a situation often criticised in the literature on corporate social responsibility (CSR).[30]

These shortcomings can partly be attributed to the governance structures of Moroccan tourism, which are characterised by top-down decision-making and limited local participation. The lack of coordination between public authorities, private investors and civil society actors weakens the enforcement of ESG standards and hinders sustainable development efforts. This fragmented governance model perpetuates ESG non-compliance by failing to establish clear accountability mechanisms or long-term sustainability benchmarks.[31]

This issue is not unique to Taghazout Bay. Nationally, only 20% of collected wastewater is treated before being discharged into the environment.[32] This low treatment rate raises serious concerns in coastal tourist zones, where seasonal population surges increase pressure on already fragile sanitation infrastructure (see Table 1).

Dissatisfaction with the deterioration of the natural resources of the local environment, particularly water resources, was also mentioned. The presence of numerous tourist structures in a region already experiencing water stress worsens environmental conditions. The inadequate management of natural resources, exacerbated by tourism development, is a major ethical problem that raises questions about business priorities.[33] Often, economic profits and market logic are prioritised

[30] Acquier and Gond (2007), p. 24.

[31] Davis (2006), p. 90.

[32] CFCIM (2014), p. 1.

[33] Arib (2005), p. 4; Butler (1974), p. 107.

Table 1 First extract from comments collected during the field survey, 2024

"We see that waste is not collected regularly, and wastewater is not treated properly, which poses major environmental problems"
"Despite the certifications obtained, the station has failed to put in place effective systems for waste collection and wastewater treatment"
"The pressure exerted by hotels on water resources is enormous, especially in a region already experiencing water stress. Promises of sustainability seem more like marketing tools than a sincere commitment"

Source: processed by authors, 2025

Table 2 Second extract from comments collected during the field survey, 2024

"We find that priority is often given to economic profits rather than environmental protection and the well-being of the local community"

Source: processed by authors, 2025

over ecological sustainability, revealing a tension between economic, social and environmental objectives.[34]

The Souss-Massa region, where Taghazout Bay is located, is officially recognised as a high water stress area. The resort is being developed in a coastal zone that combines urban and rural dynamics, in a context where water scarcity is a structural environmental constraint.[35] This raises legitimate concerns about the long-term sustainability of tourism infrastructure, particularly during peak seasons when demand for water increases significantly.

These concerns are not isolated to Taghazout Bay. Other large-scale coastal tourism projects in Morocco have also faced criticism for failing to integrate environmental constraints into their development strategies (see Table 2).

A relevant example is the seaside resort of Saïdia, which has been widely criticised for its poor integration of coastal preservation into its development strategy. Moroccan decision-makers failed to maintain a balance between tourism investment and environmental protection. The coastline has been heavily urbanised, with cafés built on sand dunes and pedestrian walkways constructed close to the shoreline, disrupting the dune ecosystem and altering the visual and ecological integrity of the area. This case illustrates how ESG principles are often sidelined in favour of short-term economic gains.[36]

The large gap between sustainability promises and their practical realisation[37] reflects the complexity of sustainability issues. Although some interviewees expressed being happy or even proud of the project, others were critical of the effective implementation of the station's social and environmental commitments. This

[34] Ben Yedder and Zrelli (2020), p. 2.

[35] Construction21 (2016), p. 1.

[36] Yabiladi (2020).

[37] Burrai et al. (2019), p. 9.

illustrates internal difficulties in the tangible applicability of ESG standards, at least at the environmental and social levels.

5.2 The Prospects of a Lasting and More Solid Territorial Anchoring

The second major ethical issue in the applicability of ESG standards is linked primarily to the level of inclusion of the local environment. To guarantee sustainable tourism in Taghazout Bay, it is crucial to establish a lasting and solid territorial anchor, which would require a deep integration of the seaside resort into its local environment, both ecologically and socio-economically. Taghazout Bay aims to transcend certifications and adopt authentic and transparent ESG practices, integrating local concerns into their management model.[38]

Despite these ambitions, this objective remains largely unfulfilled. The continued reliance on centralised, top-down governance structures restricts the effective participation of local communities. This structural limitation undermines the credibility of ESG commitments and contributes to the perception of sustainability as rhetorical rather than transformative (see Table 3).

According to interviewees, the resort must work closely with local communities to promote sustainable practices that benefit both the environment and society.

Aligning economic objectives with ESG commitments appears essential for the development of truly sustainable tourism.[39] Recent initiatives, although not directly related to Taghazout Bay, may offer valuable models for replication. In 2024, the Moroccan Society for Tourism Engineering (SMIT) launched a programme to promote rural and heritage-based tourism. This initiative includes the adaptive reuse of traditional kasbahs as eco-friendly guesthouses and the development of income-generating activities in surrounding communities. By promoting local participation and environmental stewardship, this programme reflects a governance approach more closely aligned with ESG principles.

Table 3 Third extract from comments collected during the field survey, 2024

"Often, we are not consulted or included in decisions. For Taghazout Bay to succeed in the long term, it is crucial that residents' voices are heard and taken into account. We know our environment and our needs better than anyone"
"We need jobs and opportunities, but we also want to preserve our environment and our community. Including local residents in Taghazout Bay tourism projects can help balance economic development with ecological conservation and social cohesion. We must be partners, not just spectators"

Source: processed by authors, 2025

[38] Acquier and Gond (2007), p. 29.

[39] Ben Yedder and Zrelli (2020), p. 15.

Table 4 Fourth extract from comments collected during the field survey, 2024

"Tourism can bring economic benefits, but it must not come at the expense of our culture and way of life. It is essential that the resort works hand in hand with us, the locals, to ensure that the development is beneficial for all and respects our traditions and heritage"

Source: processed by authors, 2025

This contrast between the persistent shortcomings of large-scale coastal resorts and the more inclusive models emerging in rural tourism highlights a structural paradox in Moroccan tourism governance. Although national strategies increasingly reference sustainability, operational frameworks often lack mechanisms—such as local consultation, accountability and ESG monitoring—that would support effective implementation.

In this context, the study reveals the need to implement corrective measures. Taghazout Bay must assess and mitigate the negative impacts of its activities, such as waste management and pressure on water resources. Implementing best-practice systems for waste and wastewater management would be a key step in reducing the resort's ecological footprint and restoring trust with local communities (see Table 4).

As emphasised by Berger-Douce (2011) and de Bry (2008), ethics can act as a catalyst for a sustainable strategy. This involves going beyond mere compliance with ESG standards and integrating ethical principles into all strategic decisions. An ethical approach could include initiatives to support local economies, promote local culture, preserve the natural environment and ensure the participation of local stakeholders in sustainable tourism management.[40]

More broadly, strategic dimensions must be considered for sustainable practices.[41] For Taghazout Bay, this means taking a holistic approach to sustainable development, incorporating long-term strategies that benefit both the company and local community. Collaborating with local associations, partnering with sustainable businesses and educating tourists on environmentally friendly practices are key steps.

Progressing towards these objectives may require a shift towards more decentralised governance and the gradual establishment of participatory mechanisms. Transparent ESG monitoring systems and partnerships with sustainable enterprises and civil society actors could help reinforce this trajectory towards more ethical and inclusive tourism.

6 Conclusion

In this study, we returned to practices and commitments in terms of ESG standards in the tourism sector in Morocco, particularly the case of the Taghazout Bay seaside resort in Agadir. Despite the benefits of the project, in particular local employment,

[40] Arib (2005), p. 41; Burrai et al. (2019), p. 11.

[41] Mathieu and Soparnot (2009), p. 211.

vulnerabilities and inadequacies remain in terms of the inclusion of the local community and modes of production and consumption harmful to the social and environmental balances of the local environment.

Taghazout Bay's inability to effectively apply ESG standards and implement sustainable tourism reveals significant ethical issues. The literature review highlights the importance of an authentic commitment to sustainable practices, the responsible management of natural resources and a deep integration of ethical principles into business strategies. The testimonies of local actors confirm the need to bridge the gap between discourse and practice to ensure development that is truly sustainable and beneficial for the local community and environment.

Long-term territorial anchoring of Taghazout Bay is crucial for the establishment of sustainable tourism. This requires the authentic integration of ESG standards, ethical and strategic management, attention to social and environmental impacts, active participation by local stakeholders and local ownership of sustainability initiatives. By adopting these practices, Taghazout Bay can become a successful model of a sustainable seaside resort, benefiting both the environment and local communities.

The findings of this study have a number of policy implications for the future of tourism in the Agadir region. Firstly, it is necessary for the Taghazout station to further improve its parameters to implement ESG standards by working to further mitigate risks associated with ESG factors. Furthermore, following the image according to which tourism in the Taghazout Bay resort is considered a luxury, it is necessary for public actors to promote the competitiveness of tourism by guaranteeing the stability of offerings as well as targeting other social groups. Furthermore, policymakers should focus on expanding sustainable tourism and improving infrastructure with the deliberate aim of increasing international tourism demand without neglecting local communities. This suggests that the local environment of resorts and hotel facilities is crucial for the future of sustainable tourism and that emphasis should be placed on policies to improve it in the region by integrating ESG standards.

References

Acquier A, Gond J-P (2007) Aux sources de la responsabilité sociale de l'entreprise: À la (re) découverte d'un ouvrage fondateur, Social Responsibilities of the Businessman d'Howard Bowen. Revue Finance Contrôle Stratégie 10:5–35

Aguilo E, Alegre J, Sard M (2005) The persistence of the sun and sand tourism model. Tour Manag 26(2):219–231

Arib F (2005) Le tourisme: Atout durable du développement au Maroc? Téoros 24(1):37–41. https://doi.org/10.7202/1071108ar

ASEAN Taxonomy Board (2024) ASEAN Taxonomy for Sustainable Finance – Version 3. https://asean.org/book/asean-taxonomy-for-sustainable-finance-version-3/. Accessed 27 May 2025

Baloch QB, Shah SN, Iqbal N et al (2023) Impact of tourism development upon environmental sustainability: a suggested framework for sustainable ecotourism. Environ Sci Pollut Res 30:5917–5930. https://doi.org/10.1007/s11356-022-22496-w

Ben Yedder M, Zrelli I (2020) Les finalités écologique et sociale de la responsabilité sociale de l'entreprise dans le secteur touristique: Opposition ou convergence? Téoros 39(1). https://doi.org/10.7202/1074095ar

Benattou A (2023) Station de Taghazout Bay entre projection touristique,Vécu et marges mondialisées Une approche de communication socio-territoriale. Revue Internationale du Chercheur 4(2):485–511. https://www.revuechercheur.com/index.php/home/article/view/621

Berg F, Kölbel JF, Rigobon R (2022) Aggregate confusion: The divergence of ESG ratings. Rev Financ 26(6):1315–1344. https://doi.org/10.1093/rof/rfac033

Berger-Douce S (2011) L'éthique catalyseur d'une stratégie durable en PME ? Humanisme et Entreprise n° 303(3) 9–24 https://doi.org/10.3917/hume.303.0009

Burrai E, Buda D-M, Stanford D (2019) Rethinking the ideology of responsible tourism. J Sustain Tour 27(7):992–1007. https://doi.org/10.1080/09669582.2019.1578365

Butler RW (1974) The social implications of tourist developments. Ann Tour Res 2(2):100–111. https://doi.org/10.1016/0160-7383(74)90025-5

Çakar K, Uzut İ (2020) Exploring the stakeholder's role in sustainable degrowth within the context of tourist destination governance: the case of Istanbul, Turkey. J Travel Tour Mark 37(8–9):917–932. https://doi.org/10.1080/10548408.2020.1782307

Camilleri MA (2018) The tourism industry: An overview. In: Travel marketing, tourism economics and the airline product, tourism, hospitality & event management. Springer, pp 3–27. https://doi.org/10.1007/978-3-319-49849-2_1

CFCIM (2014) L'eau au Maroc – Fiche marché. https://www.cfcim.org/wp-content/uploads/2015/02/Eau-Maroc-2014.pdf. Accessed 27 May 2025

Chen CD, Su CHJ, Chen MH (2022) Are ESG-committed hotels financially resilient to the COVID-19 pandemic? An autoregressive jump intensity trend model. Tour Manag 104581. https://doi.org/10.1016/j.tourman.2022.104581

Chen CD, Su CHJ, Chen MH (2022a) Understanding how ESG-focused airlines reduce the impact of the COVID-19 pandemic on stock returns. J Air Transp Manag 102:102229. https://doi.org/10.1016/j.jairtraman.2022.102229

Construction21 (2016) Taghazout Bay Eco-Tourism. https://www.construction21.org/belgique/data/exports/pdf/taghazout-bay-eco-tourism.pdf. Accessed 27 May 2025

Davis DK (2006) Neoliberalism, environmentalism, and agricultural restructuring in Morocco. Geogr J 172(2):88–105. https://www.jstor.org/stable/3873982

de Bry F (2008) Principes éthiques et pratiques de la responsabilité sociale des entreprises (RSE), Tome 1. Entreprise éthique, no 28, avril 2008. Cercle éthique

De Grosbois D, Fennell DA (2022) Determinants of climate change disclosure practices of global hotel companies: Application of institutional and stakeholder theories. Tour Manag 88:104404. https://doi.org/10.1016/j.tourman.2021.104404

Fatemi A, Glaum M, Kaiser S (2018) ESG performance and firm value: The moderating role of disclosure. Glob Financ J 38:45–64. https://doi.org/10.1016/j.gfj.2017.03.001

Font X, Guix M, Bonilla-Priego MJ (2016) Corporate social responsibility in cruising: Using materiality analysis to create shared value. Tour Manag 53:175–186. https://doi.org/10.1016/j.tourman.2015.10.007

George AL, Bennett A (1999) Case studies and theory development in the social sciences. MIT Press, Cambridge

Goymen K (2000) Tourism and governance in Turkey. Ann Tour Res 27(4):1025–1048

Hamilton JM, Maddison DJ, Tol RSJ (2005) Climate change and international tourism: a simulation study. Glob Environ Chang 15(3):253–266

Han H, Yu J, Lee KS, Baek H (2020) Impact of corporate social responsibilities on customer responses and brand choices. J Travel Tour Mark 37(3):302–316. https://doi.org/10.1080/10548408.2020.1746731

Ionescu GH, Firoiu D, Pirvu R, Vilag RD (2019) The impact of ESG factors on market value of companies from travel and tourism industry. Technol Econ Dev Econ 25(5):820–849. https://doi.org/10.3846/tede.2019.10294

Johannesburg Stock Exchange (2022) Sustainability disclosure guidance. https://www.jse.co.za/sites/default/files/media/documents/JSE%20Sustainability%20Disclosure%20Guidance_1.pdf. Accessed 27 May 2025

Jørgensen MT, McKercher B (2019) Sustainability and integration–the principal challenges to tourism and tourism research. J Travel Tour Mark 36(8):905–916. https://doi.org/10.1080/10548408.2019.1657054

Kim B, Lee S (2020) The impact of material and immaterial sustainability on firm performance: The moderating role of franchising strategy. Tour Manag 77:103999. https://doi.org/10.1016/j.tourman.2019.103999

Mathieu A, Soparnot R (2009) Les dimensions ontologiques, stratégiques et organisationnelles de l'appropriation du concept de développement durable en entreprise. Manag Avenir 23(3):199–218. https://doi.org/10.3917/mav.023.0199

Salihi AA, Ibrahim H, Baharudin DM (2025) Financial inclusion and environmental sustainability in african countries: role of technology innovation. In: Malik FA, Mahajan S, Yadav DK, Lone NA, Amin S (eds) Financial Resilience and Environmental Sustainability. Springer, Singapore. https://doi.org/10.1007/978-981-96-4269-4_14

SAPST (2022) Taghazout bay destination authentique écoresponsable. SAPST

Singhania M, Saini N (2023) Institutional framework of ESG disclosures: comparative analysis of developed and developing countries. J Sustain Financ Invest 13(1):1–44. https://doi.org/10.1080/20430795.2021.1964810

Su CHJ, Chen CD (2020) Does sustainability index matter to the hospitality industry? Tour Manag 81:104158. https://doi.org/10.1016/j.tourman.2020.104158

United Nations World Tourism Organization (UNWTO) (2003) Djerba declaration on climate change and tourism. Available at: http://www.travelmole.com/news_feature.php?id597591

Yabiladi (2020) Maroc: Le littoral méditerranéen saccagé par les aménagements touristiques, 28 January 2020. Available at: https://www.yabiladi.com/articles/printview/88487/maroc-littoral-mediterraneen-saccage-amenagements.html

Rachid EL Bazzim is a professor of Public Law at the Faculty of Juridical, Economic and Social Sciences, Ibn Zohr University, Agadir, Morocco. His scholarship focuses on regulatory governance, economic regulation, and the independence and accountability of competition and other regulatory authorities, with particular attention to the Arab region and the Global South. He has published on competition law and policy, liberalization and regulatory authorities, parliamentary institutions, and public action in relation to environmental governance.

Hassan Edman is a research professor at the Faculty of Legal, Economic, and Social Sciences at Ibn Zohr University, Morocco. He is a permanent researcher at the Laboratory of Studies and Applied Research in Economic Sciences (LERASE) and an associate researcher at the Moroccan Center for Studies and Policy Analysis (CEMAP). His expertise includes economics, management, territorial development, and public policy.

Global and Regional Governance Challenge

Illegal Fishing in Thailand's Food Industry

Surinrat Kaewtong, Pajon Kongmuang, and Phongsak Jehpong

Abstract Illegal, unreported, and unregulated (IUU) fishing remains one of the most persistent challenges within Thailand's fisheries sector, undermining marine sustainability, workers' rights, and international market access. This chapter traces the historical evolution of Thailand's fishing industry, from traditional small-scale practices to the rapid expansion of mechanized trawling, and shows how technological change, weak regulatory oversight, and overcapacity created conditions for systemic illegality. Drawing on the Business and Human Rights (BHR) framework and the UN Guiding Principles on Business and Human Rights (UNGPs), the chapter argues that Thailand's IUU crisis is inseparable from wider governance failures relating to state duty to protect, corporate responsibility to respect human rights, and gaps in supply chain due diligence. The EU yellow-card pressure acted as an extraterritorial regulatory trigger that compelled significant domestic reforms, including vessel registration, labor inspections, monitoring systems, and coordination with ASEAN mechanisms. However, despite progress, long-term transformation requires more than technical regulation; it demands polycentric accountability involving the state, industry, global buyers, and fishing communities. By situating Thailand's fisheries reforms within a global BHR landscape, the chapter demonstrates how strengthening human rights due diligence, labor protections, and inclusive governance are essential for achieving sustainable and rights-respecting fisheries.

S. Kaewtong · P. Kongmuang (✉) · P. Jehpong
Faculty of Law, Prince of Songkla University, Hat Yai, Thailand
e-mail: pajon.k@psu.ac.th; phongsak.j@psu.ac.th

S. Talukdar (ed.), *Law, Accountability, and Corporate Conduct*, New Approaches to Business, Human Rights and the Environment 1,
https://doi.org/10.1007/978-3-032-28714-4_8

1 Introduction

Thailand's fisheries sector has undergone rapid transformation over the past century, yet this growth has been accompanied by serious environmental and human rights challenges. It is considered a top revenue-generating agricultural industrial product for the country. Though the country is one of the world's leading exporters of aquatic products, with export values in categories such as shrimp, squid, fresh chilled fish, frozen fish, and tuna products exceeding 300 billion baht, illegal, unreported, and unregulated (IUU) fishing has depleted marine resources, undermined regulatory authority, and exposed workers—especially migrants—to widespread exploitation. Understanding Thailand's IUU problem requires an integrated perspective that considers historical fishing practices, technological changes, governance gaps, and the pressures of global seafood supply chains. This chapter adopts a Business and Human Rights (BHR) approach, guided by the UN Guiding Principles on Business and Human Rights (UNGPs), to analyze the state's duty to protect marine and labor rights, the corporate responsibility to respect these rights, and the role of international market actors in shaping accountability.[1]

While marine natural resources provide enormous fishing yields, they face deterioration issues from two main causes: natural degradation and human exploitation. Human causes stem from marine fishing aiming for high economic returns, leading to an increasing interest in the fishing industry and resulting in overfishing. Evidence of this includes the rise in numbers and efficiency of fishing vessels and gear, particularly trawl nets and push nets, which catch bottom-dwelling aquatic animals. These are considered highly destructive tools as they cannot select target aquatic species (non-selective gear).[2]

Overfishing disrupts natural balance and violates laws. When Thailand engages in illegal fishing, import leaders, such as the European Union (EU), express dissatisfaction and issue warnings about possibly suspending fishery product imports from Thailand. This compels Thailand to implement corrective measures as per Order No. 10/2558 from the head of the National Council for Peace and Order (NCPO), addressing illegal, unreported, and unregulated (IUU) fishing. Consequently, all stakeholders in the Thai fisheries sector—including the government, fishermen, and fisheries product enterprises—must collaborate and adapt to resolve these issues, leading to an agricultural sector reform. This reform is also part of the broader economic reform agenda undertaken by the National Reform Council, which has appointed a committee to study and consider sustainable agricultural systems, including the management of illegal fishing, ultimately aiming to reform Thailand comprehensively.[3]

Greenpeace Thailand (2015) references the Food and Agriculture Organization of the United Nations (FAO) and the International Plan of Action to Prevent, Deter,

---

[1] Stringer et al. (2022), p. 133645.

[2] Prompatanapak and Lopetcharat (2020), p. 735318.

[3] Wongrak et al. (2021), p. 6814.

and Eliminate Illegal, Unreported, and Unregulated Fishing (IPOA-IUU). This plan defines illegal, unreported, and unregulated (IUU) fishing as occurring when vessels violate fishing laws, whether this takes place under the jurisdiction of a coastal state, within a regional fishing management organization's area, or in international waters regulated by management organizations. This definition encompasses various illegal fishing activities, including those undertaken within a coastal state's jurisdiction as well as in regional or international waters.[4]

Illegal fishing encompasses the following types of fishing activities:

1. Fishing by vessels of any nationality in the territorial waters of any country without the authorization of said country or in violation of regulations and laws
2. Fishing vessels flying the flag of a country that is a member of a regional organization responsible for managing fisheries that violate the measures stipulated for fish conservation by that country or related measures set forth by international law
3. Violations of national and international laws, including laws under cooperative fishery agreements by regional fishery management organizations

Unreported fishing includes the following activities:[5]

1. Fishing without reporting or incorrectly reporting to national fisheries regulatory authorities, as required by law or regulations
2. Fishing in areas where fishing is permitted within the region but failing to report or incorrectly reporting as required by law or regulations set forth by the organization

Unregulated fishing includes the following activities:

1. Fishing in areas managed by regional fisheries management organizations by vessels without nationality or by vessels flying the flag of a nonmember country or by other fishing entities that violate conservation and management measures set by the organization
2. Fishing that is inconsistent with the responsibilities of states in reserve areas for increasing fish populations, which are not yet designated conservation measures, for the conservation of aquatic resources under international law

For Thailand, the scope of illegal fishing also includes fishing that violates regulations and laws within Thailand's territorial waters. This means illegal fishing near coastal areas reserved for local or small-scale fisheries only, without authorization for industrial fishing, such as using trawl nets or using lighted nets to attract fish. Such illegal fishing not only steals fish, which are national resources, but also damages fishing equipment crucial for local fishermen's livelihoods.[6]

---

[4] Subnawin and Singchai (2024), pp. 449–460.

[5] Mutaqin (2021), pp. 461–480

[6] Thammachote and Trochim (2023).

In addition, Thai fishing vessels that are not registered legally and operate in Thai waters are considered illegal, even without further violations. Illegal fishing also includes cross-border illegal fishing, where Thai fishing vessels fish unlawfully outside Thai waters or other nations' vessels fish unlawfully within Thai waters.

1.1 The European Union's Strict Measures Against Illegal Fishing

The European Union has issued regulations to prevent, deter, and eliminate illegal, unreported, and unregulated (IUU) fishing. Countries exporting marine products to the EU must establish systems to prevent, deter, and eliminate IUU fishing and must provide a catch certificate for every export to the EU, certifying that the products do not originate from IUU fishing. This regulation has been in force since January 1, 2010.

Under this regulation, Thailand's Department of Fisheries, Ministry of Agriculture, and Cooperatives has implemented measures to control the fishing activities of Thai fishing vessels to prevent IUU fishing, established a certification system for caught aquatic animals, and set up a traceability system within the existing legal and regulatory framework. The European Union representatives have conducted three assessments of Thailand's control measures and IUU compliance: in July 2011, October 2012, and most recently on October 8, 2014. After the most recent assessment in October 2014, the European Union decided to issue a yellow card to Thailand due to inadequate progress in addressing illegal fishing, or IUU fishing, in compliance with EU IUU regulations.[7]

Later, in April 2015, the European Union issued a warning, or a "yellow card," to Thailand regarding insufficient measures to combat illegal fishing. Thailand was given until July 2015 to address the IUU fishing issues and comply with the EU's IUU regulations to have the yellow card lifted. Failure to comply might result in a red card, prohibiting Thailand from exporting fishery products to the EU, which would significantly impact seafood exports.[8]

The Thai Public Relations Department (2015) reported that the EU recommended the following improvements for Thailand to tackle IUU fishing:

- Revising national fisheries laws to align with international standards
- Developing a National Plan of Action to Prevent, Deter, and Eliminate Illegal, Unreported, and Unregulated Fishing (NPOA-IUU) for 2015–2019 that is practical for implementation
- Installing vessel monitoring system (VMS) equipment, especially on large fishing vessels, to effectively control illegal activities in foreign waters

---

[7] Wilcox et al. (2021).

[8] Sampantamit et al. (2021), p. 880.

– Establishing a traceability system to identify which vessel caught the fish, in which waters, such as with legally compliant catch certificates

When the EU issued a warning to prevent, deter, and eliminate IUU fishing, Thailand needed to address the problem urgently. This was mandated by the decree of the Head of the National Council for Peace and Order No. 10/2015 on the resolution of illegal, unreported, and unregulated (IUU) fishing issues. Various sectors of Thailand's fishing industry, including government agencies, fishermen, and fisheries product operators, had to adapt and join forces to resolve the issue, effectively reforming the fishing and agricultural sectors.[9]

The Thai Ministry of Foreign Affairs emphasized that the Thai government recognized the importance of marine resource conservation and deemed the resolution of IUU fishing as a national priority, requiring collaboration among relevant agencies. The Department of Fisheries, as the leading agency, collaborated with other government and private sector entities to implement six key plans consistently, as reported by Thai PBS (2015):

1. Revising the Fisheries Act and related subordinate laws
2. Creating a national plan to prevent, deter, and eliminate IUU fishing
3. Expediting the registration of fishing vessels and issuing fishing licenses
4. Enhancing the fisheries control and monitoring system, especially monitoring fishing vessel entry and exit at ports
5. Procuring a vessel monitoring system (VMS)
6. Improving the traceability system

In regard to revising the Fisheries Act, the National Legislative Assembly considered the Fisheries Act B.E. 2558 which was enacted on April 28, 2015. This Act includes provisions for managing illegal fishing and promoting community participation. Local fishing groups now have the opportunity to send representatives to provincial committees, allowing them to influence national policies and participate more actively in problem-solving.[10]

Mr. Pitipong Pungboon Na Ayudhya, the Minister of Agriculture and Cooperatives, discussed the progress in addressing issues related to Thai fishery products identified as illegal by the EU since October 2014. An assessment was scheduled for August of that year. Consequently, Thailand expedited three measures: specific legislation, a comprehensive fisheries plan, both of which were completed, and registering illegal fishing vessels to operate legally, enforced since July 1, 2015, with no extensions. Failure to meet the assessment could severely impact Thai fishery exports.[11]

In September 2015, the Ministry of Agriculture and Cooperatives planned to discuss with the EU the government's actions to address illegal fishing. Initially, this would involve enacting a royal decree (RD) on IUU. The Ministry would draft new IUU legislation to replace the provisional decree, if passed and enacted, to align

[9] Song et al. (n.d.).

[10] Khan et al. (2024), p. 105936.

[11] Tsolakis et al. (2021), pp. 495–519.

with the EU's recommendations for specific IUU legislation in Thailand (Deep Sea Fisheries, 2015).

The Department of Fisheries, under the Ministry of Agriculture and Cooperatives, has undertaken the task of controlling Thai fishing vessels to prevent IUU fishing. They have established a system for issuing catch certificates, regulating fishing activities to ensure they are not IUU, and implementing traceability systems within the existing legal and regulatory framework.[12]

Efforts to prevent IUU fishing begin with ensuring that Thai-flagged vessels operating in both Thai and international waters are not involved in IUU activities. This involves registration for Thai vessels and obtaining licenses for marine fishing and fishing activities. According to the 2015 fishing database, out of the total 57,141 fishing vessels across 23 coastal provinces, 10,001 vessels have valid registration, vessel usage licenses, and fishing permits. This data was summarized from the Thai Fishery Information System (Fishing Info) by the Information and Communication Technology Center on July 6, 2015.

The approach to seriously addressing illegal fishing includes controlling fishing vessels that are not registered or lack permits, known as "fishing licenses," which will prevent them from going out to sea. It also includes banning trawling, installing tracking devices on fishing vessels over 60 gross tons operating outside territorial waters, implementing an entry-exit control system for fishing vessels over 30 gross tons, and other measures totaling 15 in all, with no more leniency from July 1, 2015. This aligns with the EU's demands to solve illegal fishing issues. Strict law enforcement by the government has led to protests by thousands of Thai fishing vessels in various provinces since the beginning of the month. This issue has become a hot topic, raising concerns about potential seafood shortages and price increases. Conversely, it has benefited legal and small-scale local fishing boats, allowing them to work and catch more fish, positively impacting the aquatic ecosystem by allowing juvenile fish to survive. Coastal fishing, which employs about 85% of fishermen, has thrived, while the protesting commercial fishers constitute about 15% of the industry.[13]

Over the past 50 years, fishing vessel owners have often neglected to comply with the law, partly due to lax enforcement. Most vessels operated without obtaining fishing licenses. To legalize their operations and acquire fishing licenses, these vessels need to invest between 200,000 and 500,000 baht per vessel. Consequently, many vessels are docking not as a protest against the government or to negotiate leniency with the Department of Fisheries but due to fear of arrest by authorities. For instance, in southern provinces like Songkhla, out of approximately 1000 fishing vessels, only about 100 are legally compliant, leaving around 800 docked. Similar situations are seen in Pattani, Nakhon Si Thammarat, Satun, Trang, and other provinces, where approximately 80% of vessels have ceased operations, while only 20% are legally compliant and continue fishing.[14]

[12] Djunarsjah et al. (2021), p. 012018.

[13] Zwoelfer (2020), p. 012019.

[14] Panyarux (2020).

The solution for commercial illegal fishing is to rectify and legalize operations. The government has urged fishermen and fisheries operators to register their vessels, obtain fishing licenses, and use legal fishing equipment, also ensuring that crew members have proper labor permits. Those who comply with all three requirements can resume fishing as usual. Others can still visit the One-Stop Service Centers until July 15, 2015, and contact the Marine Department and Department of Fisheries until July 31, 2015.[15]

2 Illegal Fishing: A Regional Issue for the ASEAN

The problem of illegal fishing in the ASEAN involves violations of laws within member countries, such as Cambodian fishing vessels infringing on Thai waters, as well as violations involving ASEAN members and other countries. Indonesia and the Philippines had previously been at risk of receiving yellow cards, and in April 2015, Thailand received a yellow card while Cambodia received a red card, barring it from exporting fishery products to the EU. This situation underscores the need for the ASEAN to address the entire seafood supply chain to maintain the EU market. The ASEAN Fisheries Consultative Forum Body (AFCFB) was established to promote and develop sustainable marine resource management as a solution to this issue. AFCFB proposed measures and practices to combat illegal, unreported, and unregulated (IUU) fishing.

The ASEAN's efforts against IUU fishing will be recognized internationally only if the measures are effectively enforced among member countries. Successfully combating IUU fishing will not only preserve the fishery market but also ensure the sustainability of marine resources, supporting ASEAN's food security policy as well.[16] However, ASEAN's cooperative mechanisms is largely voluntary, in contrast with the EU's mandatory due diligence approach. This highlights the need for regional harmonization of labor standards, transparency, and human rights due diligence obligations to prevent regulatory arbitrage between Southeast Asian states.

3 Fisheries Reform

Since the National Council for Peace and Order (NCPO) issued Order No. 10/2015 on addressing illegal, unreported, and unregulated (IUU) fishing, significant emphasis has been placed on tackling illegal fishing as urgent reforms are crucial to avoid future impacts on the nation's seafood exports and overall security.[17]

Beginning July 1, 2015, the Ministry of Commerce dispatched officials to survey markets and monitor potential impacts. The Department of Internal Trade observed

[15] Busaranuvong and Khumwang (2020), pp. 01–27.

[16] Song et al. (n.d.).

[17] Arnason (2023), pp. 263–283.

a slight decline in seafood entering Thai markets like the one in Samut Sakhon, with prices rising marginally. However, on July 6, 2015, Mr. Bunyarit Kalyanamitra, Director-General of the Department of Internal Trade, confirmed that seafood shortages were not as feared.[18]

This corresponds with a Master Poll survey on community leaders' views regarding lifting the EU yellow card and seafood shortage concerns. The EU yellow card system represents a form of extraterritorial regulatory leverage, whereby importing states impose human rights and sustainability conditions on foreign producers. In the context of the fisheries sector, this mechanism extends the accountability of European retailers and consumers across global supply chains.

Surveying 1079 community leaders nationwide from July 3 to 5, 2015, revealed that almost all (91.2%) felt stringent law enforcement by the government would have positive outcomes. These include easing the EU yellow card, enhancing national image, and resolving multiple issues like illegal fishing, human trafficking, undocumented labor, and curbing influential figures' control. A minor percentage (8.8%) believed it would result in higher seafood prices and potential shortages. On the flip side, local fishing networks sought to address seafood shortages and rising prices by establishing nationwide distribution centers, thereby turning a crisis into an opportunity for local fishermen.[19]

3.1 A History of Thai Fisheries

Researching the history of something requires evidence, documents that have been recorded, and accounts from people involved in those activities during relevant times. For Thai fisheries, which have been intertwined with the Thai way of life since ancient times, there is a well-known saying from the early twenty-fifth century, "In water, there are fish; in fields, there is rice." This reflects the abundance of Thailand and the main livelihoods of the Thai people historically, which are agriculture and fishing.[20]

One of the important old documents that can be referenced to trace the history of Thai fisheries is titled "A Review of Aquatic Resources of Siam with Plan and Recommendations for their Administration, Conservation and Development." This document was compiled by Dr. Hugh McCormick Smith, an advisor to the Siamese government's aquatic department, and was published by the Ministry of Agriculture of Siam in 1925 (BE 2468). It was translated by Luang Chulasakphitchathorn. The Southeast Asian Fisheries Development Center later republished this document based on the original text in 1983 (BE 2526).[21]

---

[18] Johnston (2023).

[19] Paniagua and Rayamajhee (2024), p. 106182.

[20] Kadfak and Widengård (2023), pp. 1322–1342.

[21] Satumanatpan et al. (2024), pp. 167–187.

Both the compiler and the translator held significant positions, with the former serving as the Director-General of the Department of Fisheries and the latter becoming the first Director-General of the Department of Fisheries in Thailand from BE 2468 and from BE 2474 to BE 2485. The Department of Aquatic Animals was officially established on September 21, BE 2469, and later its name was changed to the Department of Fisheries, which it retains to this day. The latter served as the first Director-General of the Department of Fisheries in Thailand from 1925 until 1942. The Department of Aquatic Animals was formally established on September 21, 1926, and later changed its name to the Department of Fisheries, as it is known today.[22]

Fishing has been a way of life for Thai people in tandem with agriculture since ancient times. The traditional methods of catching aquatic animals have been simple and required no special tools, evolving only as necessary. Initially, methods like catching, hitting, spearing, scooping, and draining were used when aquatic animals were visible. Over time, strategies such as trapping, baiting, and creating simple tools from natural materials were developed, aligning with the habits and habitats of the aquatic animals.

3.2 Thai Coastal Fisheries Before the Use of Synthetic Fibers in Fishing Gear (Before BE 2495/1952 AD)

Before World War II, economic activity centered around large rivers and river mouths, with travel mainly by boat. Fishing at this time was primarily for household and local consumption due to limited market needs, and aquatic resources were abundant. Simplistic fishing methods were using natural materials such as branches, bamboo, flax, jute, raw cotton, vines, and coconut fibers. Traditional implements included spears, hooks, traps, nets, and various handmade devices.[23]

Freshwater fishing was conducted in rice fields, streams, canals, rivers, and waterfalls using a similar assortment of simple tools. Coastal sea fishing was carried out in river mouths, mangrove forests, and along the coast, targeting a variety of aquatic species such as shrimp, shells, crabs, fish, and seaweed. Given the diverse and extensive fishing grounds, fishermen invented diverse methods and gear for different species and sizes, such as hooks, spears, nets, and traps of various kinds.[24]

In the early days, the fishing boats used were mainly oar driven or sailboats made entirely from wood and other natural materials, powered by human effort and wind. High skill and experience were required for navigating and fishing, necessitating a deep understanding of the sea and marine life. The person in charge of the fishing operations on these boats was known as the "captain," and some fishing methods

---

[22] Noranarttragoon et al. (2023), p. 177.

[23] Suwankiri (n.d.).

[24] Bauer et al. (2023), pp. 277–302.

also required specialized skills like detecting underwater sounds, a role often filled by experienced southern fishermen, particularly for purse seine fishing.[25]

Fishing with nets involved various coastal methods such as trawling, surrounding nets, and lift nets. These operations relied on good visual observation of sea conditions and creating habitats, such as hanging coconut fronds in the sea, to attract marine life, a technique known locally as "setting" or, in southern dialect, "unuh" (from Malay). Therefore, the early fishing practices were predominantly traditional or small scale. Major fishing tools included fish traps, fishing rafts, and weirs, as recorded by the Department of Fisheries in 1940, with counts of 280, 340, and 106, respectively. These numbers increased in 1947 to 823, 1286, and 287, respectively. At that time, there were also 16 records of trawl nets and 161 records of seine nets as of 1925.[26]

One of the early documented types of nets, so significant that the Siamese government enacted laws to regulate and manage their use, might be considered the first aquatic resource conservation law in Thailand. This was the "long-winged bag net," believed to be a type of barrier net that is pulled (also known as the seine or dragging net). This type was popular along the coast and around Songkhla Lake. This led officials to propose the Water Tax Act in 1933 by the Ministry of Finance to conserve and protect marine life in the lake and along the coast. During this period, there was also an increase in foreign nationals engaging in fishing in Thailand, prompting officials to propose the 1934 Aquatic Animal Capture Rights Act, which barred foreigners from fishing in Thai waters.[27]

Fishing tools of that era, such as fish traps, fishing rafts, weirs, trawl nets, seine nets, cast nets, and Japanese seine nets, were made from natural fibers like raw cotton, jute, and flax. These materials required treatment with natural extracts to increase their durability and lifespan. The extract, known as "Nam Ngoob," was obtained by fermenting mangrove bark, which was then used to dye the raw cotton nets every 2–4 weeks. The nets also needed to be dried after each use, which was a time-consuming maintenance process. Additionally, natural fibers were not very durable. In 1952, a Japanese company introduced synthetic fiber (nylon) nets to the Thai fishing industry. These nets proved highly effective and quickly gained widespread popularity.[28]

Toward the end of this period, the first surveys and studies of Thai fishing tools were conducted by the Department of Fisheries in 1949–1950. Surveys of saltwater fishing tools on Thailand's Indian Ocean coast (the Andaman Sea) were conducted by Mr. Sanan Ruamarak and Lt. Swang Jarernphon (RN) (Department of Fisheries, 1950, 1951), and the survey of saltwater fishing tools in the Gulf of Thailand was conducted in 1951–1952 by Lt. Swang Jarernphon (RN) and Mr. Prakob Rodphotong (Department of Fisheries, 1953). These efforts marked the beginning of historical

[25] Prabakaran et al. (2024), p. 115864.

[26] Haritavorn (2023), p. 4816.

[27] Ainsworth et al. (2023), pp. 263–278.

[28] Galam et al. (2024), p. 01171968241245382.

documentation and development of Thai fishing tools. This era saw collaboration with foreign nationals and a serious advancement in marine fisheries in Thailand, with technology adoption from abroad. Foreign nationals, particularly from Japan and China, began participating in fisheries through joint fishing companies.

3.3 Evolution of Thai Sea Fisheries: From Natural Materials to Synthetic Fibers (1952–1962)

Thai fisheries began to develop rapidly and extensively in the late twentieth century (1952). This period marked a collaboration with foreign nations, particularly when Japanese companies introduced fishing tools made from synthetic fibers, specifically "nylon nets" (nylon), chemically known as polyamide (PA), to Thailand in 1954 (Department of Fisheries, 1969).[29]

Nylon fishing materials made fishing tools more durable, strong, easier to maintain, and more efficient at catching fish. Initially, nylon drift nets were used for fishing Spanish mackerel and other surface fish like king mackerel and queenfish. Nylon nets quickly spread to purse seines, trawl nets, fish traps, bamboo rafts, and other types of fishing gear. The introduction of synthetic fibers in fishing gear led to rapid advancements in fishing tools and methods in Thailand, resulting in a significant increase in the country's fishery production.[30]

During this era, the Thai aquatic market remained focused on local and domestic consumption. Targeted aquatic species included surface fish like mackerel, Spanish mackerel, king mackerel, queenfish, and other commonly consumed household fish. There was also a shift from traditional stationary fishing tools like fish traps and bamboo rafts to more mobile equipment such as purse seines, drift nets, and trawl nets. Notably, this era marked the beginning of bottom trawling in Thailand. Between 1953 and 1960, Chinese pair trawlers were introduced to experiment with this fishing method in the Gulf of Thailand, though initial efforts were not very successful. Subsequently, the Department of Fisheries introduced the German Othello otter trawl for bottom trawling in the Gulf of Thailand, which proved to be successful and gradually gained popularity.[31]

3.4 The Era of Bottom Trawl Expansion (1962–1972)

Following the introduction and rapid adoption of bottom trawling equipment in the Gulf of Thailand since 1960, the popularity of this fishing method surged. The number of trawling fishing vessels increased from 99 in 1960 to 2606 in 1965 (Department

---

[29] Avakiat and Rooppsuwankun (2024), pp. 67–75.

[30] Moazzam and Moazzam (2023).

[31] Deb and Dey (2024), p. 165.

of Fisheries, 1997). During the initial expansion phase, the Department of Fisheries built survey trawlers for coastal and deep-sea areas, like the "Pramong 2," "Kittikachorn," and "Thanarat" ships. "Pramong 2" and "Kittikachorn" were assigned to survey fishery resources in the Gulf of Thailand, while "Thanarat" focused on areas outside Thai waters and in the Andaman Sea (during this era, territorial waters extended up to 12 nautical miles from the coastline according to international norms). These survey ships not only conducted research but also promoted modern fishing techniques to local fishermen across the country.[32]

The simplicity of bottom trawl equipment, combined with the relatively shallow and abundant waters of the Gulf of Thailand and the Andaman Sea, made bottom trawling highly efficient. Consequently, trawling quickly became popular and widely adopted; it began to negatively impact traditional coastal fishing methods like fish traps across the Gulf of Thailand, causing their numbers to decline steadily. This led the government to introduce its first trawling regulations in 1963, mandating that trawlers operate more than 10 nautical miles from the shore and over 1 nautical mile from fish traps. By 1972, this was updated to prohibit trawling within 3000 meters (approximately 1.6 nautical miles) from the shore and more than 400 meters from fish traps, under the Fisheries Act of 1947.[33]

Law of the Sea (1982) came into effect, establishing full exclusive economic zone (EEZ) regulations whereby coastal states had sovereign rights over exploration, exploitation, conservation, and management of natural resources within 200 nautical miles of their shores. This heightened enforcement and stricter regulations among countries exacerbated the challenges for Thai trawlers operating abroad. Many Thai trawlers that failed to secure agreements with neighboring countries returned to fish in Thai waters, severely impacting local marine resources. As a result, the government introduced measures to reduce the number of trawling vessels in the Gulf of Thailand, starting with a Cabinet resolution in 1978.

The initial impact of bottom trawling on marine resources led to a rapid increase in fishery production, particularly of demersal (bottom-dwelling) species. However, this also caused ecological shifts and affected other fishing methods. Initially, bottom trawling targeted large demersal fish like groupers, snappers, and large jacks, which occupy the top levels of the marine food chain. As their populations declined, the biomass of lower-tier aquatic species like shrimp and squid increased, and fishermen adjusted their focus accordingly, emphasizing shrimp trawling from 1967 to 1977.[34]

During this period, purse seine fishing also evolved, with advancements in tools, equipment, and fishing techniques, such as the use of lighted purse seines. Initially, skipjack tuna, which was not popular locally and sold for only 1.50–5 baht per kilogram, became highly sought after due to international demand, particularly from Japan. The establishment of tuna-smoking factories in Thailand increased demand

[32] Pauly and Chuenpagdee (2003), pp. 337–354.

[33] Stobutzki et al. (2006b), pp. 130–142.

[34] Vandergeest and Marschke (2020), pp. 291–315.

and prices, elevating the price of tuna to over 10 baht per kilogram. Consequently, many purse seine fishers began targeting skipjack tuna more, leading to developments in nets and fishing vessels to enhance efficiency. Larger nets, bigger and more advanced boats, and modern electronics were integrated into fishing operations, marking the start of intensive skipjack tuna fishing by Thai fishers during this period.[35]

3.5 *The Early Period of Fishing with Light (1977–1987)*

In the past, light was used in fishing primarily for visibility, using natural fuel like bark and tree resin to make torches. This light was used to spot and catch aquatic animals such as crabs, shrimp, squid, and various fish. Additionally, light served as a signal for the position of fishing gear at sea and for navigation at night. Later, different types of lamps utilizing fuel like kerosene and acetylene gas from calcium carbide (CaC) came into use. These lamps were then used to attract aquatic animals, which would gather around the light, allowing fishermen to catch them using tools like lift nets, shrimp traps, swing nets, and encircling nets for squid.[36]

Around 1977, there was an initiative to install dynamos on the engines of fishing boats that used bait, swing nets, and cast nets for squid fishing. This created electricity to attract groups of squid, which proved highly effective and quickly gained widespread popularity. This innovation led to the commonly known names "Dai Boats" or "Squid Dai Boats." The technique of using electric lights to attract aquatic animals spread to various other types of fishing gear, including scoop nets, encircling nets (or surround nets), cast nets, encircling lantern nets, and even today's large purse seines.[37]

Traditional purse seine fishing involved visually searching for fish schools and using natural materials like coconut fronds. In contrast, fishing using light as an attractant has severely destructive impact on fishery resources. Simultaneously, encircling nets have been significantly developed, especially the encircling nets for catching tuna. The nets have been designed to catch large surface fish, leading to excessive exploitation of the tuna resources in the Gulf of Thailand, causing the tuna population to decline. This has also started affecting other marine species in the Gulf of Thailand, notably the anchovy, which was previously the best raw material for producing top-quality Thai fish sauce and is a primary food source in the food chain for tuna and squid. As more predators (like tuna) are caught, the numbers of prey (like anchovies) increase and are subsequently caught by humans. This marks the beginning of diverse methods of anchovy fishing in Thailand in later periods.[38]

---

[35] Baran (2005).

[36] Stobutzki et al. (2006a), pp. 109–118.

[37] Marschke and Vandergeest (2016), pp. 39–46.

[38] Butcher (2004), pp. 234–292.

The impact of fishing using light attractants on aquatic resources is significant, as most aquatic animals respond positively to light to varying degrees depending on the species. This makes light-based fishing widely popular among fishermen, which in turn greatly affects aquatic resources in various ways, including:[39]

1. The rapid decline in aquatic populations as they are easily caught and consumed
2. Increased opportunities for the mating and propagation of certain aquatic species, such as the big fin reef squid (*Sepia* spp.), which naturally mate during the full moon
3. The widespread dispersion of various aquatic species

Overall, it can be considered that fishing using light attractants is another hazardous fishing method to aquatic resources if not managed properly and without a conscious effort to conserve resources for sustainable use.

3.6 The Era of Overfishing Beyond the Capacity of Thailand's Fishing Resources (BE 2535–BE 2545)

The development in all sectors of Thailand has also impacted its fishing practices. During this era, Thai people struggled to survive, needing jobs to support themselves and their families. As transportation, communication, and information dissemination became more convenient, it led to increased exploitation of fishery resources. Fishing areas were limited and continually dwindling, exacerbating the severe impact on aquatic resources in Thai waters during this period.[40]

1. Reduction of Thai Fishing Areas: The growing population demanded more living space, and naturally, humans prefer to live near water bodies and lowland areas. Economic and industrial development further stimulated encroachment and destruction of water bodies, which are critical fishing areas. Waste from various activities, whether intentionally discharged or not, led to the widespread degradation of these fishing areas, including the sea.
2. Characteristics of Multi-Species Fishery Resources: The presence of diverse species and the varied fishing gear (multi-gear) used for catching both the same and different target aquatic groups, along with different boat sizes, made resource management challenging.
3. Increase in Fishing Units in Thai Waters: The establishment of exclusive economic zones (EEZ) by neighboring countries and stricter enforcement measures caused Thai fishing vessels, which had been operating in neighboring countries both legally and illegally, to return and increase their fishing activities in Thai waters. This increased the cost of resource management for the state, such as patrol boats, joint management measures with fishermen, and surveys and assessments of new fishing grounds.

---

[39] Pauwels et al. (2003), pp. 23–53.

[40] Falvey (2000).

4. Common Property Resources: The Department of Fisheries (2008) explained that Thailand's marine fishery resources are a common property resource, meaning no single entity owns the fisheries exclusively. It can also be said that the fisheries resources of a country belong to its people. Therefore, no one has absolute rights to use or prevent others from using these resources. This led to an open access scenario, allowing anyone with capital and capability to enter the fishery profession freely. Unregulated increases in local fishing units, driven by economic pressures, further intensified the exploitation of fishery resources. The economic downturn in BE 2540 (1997) caused many factory workers who had lost their jobs to turn to local fishing as a new livelihood.
5. The development of small-scale fishing boats has progressed significantly by replacing their original engines—which were water pumps, generators, or small gasoline engines with 8–20 horsepower—with high-speed diesel engines. These new engines, which are repurposed from old small truck engines (pickup cars), are small in size but have high horsepower ranging from 40 to 80 HP. This upgrade increases the boats' speed and shortens the travel time to fishing areas, allowing fishermen to spend more time fishing and use more fishing gear such as crab nets, squid traps, fish traps, mackerel fishing hooks, and squid trolling hooks, among others.
6. The development of the food and agricultural industries, including related sectors, has increased the demand for raw materials to supply factories, such as fresh seafood, frozen foods, and animal feed. This has led to an increase in commercial fishing activities, and fishery operators have started employing more foreign labor.
7. The increased fishing time using various types of equipment, such as trawl nets, encircling nets, and drift nets, is further supported by modern electronic devices. These devices include fish finders, echo sounders, sonar, and radar, making fishing more efficient. However, as water resources decrease, fishermen need to spend more hours per fishing trip, increase the number of trips per day, and extend the number of fishing days per month. This intensifies the exploitation of aquatic resources.
8. The use of advanced tools and equipment in fishing, along with better communication and information dissemination, has led to enhanced awareness and skills in fishing. This includes the improvement and modification of fishing tools and methods, resulting in higher efficiency. For instance, the use of nylon monofilament nets by both small-scale local fishers and large commercial fishing operations—ranging from small coastal boats to large fishing vessels over 100 tons in the Gulf of Thailand—is prevalent. Additionally, various traps have incorporated winches to reduce labor, and trawlers have adopted high-opening trawl techniques from neighboring countries.

However, the Department of Fisheries (2008) concluded that the general state of marine aquatic resources, particularly in the Gulf of Thailand, has been fully exploited to its maximum production capacity. Consequently, the opportunity for increasing marine fishery production is quite limited. On the other hand, the

Andaman Sea still presents some areas with potential for expansion, such as the continental shelf, deeper water areas, and tuna fishing in the Indian Ocean.[41]

Due to the limited territory of fishing grounds and aquatic resources, there has been increased competition for resources and conflicts over fishing areas. This era of Thai fisheries has seen the enactment of numerous fishing laws for enforcement, which have posed challenges in terms of effective implementation. Fishermen have adapted by seeking a more diverse range of resource areas, from domestic waters to international fisheries and international waters. Tuna purse seining in the Indian Ocean represents one of the largest and most complex fishing operations, yet it yields significant income.[42]

Additionally, the government has established policies aimed at sourcing raw materials to supply tuna canning factories, which have seen substantial growth in Thailand's tuna processing industry. Thailand ranks among the top exporters of canned tuna worldwide. The government built two large deep-sea research vessels.

At the same time, the regional international organization based in Thailand, the Southeast Asian Fisheries Development Center (SEAFDEC), received partial budget support from the Thai government to build a large deep-sea fishing training and research vessel. This vessel aims to meet the needs and interests in deep-sea fishing of the SEAFDEC member countries. The vessel, named "M.V. SEAFDEC," joins the fleet of three survey/training ships, which are equipped with main fishing tools including tuna purse seines.[43]

In response, the private sector has established the Thai Deep Sea Tuna Fishing Cooperative Group, which engages in offshore fishing through joint ventures among groups of fishermen. They have also received support in the form of low-interest loans (soft loans) from the government. This funding enabled them to purchase an older tuna purse seiner with a capacity of about 1800 gross tons from Japan. The vessel, named "Mukmanee," operated out of Phuket in the Indian Ocean for around 5 years, but it ultimately did not succeed, possibly due to non-standardized internal management. Therefore, the operations were eventually discontinued.[44]

3.7 *Era of Responsible Fishing Awareness (2002–2013)*

The results of overfishing beyond the capacity of fisheries resources in Thai waters and neighboring regions in past years have created repercussions that put various pressures on Thai fishermen and the fishing industry, which continue to intensify. Examples of these impacts include:[45]

---

[41] Kongprasertamorn (2007), pp. 1–10.

[42] Van Zalinge et al. (2000).

[43] Choo (2008).

[44] Baran et al. (2007), pp. 227–290.

[45] Chuenpagdee and Jentoft (2009), pp. 109–120.

1. Conflicts Among Fishermen: There have been conflicts among fishermen in coastal areas due to competition for resources. This includes conflicts between local fishermen and commercial fisheries and the utilization of government measures as tools to protect individual benefits. Additionally, there have been conflicts between fishermen and other sea activities such as tourism and oil and natural gas exploration and drilling. These disputes have become more frequent and severe, compelling fishermen to comply with regulations and laws governing the shared use of marine and water resources.
2. Decreased Fishery Production: There has been a decline in fishery production, leading to reduced income for fishermen. Revenue from selling aquatic animals has decreased due to quality and quantity issues (smaller size and lower quantity of aquatic animals). This is while the costs of essential fishing factors have increased. Expenses for each fishing trip (fuel), maintenance costs for fishing boats, and fishing gear (equipment degradation) have risen, making traditional fishing methods economically unviable. Consequently, fishermen have had to devise ways to sustain their income and keep their fishing activities afloat. Examples include:
   - Converting Boat Engines to Use Liquefied Natural Gas: Modifying boat engines and propellers to be more efficient.
   - Purchasing Oil in Offshore Areas: Buying fuel from areas beyond the jurisdiction of customs laws.
   - Reducing Fuel Consumption: By minimizing trips between the port and fishing areas, some fishermen opt to stay at sea until they have fully loaded their catch.
   - Shared Fish Transport Services: Utilizing so-called carrier boats or tour boats to transport catches collectively. Additionally, they focus on methods to increase the value of the caught aquatic animals by employing various suitable preservation techniques immediately after capture.
3. The continued pressure from exporting aquatic products to various regions, including Europe, America, Japan, Australia, and others, has forced Thai fisheries to increasingly comply with international regulations. The buyers from these countries have established rules for the purchase of aquatic products from Thailand that require responsible fishing practices that are environmentally friendly. Additionally, the products must be clean, safe, and hygienic according to international standards. Although these rules may sometimes serve as a pretext for protecting their own trade activities, such as requiring Thai trawlers to have devices and methods to prevent the capture of sea turtles and nontarget aquatic animals, and recently raising the issue of human trafficking related to the use of foreign labor on fishing boats.

This international scrutiny provides a valuable opportunity for the Thai fishing industry to evolve responsibly regarding resources, the environment, and society. Moreover, the pressure related to export issues has led to stricter adherence to international fishing regulations, even in international waters. For aquatic products to be accepted, their source must be verified, demonstrating that the raw materials used in production are responsibly sourced.

This means that cooperation in fishing with neighboring countries or other regions must follow strictly signed agreements and comply with international principles.

4. Thailand's Participation in Agreements and Joint Fisheries Action Plans with Southeast Asian Member Countries:

Thailand has endorsed agreements and joint action plans on fisheries with member countries in the Southeast Asian region. Fisheries are an important economic sector for the country, both for domestic consumption and export purposes. Thailand's geographic and biological diversity offers a wide range of resource utilization opportunities. As a result, it is not feasible for Thai fisheries to develop and implement plans to address challenges independently. Consequently, member countries in the Southeast Asian region convened meetings to draft joint agreements and action plans for regional fisheries management during the Millennium Conference in Bangkok in November 2001, under the theme "Fish for the People."[46]

These discussions culminated in action plans that member countries can implement to ensure coordinated efforts toward sustainable fisheries for regional food security. The focus areas include:

- Decentralized fisheries management
- Fishing rights
- Fisheries statistics and sustainable fishing indicators
- Responsible fishing technology
- Resource restoration and efficient use
- Quality and safety management systems for fishery products

In this modern era of fisheries, there has been a formation of cooperative groups and integrated efforts to reduce costs and increase efficiency, value, and quality of various fishery activities. Both public and private sectors have engaged in numerous activities, ranging from commercial to small-scale fisheries, driven by governmental promotion and private sector adaptation. Examples include:

- International Fisheries Cooperation: Conducting joint fishing operations with neighboring countries following regulations and agreements, establishing companies to manage joint and offshore fisheries more effectively according to international standards.
- Monitoring and Certification: Export products are subject to official checks and certifications to meet standards.
- Community-Based Fisheries Management: Local fishermen engage in various activities to conserve and restore local resources, such as crab banks, artificial reef projects, and community-based fisheries management initiatives. For

[46] Khemakorn (2006), p. 14.

instance, joint studies with the Department of Fisheries on "rope traps for sustainable coastal fisheries management."

The government places importance on restoring fishery resources by enacting the Fisheries Act, implementing conservation measures, and developing coastal fishing grounds. Measures have included seasonal closures in the Upper Gulf of Thailand for resource conservation, deploying artificial reefs, and promoting diverse types of aquaculture such as freshwater, brackish water, and marine farming. This approach has broadened Thailand's aquatic products market globally while also bringing diverse aquatic products from various regions of the world to domestic markets.[47]

Most recently, in 2011 (2010), there was another regional meeting in Southeast Asia to discuss and agree on fisheries cooperation and research leading up to the year 2020 (2021). The key conclusion emphasized regional cooperation. Modern fisheries are increasingly interconnected with various issues. Global environmental changes have worldwide implications, and Thailand and its waters are not exempt from these influences. Beyond overfishing, environmental and climatic changes and advancements in energy exploration have significantly impacted Thai fisheries. Natural disasters like floods, tsunamis, El Niño phenomena, and others have altered the environmental conditions of Thai waters. This includes events like red tides, low-oxygen water layering (hypoxia), and the expansion of oil and natural gas exploration and drilling in the Gulf of Thailand. Meanwhile, the growth and expansion of neighboring countries' fishing industries, which have developed significantly, have led to more frequent incursions into Thai waters by their fishing vessels.[48]

3.8 *Era of Fisheries Reform (or Crisis) in Thai Marine Fisheries (Since 2013)*

The evolution of fishing technology shaped not only ecological pressures but also labor relations and corporate practices. As mechanization expanded, the industry increasingly depended on larger crews and migrant labor, creating new vulnerabilities that later became central to Thailand's human rights challenges. A Business and Human Rights (BHR) perspective allows us to understand how historical development laid the foundation for current governance and accountability gaps.

In 2013, the global economic pressure (recession or stagnation), especially in Europe and America, significantly affected the volume of Thai fishery products entering these markets. This had an impact on the internal economies of these countries. To protect their domestic entrepreneurs, issues of illegal fishing according to the practices of the Food and Agriculture Organization (IUU Fishing/FAO Code of Conduct) were raised to halt or slow the import of Thai fishery products. Additionally,

[47] Christensen and Walters (2004), pp. 549–562.

[48] Pauly and Chuenpagdee (2003), pp. 337–354.

several countries used the issue of human trafficking as an excuse to stop importing fishery products from Thailand. For example, the United States placed Thailand on the Tier 3 Watch List, which the Thai government was already trying to address by updating the 1947 Fisheries Act. However, the European Union issued a yellow card against Thai fishery imports before any amendments were made.[49]

When a new Thai government was formed, it swiftly enacted the new Fisheries Act of 2015 on April 28, 2015. This was followed by further amendments and the proclamation of the Fisheries Ordinance on November 13, 2015, which introduced stricter penalties and immediate, rigorous enforcement of the law.[50] Simultaneously, efforts to address human trafficking and illegal labor on fishing boats and in the fishing industry were also intensified.

These actions had significant direct impacts on Thai marine fisheries in various aspects. Notable impacts from stringent law enforcement in the marine fisheries sector included:

1. Immediate Reduction in Fishing Effort: There was a significant drop in the number of active fishing vessels, particularly in offshore areas.
2. Increased Coastal Fishing: There was a surge in fishing activities in coastal areas.
3. Decreased Overall Fishery Production: The total fishery yield declined.
4. Increased Domestic Seafood Prices: The prices of seafood in local markets rose.
5. Economic Slowdown in Coastal Fishing Communities: There was an economic downturn in local marine fishing economies.
6. Improvement in Marine Fishery Resources: Natural fishery resources showed potential signs of recovery.
7. Increased Conflicts: There were heightened conflicts among different stakeholders involved in marine fisheries.
8. More Intrusions by Neighboring Fishing Vessels: There were increased incursions into Thai waters by fishing boats from neighboring countries.
9. Growth in Imported Fishery Products: There was a rise in the diversity and quantity of imported fishery products.
10. Potential for Increased Corruption: There may have been an uptick in unlawful benefits taken by officials.

It is noteworthy that since the enactment of the Fisheries Ordinance in November 2015, there has been no concrete report summarizing the economic and social impact resulting from this ordinance. The most tangible outcome has been the lifting of the yellow card status of Thai fisheries by the European Union in 2019. Therefore, it remains unclear whether the period following the enactment of the 2015 Fisheries Ordinance marks an era of reform for Thai fisheries or poses a crisis for Thai marine fisheries and fishermen.[51]

---

[49] Lunn and Dearden (2006), pp. 60–71.

[50] Nasuchon and Charles (2010), pp. 163–169.

[51] Anuchiracheeva et al. (2003), pp. 1049–1068.

Currently, the export value of Thailand's fishing industry is immense. Thailand is recognized as a country with high potential in producing and processing seafood and fishery products. It is among the world's top exporters of aquatic animals such as shrimp, squid, frozen fish, and tuna products. The export of fishery and seafood products significantly contributes to the national revenue. The fishing profession is vital to the country's economy, providing employment and generating numerous ancillary industries.[52]

After the European Union (EU) issued an official yellow card warning for Thailand's lack of concrete action in addressing illegal, unreported, and unregulated (IUU) fishing in compliance with international laws, the issue needed urgent and appropriate resolution. Failure to do so could lead to a ban on Thai fishery product imports, which might devastate the entire Thai fishing industry.[53]

4 Impact of IUU Fishing on Thailand

The yellow card signifies that Thailand is at risk of being identified as a non-cooperating country under the EU's IUU regulations. While the yellow card currently serves as a warning without stopping imports of seafood caught by Thai vessels into the EU market, a red card would result in a complete ban on importing all fishery products caught by Thai-flagged vessels into the EU, except for certain exempted items such as aquaculture products. For fishery and processed fishery products that use imported raw materials for processing within Thailand, there could be impacts, particularly on canned tuna. Thailand would need to improve its traceability system to assure the EU that no seafood caught by IUU fishing vessels enters the supply chain. If the EU lacks confidence in Thailand's traceability system, it could deny imports of such products.[54]

The resulting impact from the ban on fishery industry products sold in Europe would cause an estimated loss of 100 billion baht in exports. The entire fishing industry would face a crisis, affecting fishing vessel owners within the country, as well as over 100,000 Thai and foreign workers. It would also impact upstream operators such as ice producers, packaging manufacturers, and fishing equipment suppliers and downstream operators like exporters and distributors. Although the Thai government has played a role in addressing illegal fishing, it seems to have created new problems. Fishery product prices within the country have surged due to higher production costs, causing many operators to cease their business activities. Over 60,000 workers have been affected, and the processing industry is experiencing raw material shortages as some fishermen can no longer operate.[55] There is significant

[52] Teh and Pauly (2018), p. 44.

[53] Barbier et al. (2002), pp. 343–365.

[54] Wongrak et al. (2021), p. 6814.

[55] Zwoelfer (2020), p. 012019.

attention on whether the current measures to address IUU fishing will be effective. These reforms address procedural compliance but only partially fulfil the state's duty to protect under the UNGPs. Effective human rights protection requires ensuring that both state and corporate actors prevent labor exploitation, provide remedy mechanisms, and integrate human rights due diligence into the seafood supply chain. The direction of future solutions remains in question, and there is concern about whether new issues will arise, further harming the Thai fishing industry and negatively impacting the people in the country as has happened previously.

Greenpeace Thailand (2015) refers to the Food and Agriculture Organization of the United Nations (FAO) and its International Plan of Action to Prevent, Deter, and Eliminate Illegal, Unreported, and Unregulated Fishing (IUU Fishing). This plan states that illegal fishing occurs when vessels violate fishing laws. This can include fishing activities conducted under the jurisdiction of coastal states or in international waters governed by regional fisheries management organizations.[56]

Illegal fishing encompasses the following types:

1. Fishing Without Authorization: This includes any vessel of any nationality engaging in fishing activities in the waters of a country without permission from that country or in defiance of its regulations and laws.
2. Violation by Member Country Vessels: This refers to fishing vessels flying the flag of a member country of a regional organization responsible for fisheries management, which violate the conservation measures set by that country or related international laws.
3. Infringement of National and International Laws: This includes breaches of both domestic and international laws, as well as laws under cooperative fishing agreements established by regional fisheries management organizations.

Unreported fishing encompasses the following:

1. Fishing Without Reporting or Misreporting: This occurs when fishing activities are not reported or are incorrectly reported to the national regulatory authorities as required by laws or regulations.
2. Fishing in Reportable Areas Without Reporting: This includes fishing in areas where fishing is permissible within a region, but the activities are not reported or are incorrectly reported, as required by the laws or regulations established by the relevant organization.

Unregulated fishing encompasses the following:

1. Fishing in Areas Managed by Regional Organizations: This involves fishing within the jurisdiction of a regional fisheries management organization by vessels without nationality, vessels flying the flag of a nonmember state, or other fishing entities violating the conservation and management measures established by the organization.

[56] Kadfak and Linke (2021), p. 104445.

2. Fishing Inconsistent with State Responsibilities: This includes fishing activities that do not align with the responsibilities of states in areas reserved for increasing fish populations, particularly where no specific conservation measures have been established under international law for the conservation of aquatic resources.

5 Scope of Illegal Fishing in Thailand

For Thailand, the scope of illegal fishing also includes activities that violate laws and regulations within Thailand's territorial waters. This includes illegal fishing in coastal waters reserved for small-scale or local fisheries, where industrial fishing is not permitted. Such activities might involve using trawlers or light-luring techniques with purse seines. Illegal fishing not only resembles stealing fish from the sea, which are national resources, but also destroys fishing gear that local fishermen use for their livelihood.[57]

Furthermore, Thai fishing vessels that are not legally registered but operate within Thai waters are considered illegal, even if they do not violate any additional laws. Illegal fishing also encompasses cross-border illegal fishing, where Thai fishing vessels operate unlawfully beyond Thailand's territorial waters without legal rights. Conversely, it also includes foreign vessels of any nationality fishing illegally within Thai waters.[58]

6 Crisis of the Yellow Card Situation in Thai Fisheries and the EU's Strict Inspection on Illegal Fishing

The European Union (EU) has implemented regulations to prevent, deter, and eliminate illegal, unreported, and unregulated (IUU) fishing. Countries exporting marine products to the EU must establish systems to prevent, deter, and eliminate IUU fishing and must provide a catch certificate with every export of marine products to certify that these products are not sourced from IUU fishing. These regulations have been in effect since January 1, 2010.[59]

Under these regulations, the Department of Fisheries, Ministry of Agriculture and Cooperatives, has overseen Thai fishing vessels to prevent IUU fishing, established a system for issuing catch certificates, and developed traceability systems within the existing legal and regulatory frameworks. The EU has sent delegations to inspect and assess Thailand's control over fishing and IUU operations three times:

[57] Torell et al. (2010).

[58] Kadfak and Linke (2021), p. 104445.

[59] Kadfak and Linke (2021), p. 104445.

in July 2011, October 2012, and most recently on October 8, 2014. After the latest evaluation in October 2014, the EU decided to issue a yellow card warning to Thailand, stating that Thailand's efforts to tackle illegal or IUU fishing did not align with EU IUU regulations.[60]

In April 2015, the EU officially issued a yellow card to Thailand, warning that the measures taken against illegal fishing were insufficient to address the problem. Thailand was given a deadline until July 2015 to resolve IUU fishing issues and comply with EU IUU regulations to have the yellow card lifted. Failure to do so could result in a red card, which would ban Thai fishery product exports to the EU, adversely affecting seafood exports significantly.[61]

Thai Publica News Agency (2015) reported that the EU recommended Thailand make the following improvements to address IUU fishing:

- Improve domestic fishing laws to align with international principles
- Update the National Plan of Action to Prevent, Deter, and Eliminate Illegal, Unreported and Unregulated Fishing (NPOA-IUU) for 2015–2019 to be practically applicable
- Install vessel monitoring systems (VMS) on large fishing vessels operating in international waters to effectively control illegal activities
- Develop traceability systems for fishery products to identify the originating vessel and waters, including issuing legal catch certificates

Measures Against Illegal Fishing

When the European Union issued a warning to implement measures to prevent, deter, and eliminate illegal, unreported, and unregulated (IUU) fishing, Thailand had to address the issue urgently and seriously under the directive of the Head of the National Council for Peace and Order (NCPO), Order No. 10/2015, concerning the resolution of IUU fishing issues. The Thai fishing sector, including government officials, fishermen, and fishery product entrepreneurs, had to adapt and collaborate to solve this problem and reform the fishing and agricultural sectors.[62]

The Ministry of Foreign Affairs stated that the Thai government recognizes the importance of conserving marine resources and has designated the resolution of IUU fishing as a national priority. This requires the cooperation of relevant agencies. The Department of Fisheries, Ministry of Agriculture and Cooperatives, as the primary agency, has led the integration efforts with relevant public and private sectors to expedite the implementation of six key action plans to achieve tangible results continuously:[63]

1. Amendment of the Fisheries Act and related subordinate laws
2. Development of a National Plan of Action to Prevent, Deter, and Eliminate IUU Fishing
3. Accelerating the registration of fishing vessels and issuance of fishing licenses

---

[60] Dharmasaroja (2019).

[61] Kadfak (2023), p. 19.

[62] Song et al. (n.d.).

[63] Aussawarangkul and Wongbandit (2014).

4. Development of a control and monitoring system for fishing activities, particularly the control of entry and exit of fishing vessels at ports
5. Implementation of a vessel monitoring system (VMS)
6. Improvement of the traceability system

In action 1, the amendment of the Fisheries Act, the National Legislative Assembly considered the Fisheries Act of 2015, which was enacted on April 28, 2015. The provisions of this Act align with the management of illegal fishing and enhance community participation. This allows local fishing communities to form groups and have the opportunity to send representatives to serve on provincial committees, which can influence national policy. It opens up the opportunity for communities to participate more in resolving the issues.

Piti Pongsakorn, Minister of Agriculture and Cooperatives, discussed the progress in resolving the issue of Thai fishery products being considered illegal by the European Union (EU) since October 2014, with a reevaluation scheduled for August. Thailand has urgently implemented three measures: specific legislation, a comprehensive fisheries plan (both of which are completed), and legalizing unregistered fishing vessels, effective July 1, 2015. No further extensions will be allowed as failing the assessment could affect all Thai fishery exports, necessitating strict enforcement (Department of Public Relations, 2015). In September 2015, the Ministry of Agriculture and Cooperatives plans to discuss government actions with the EU to resolve illegal fishing issues. Initially, they will issue a decree or act through the Ministry, drafting a new act that, once approved, will replace the old decree to align with the EU's recommendation for specific IUU legislation.[64]

The Department of Fisheries, Ministry of Agriculture and Cooperatives, has established control measures for Thai fishing vessels to prevent IUU fishing. This includes the creation of a catch certification system, control systems to prevent IUU fishing, and a traceability system within the existing legal and regulatory frameworks. Measures to ensure that Thai fishing vessels are not engaging in IUU fishing include requiring Thai-flagged vessels fishing domestically and internationally to register and obtain proper fishing licenses. As of 2015, data from the fishing database covering 23 coastal provinces show a total of 57,141 fishing vessels, of which 10,001 are legally registered, have valid vessel licenses, and hold fishing permits. This information is summarized from the Thai Fisheries Information System (Fishing Info) by the Information Technology and Communication Center as of July 6, 2015.[65]

Key measures to tackle illegal fishing seriously include:

1. Controlling unregistered vessels or those without permits (known as "criminal certificates") from fishing
2. Prohibiting the use of trawlers
3. Installing vessel monitoring systems (VMS) for vessels of 60 gross tons and above operating in international waters

[64] Wilhelm et al. (2020), p. 103833.

[65] Dasilva (2020).

4. Implementing entry-exit notification systems for vessels of 30 gross tons and above
5. Enforcing 15 other regulations without any leniency from July 1, 2015, onwards, to address illegal fishing issues as demanded by the EU

Strict enforcement of these laws led to protests, with thousands of fishing vessels in various provinces halting operations from the beginning of the month. This has become a hot issue, raising concerns that it could lead to a chain reaction, particularly in seafood shortages and rising prices. However, on the flip side, this situation benefits small-scale and legal fishing operations, as they can work and catch more fish, which is also advantageous for marine resources, allowing young fish to grow to maturity. Coastal fisheries, which make up 85% of the fishing industry, see improvement. Meanwhile, the commercial fishing sector, which comprises about 15% of the industry, is the majority of those protesting.

For more than 50 years, boat owners in the fishing industry have not adhered to the laws nor have the laws been strictly enforced. Consequently, most of the boats have not received lawful certification. To make these boats legal and obtain the necessary permits for operating legally, an investment of approximately 200,000–500,000 baht per boat is required. Thus, the fishing vessels needing to dock may not necessarily be protesting against the government or negotiating with the Department of Fisheries for leniency and exemptions but may instead be fearing arrest by the authorities.[66]

Based on surveys in various southern provinces, it was found that in Songkhla, where there are about 1000 fishing boats, only a little over 100 boats are legally compliant, resulting in more than 800 boats docked. Similar situations are observed in Pattani, Nakhon Si Thammarat, Satun, Trang, and other provinces, where about 80% of the boats have stopped fishing activities, with only 20% of the boats being legal and able to fish.

The solution for illegal commercial fishing is to amend and correct the practices to comply with the law. The government has asked for cooperation from fishermen and fisheries operators to register their boats, obtain fishing permits using legal fishing gear, and ensure that crew members hold valid labor permits. Once these three requirements are met, they can continue their fishing activities as usual. Those who have not yet registered can do so at the One-Stop Service Centers until July 15, 2015, and can still contact the Department of Marine and Coastal Resources and the Department of Fisheries until July 31, 2015.[67]

7 The Reform of Thai Fisheries

Since the National Council for Peace and Order (NCPO) issued the NCPO Head Order No. 10/2015 on tackling illegal, unreported, and unregulated (IUU) fishing, it has highlighted the critical importance of addressing illegal fishing

[66] Stephens (2016), p. 477.

[67] Landry (2023), p. 14.

problems. This is because, without serious and urgent fisheries reform in Thailand, it could impact the country's future aquatic product exports and Thailand's security. From July 1, 2015, onwards, the Ministry of Commerce sent officials to survey the market to monitor potential impacts. The Department of Internal Trade found that at the Thai Sea Market in Samut Sakhon province, the quantity of seafood entering the market had decreased slightly, and prices had increased. However, on July 6, 2015, Boonyarit Kalayanamit, Director-General of the Department of Internal Trade, confirmed that there was no shortage of seafood as previously feared.[68]

This aligns with the exploratory research results from the Master Poll, titled "Community Leaders' Views on the EU Yellow Card and Concerns about Seafood Shortages," by the Thai Researchers Association for Community Happiness. The survey interviewed 1079 community leaders nationwide from July 3 to 5, 2015, and found that almost all community leaders (91.2%) believe that the government's strict enforcement of the law will have positive effects. Besides potentially lifting the EU yellow card and improving the country's image, it could also address multiple issues simultaneously, including illegal fishing, human trafficking, illegal labor, and the suppression of influential figures. A minority (8.8%) feels that it will have more negative effects, such as increasing the price of seafood or causing shortages. In response to the same issue, the network of local fishing boats has attempted to contribute to solving seafood shortages and price hikes by establishing distribution centers nationwide. This approach turns the crisis into an opportunity to enhance local fishery operations.[69]

Considering that the existing fisheries law has been in effect for a long time, some of its provisions are not suitable for the current situation, where aquatic resources are limited, while fishing technology has significantly developed and is being used as a tools to conduct fishing, leading to a rapid decline in aquatic species. Therefore, it is appropriate to improve the management of the country's aquatic resources and fisheries to align with international laws and standards, the advancements in fishery technology, and the current social conditions. This Act sets forth measures for promoting and developing the management and maintenance of aquatic resources, their utilization, and other related operations. It also encourages the public or local fishing communities to participate in the management, maintenance, and balanced utilization of aquatic resources. The aim is to ensure that the existing aquatic resources can be used sustainably. Moreover, the Act specifies measures to promote the quality standards of aquatic animals and products derived from fishing or aquaculture concerning hygiene, consumer safety, and environmental impact. It also includes measures to control and regulate the use of Thai fishing vessels in domestic and international waters. Therefore, it is necessary to enact the Act.[70]

[68] Wongrak et al. (2021), p. 6814.

[69] Ratner et al. (2014), pp. 120–130.

[70] Sylwester (2014), p. 423.

8 Conclusion

The crisis of illegal, unreported, and unregulated (IUU) fishing in Thailand highlights the complex intersection of economic dependency, environmental degradation, international pressure, and legal reform. While Thailand has long benefited from its abundant marine resources and a thriving export-based seafood industry, decades of overfishing, weak enforcement, and noncompliance with international standards culminated in the EU's issuance of a yellow card warning. This moment acted as a catalyst for sweeping regulatory reform, including the enactment of the Fisheries Act B.E. 2558 (2015), the development of traceability systems, the enforcement of vessel registration and licensing, and regional cooperation through ASEAN platforms. Nevertheless, enforcement alone is not sufficient. The long-term sustainability of Thai fisheries demands a paradigm shift—from viewing marine resources as limitless economic assets to recognizing them as shared ecological wealth requiring stewardship. Empowering local fishing communities, implementing community-based resource management, enhancing regional cooperation, and adapting to global environmental challenges are critical to this shift. Thailand's journey from exploitation to responsibility offers not only lessons for domestic governance but also a model for the wider Southeast Asian region, where similar pressures and challenges persist. Ultimately, Thailand's progress since the EU yellow card is significant, yet the persistence of IUU fishing and labor abuses indicates true reform must be rooted in long-term commitment, inclusive governance, and adaptive policy design—balancing economic, environmental, and social needs to ensure the sustainability of Thailand's fisheries for generations to come.

References

Ainsworth RF, Cowx IG, Funge Smith SJ (2023) Putting the fish into inland fisheries–a global allocation of historic inland fish catch. Fish Fish 24(2):263–278

Anuchiracheeva S, Demaine H, Shivakoti GP, Ruddle K (2003) Systematizing local knowledge using GIS: fisheries management in Bang Saphan Bay, Thailand. Ocean Coast Manag 46(11–12):1049–1068

Arnason R (2023) Improving fisheries management in developing countries. Mar Resour Econ 38(3):263–283

Aussawarangkul T, Wongbandit A (2014) Thailand's compliance with international standards against illegal, unreported and unregulated fisheries. Master's thesis, Thammasat University. http://ethesisarchive.library.tu.ac.th

Avakiat S, Rooppsuwankun P (2024) The important factors for Thai frozen shrimp exporting to The United States of America and Japan. APHEIT Int J Interdiscip Soc Sci Technol 13(1):67–75

Baran E (2005) Cambodian inland fisheries: facts, figures and context, vol 1751. WorldFish

Baran E, Jantunen T, Chong CK, Kang SBK, Puchong PB (2007) Values of inland fisheries in the Mekong River Basin. In: Tropical river fisheries valuation: background papers to a global synthesis, pp 227–290

Barbier EB, Strand I, Sathirathai S (2002) Do open access conditions affect the valuation of an externality? Estimating the welfare effects of mangrove–fishery linkages in Thailand. Environ Resour Econ 21:343–365
Bauer NR, Kittel IJ, Schoenig E, Ferse SC, Wild C (2023) Thailand case study: artificial reefs as a fishery management tool. In: Challenges in tropical coastal zone management. Springer, pp 277–302
Busaranuvong P, Khumwang W (2020) System dynamic model of exploited labor in Thailand's fishing industry. System 2020:01–27
Butcher JG (2004) The closing of the frontier. Brill
Choo PS (2008) Population status, fisheries and trade of sea cucumbers in Asia
Christensen V, Walters CJ (2004) Trade-offs in ecosystem-scale optimization of fisheries management policies. Bull Mar Sci 74(3):549–562
Chuenpagdee R, Jentoft S (2009) Governability assessment for fisheries and coastal systems: a reality check. Hum Ecol 37:109–120
Dasilva B (2020) Freedoms and (un) freedoms: migrant worker experiences in the Thai and Vietnamese fishing industries. Doctoral dissertation, University of Ottawa
Deb U, Dey M (2024) The crisis of fisheries and prospects for fish as food in Asia. In: Food security issues in Asia, p 165
Dharmasaroja C (2019) The socio-economic impact of IUU-fishing: The case of EU give yellow card to Thailand
Djunarsjah E, Kusumadewi D, Chairuniza G (2021) The effectiveness of Indonesia's fisheries policy to reduce illegal fishing. In: IOP conference series: earth and environmental science, vol 805(1), p 012018
Falvey L (2000) Thai agriculture: golden cradle of millennia. Kasetsart University
Galam R, Acejo I, Turgo N (2024) Asia Pacific and the global maritime industry: hierarchies, vulnerabilities, solidarities. Asian Pac Migr J:01171968241245382
Haritavorn N (2023) 'Boat quarantine': lessons learned from SARS-CoV-2 prevention and control measures in fishing communities in Thailand. Int J Environ Res Public Health 20(6):4816
Johnston DM (2023) The international law of fisheries: a framework for policy-oriented inquiries, vol 3. Martinus Nijhoff Publishers
Kadfak A (2023) How is unilateral trade-based policy adopted and integrated from the perspective of receiving countries? Applying EU IUU regulation in Thailand. In: EU trade-related measures against illegal fishing, p 19
Kadfak A, Linke S (2021) More than just a carding system: labour implications of the EU's illegal, unreported and unregulated (IUU) fishing policy in Thailand. Mar Policy 127:104445
Kadfak A, Widengård M (2023) From fish to fishworker traceability in Thai fisheries reform. Environ Plan E Nat Space 6(2):1322–1342
Khan AM, Jiang MG, Yang XQ, Apriliani IM, Purba NP, Wiryawan B, Pasaribu B (2024) Illegal fishing threatens the sustainability of future tuna commodities in Indonesia. Mar Policy 159:105936
Khemakorn P (2006) Sustainable management of pelagic fisheries in the South China Sea region. United Nations—The Nippon Foundation
Kongprasertamorn K (2007) Local wisdom, environmental protection and community development: the clam farmers in Tambon Bangkhunsai, Phetchaburi Province, Thailand. Manusya: Journal of Humanities 10(1):1–10
Landry M (2023) Fish better have my money: efforts to combat illegal, unregulated, and unreported fishing in the gulf and beyond. LSU J Energy Law Resources 11(1):14
Lunn KE, Dearden P (2006) Monitoring small-scale marine fisheries: an example from Thailand's Ko Chang archipelago. Fish Res 77(1):60–71
Marschke M, Vandergeest P (2016) Slavery scandals: unpacking labour challenges and policy responses within the offshore fisheries sector. Mar Policy 68:39–46
Moazzam M, Moazzam N (2023) An assessment of razor clam fisheries of Pakistan: history, species composition, population and export

Mutaqin ZZ (2021) Modern-day slavery at sea: human trafficking in Thai fishing industry. In: ASEAN international law. Springer Nature, Singapore, pp 461–480
Nasuchon N, Charles A (2010) Community involvement in fisheries management: experiences in the Gulf of Thailand countries. Mar Policy 34(1):163–169
Noranarttragoon P, Koolkalaya S, Thitipongtrakul W, Avakul P, Phoonsawat R, Jutagate T (2023) Trawl fisheries in the Gulf of Thailand: vulnerability assessment and trend analysis of the fish landings. Fishes 8(4):177
Paniagua P, Rayamajhee V (2024) Governing the global fisheries commons. Mar Policy 165:106182
Panyarux S (2020). The outlook of the fishing industry under the limitation of the labour force in Thailand
Pauly D, Chuenpagdee R (2003) Development of fisheries in the Gulf of Thailand large marine ecosystem: analysis of an unplanned experiment. In: Large marine ecosystems of the world: change and sustainability, pp 337–354
Pauwels OS, David P, Chimsunchart C, Thirakhupt K (2003) Reptiles of Phetchaburi Province, Western Thailand: a list of species, with natural history notes, and a discussion on the biogeography at the Isthmus of Kra. Tropical Natural History 3(1):23–53
Prabakaran K, Sompongchaiyakul P, Bureekul S, Wang X, Charoenpong C (2024) Heavy metal bioaccumulation and risk assessment in fishery resources from the Gulf of Thailand. Mar Pollut Bull 198:115864
Prompatanapak A, Lopetcharat K (2020) Managing changes and risk in seafood supply chain: a case study from Thailand. Aquaculture 525:735318
Ratner BD, Åsgård B, Allison EH (2014) Fishing for justice: human rights, development, and fisheries sector reform. Glob Environ Chang 27:120–130
Sampantamit T, Ho L, Lachat C, Hanley-Cook G, Goethals P (2021) The contribution of Thai fisheries to sustainable seafood consumption: national trends and future projections. Foods 10(4):880
Satumanatpan S, Chuenpagdee R, Traesupap S, Yeemin T, Juntarashote K (2024) Policy realignment for the implementation of the small-scale fisheries guidelines in Thailand. In: Implementation of the small-scale fisheries guidelines. Springer, pp 167–187
Song AM., Barclay K, Kadfak A (n.d.) EU trade-related measures against illegal fishing: policy diffusion and effectiveness in Thailand and Australia
Stephens S (2016) Show, don't tell: how Thailand can and must make advancements in the fight against human trafficking in the Thai fishing industry. Emory Int Law Rev 31:477
Stobutzki IC, Silvestre GT, Garces LR (2006a) Key issues in coastal fisheries in South and Southeast Asia. Fish Res 78(2–3):109–118
Stobutzki IC, Silvestre GT, Talib AA, Krongprom A, Supongpan M, Khemakorn P et al (2006b) Decline of demersal coastal fisheries resources in three developing Asian countries. Fish Res 78(2–3):130–142
Stringer C, Burmester B, Michailova S (2022) Modern slavery and the governance of labor exploitation in the Thai fishing industry. J Clean Prod 371:133645
Subnawin S, Singchai A (2024) Network construction food security of local fishing community in Thailand. Open J Soc Sci 12(2):449–460
Suwankiri D (n.d.) Labor motivation in the fisheries industry in Thailand. Available at SSRN 4852124
Sylwester JG (2014) Fishers of men: the neglected effects of environmental depletion on labor trafficking in the Thai fishing industry. Pac Rim Law Policy J 23:423
Teh LC, Pauly D (2018) Who brings in the fish? The relative contribution of small-scale and industrial fisheries to food security in Southeast Asia. Front Mar Sci 5:44
Thammachote P, Trochim JI (2023) Thailand seafood trade flow and its challenges
Torell M, Ekmaharaj S, Siriraksophon S, Wanchana W (2010) Illegal fishing. Southeast Asian Fisheries Development Center

Tsolakis N, Niedenzu D, Simonetto M, Dora M, Kumar M (2021) Supply network design to address United Nations Sustainable Development Goals: a case study of blockchain implementation in Thai fish industry. J Bus Res 131:495–519
Van Zalinge N, Nao T, Touch ST, Deap L (2000) Where there is water, there is fish? Cambodian fisheries issues in a Mekong River Basin perspective
Vandergeest P, Marschke M (2020) Modern slavery and freedom: exploring contradictions through labour scandals in the Thai fisheries. Antipode 52(1):291–315
Wilcox, C., Mann, V., Cannard, T., Ford, J., Hoshino, E., & Pascoe, S. (2021). A review of illegal, unreported and unregulated fishing issues and progress in the Asia-Pacific Fishery Commission region
Wilhelm M, Kadfak A, Bhakoo V, Skattang K (2020) Private governance of human and labor rights in seafood supply chains–the case of the modern slavery crisis in Thailand. Mar Policy 115:103833
Wongrak G, Hur N, Pyo I, Kim J (2021) The impact of the EU IUU regulation on the sustainability of the Thai fishing industry. Sustainability 13(12):6814
Zwoelfer R (2020) The economic impact of IUU-fishing and its countermeasures on small-scale fishermen in Thailand: a case study of Baan Khan Kradai. In: IOP conference series: earth and environmental science, vol 416(1), p 012019

Surinrat Kaewtong is an assistant professor at the Faculty of Law, Prince of Songkla University, Thailand. His expertise spans international law, international business law, criminal law, and civil and commercial law, with a primary focus on private law and its role in economic and commercial development. With over 20 years of academic experience, he has contributed extensively to legal scholarship and education in Thailand. His work emphasizes the application of private law principles in addressing complex legal and economic issues, and he has been actively involved in promoting the development and modernization of private law frameworks. His research and teaching have been widely recognized for their contribution to strengthening legal understanding and practice across multiple sectors in Thailand.

Pajon Kongmuang is an assistant professor at the Faculty of Law, Prince of Songkla University, Thailand. He specializes in public law, with particular expertise in environmental law and regulatory governance. With over two decades of academic and professional experience, he has played a significant role in advancing legal scholarship and contributing to legislative development in Thailand. Before his academic career, he served as a legal officer at the Council of State, where he was involved in the drafting and review of legislation. His combined experience in government service and academia has enabled him to bridge theory and practice, and his research has informed policy discussions across multiple sectors. His work focuses especially on public environmental law and legal frameworks relating to animal protection.

Phongsak Jehpong is a lecturer at the Faculty of Law, Prince of Songkla University, Thailand. His areas of expertise include Animal Law and Civil and Commercial Law. He is an emerging scholar whose academic work focuses on the development of legal frameworks for animal protection in Thailand, as well as broader issues in private law. He has actively contributed to academic discourse through research and conference presentations and has been involved in efforts to promote legal reforms, particularly in relation to animal welfare and rights. His work seeks to strengthen the legal recognition and protection of animals within the Thai legal system while integrating comparative perspectives.

AI, Environmental Damage, and Regulatory Divides: Fragmented Governance and the Latin American Response

Sebastian Smart and Danny Rayman Labrin

Abstract The environmental impact of artificial intelligence (AI) technologies is increasingly significant, particularly in terms of energy consumption, water usage, and mineral extraction, while also deepening community divides. While AI is often promoted as a tool for sustainability, its life cycle—from training models to the operation of data centres—imposes severe ecological costs, disproportionately affecting people in Global South regions, like Latin America. Existing international AI governance initiatives, such as the EU AI Act and the UNESCO Recommendation on AI Ethics, acknowledge these challenges but lack binding global commitments to mitigate them. This regulatory gap enables technology companies to engage in "forum shopping" by exploiting less-regulated jurisdictions, exacerbating environmental harm, and undermining sustainability goals in the Global South. Through an analysis of 5 key international AI governance initiatives and over 77 emerging AI regulations across Latin America, this chapter contends that without a more cohesive and inclusive global mandatory framework integrating environmental concerns, technology companies will continue to circumvent business and human rights principles, further contributing to environmental degradation, human rights harms, and irresponsible business practices in the Global South.

1 Introduction

The rapid expansion of artificial intelligence (AI) technologies has generated significant environmental concerns, particularly regarding energy consumption, water usage, and the extraction of minerals, all of which have direct implications for

S. Smart
Anglia Ruskin University, Cambridge, UK

D. Rayman Labrin (✉)
Santiago, Chile
e-mail: danny@rayman.legal

S. Talukdar (ed.), *Law, Accountability, and Corporate Conduct*, New Approaches to Business, Human Rights and the Environment 1,
https://doi.org/10.1007/978-3-032-28714-4_9

internationally recognized human rights. Under the UN Guiding Principles on Business and Human Rights (UNGPs), companies developing and deploying AI systems are responsible for identifying, preventing, and mitigating adverse human rights impacts across their entire value chains. However, while AI is often promoted as a tool for enhancing sustainability and addressing environmental challenges,[1] its life cycle continues to generate ecological and social harms that disproportionately fall on communities in the Global South. Latin America, despite being a major provider of critical minerals for AI development, bears the brunt of these environmental consequences without reaping the economic benefits associated with AI innovation. This imbalance deepens pre-existing vulnerabilities and amplifies the adverse consequences for the fundamental human rights of affected communities.

Recognizing environmental challenges, international regulatory frameworks have begun addressing AI governance. The European Union (EU) has led regulatory efforts with the AI Act, which aims to set global standards for AI governance through expansive jurisdictional reach. Similarly, global initiatives such as the UN Global Digital Compact and the UNESCO Recommendations on AI Ethics have sought to incorporate human rights and sustainability into AI governance. However, despite the proliferation of these international regulations and policy frameworks, a comprehensive and binding global regulatory regime for AI remains absent. This fragmented regulatory landscape allows technology companies to engage in "forum shopping", exploiting jurisdictions with weaker environmental and human rights protections. Consequently, the environmental impact of AI remains largely unaddressed in global governance discussions, disproportionately affecting regions like Latin America, which are primarily recipients rather than producers of AI technologies.

Today, several voices warn about the negative impact of AI, going so far as to say, for example, that AI poses an "existential threat" to the human species,[2] that it is already "too late" to regulate its consequences,[3] or that the competition for the development of these new technologies is assimilated to an "arms race" that is very difficult to stop.[4] According to a poll with over 400 experts developed by the multi-stakeholder High-level Advisory Body on Artificial Intelligence (formed in October 2023) to undertake analysis and advance recommendations for the international governance of AI, most of the respondents argued that "the race to develop and deploy AI systems defies traditional regulatory systems and governance regimes. Most experts polled for the AI Risk Global Pulse Check expect AI acceleration over the next 18 months, both in its development/technical change (74%) and adoption/application (89%)".[5]

[1] Rolnick et al. (2019); Vinuesa et al. (2020), p. 233; Spencer (2018).

[2] Cowen (2023).

[3] Schwartzentruber (2023).

[4] Roff (2019), p. 95.

[5] UN High-Level Advisory Board on AI (2024), p. 34.

Also, when it comes to risks, seven in ten experts polled were concerned or very concerned that harms (existing or new) resulting from AI will become substantially more serious and/or widespread in the next 18 months. From a list of example AI-related risk areas, a plurality of experts were concerned or very concerned about harms related to societal implications of AI, including 76% related to damage to information integrity, 74% related to inequalities such as concentration of wealth and power in a few hands, and 67% regarding discrimination and disenfranchisement, particularly among marginalized communities. Regarding the intentional use of AI that harms others, 75% were concerned about risks related to armed conflict by state actors, 72% regarding malicious use by non-state actors, and 65% regarding state actors using AI in ways that harm individuals. Additionally, 55% are concerned or very concerned about the environmental impacts of AI.[6]

AI technologies are often presented as tools capable of enhancing efficiency and contributing to sustainability goals. However, the environmental impact of AI throughout the value chain is a significant concern. Training AI models, especially deep learning algorithms, requires substantial computational power and energy, leading to considerable greenhouse gas (GHG) emissions and further human rights violations, particularly over peasants and indigenous communities affected by water consumption and mineral extraction.[7] The significant energy consumption associated with training AI models can result in GHG emissions comparable to hundreds of transcontinental flights.[8] For instance, training a single large AI model can consume as much electricity as a hundred US homes use in a year.[9] These impacts highlight the importance of considering not just the operational phase but also the energy costs embedded in the development and training of AI models.

The production and deployment of AI technologies also involve significant environmental costs. The extraction of minerals necessary for manufacturing AI hardware, such as lithium, cobalt, and rare earth elements, leads to environmental degradation and socio-economic disruptions, particularly in the Global South. Additionally, the expansion of data centres, which house the servers necessary for AI operations, exacerbates energy and water consumption. These facilities require continuous power and cooling, leading to substantial energy use and water stress in regions already facing environmental challenges.

Water scarcity is another significant issue exacerbated by the expansion of AI and data centres, particularly in Latin America. The region, already vulnerable to climate change-induced droughts, faces additional pressures from the water-intensive operations of data centres. Data centres require vast amounts of water for cooling their servers, a necessity that competes directly with local communities' needs for drinking and agriculture. The situation is particularly dire in countries like Uruguay and Chile, which have experienced severe droughts in recent years. In

---

[6] Ibid. p. 29.

[7] Ligozat et al. (2022), p. 5172.

[8] Strubell et al. (2019).

[9] Saul and Bass (2023).

Uruguay, the worst drought in seven decades led to the capital, Montevideo, reaching "day zero" and running out of potable water.[10] In Chile, over half the population faced severe water scarcity by early 2022, prompting unprecedented water rationing measures in Santiago.[11]

Considering these challenges, this chapter evaluates how environmental concerns are reflected in international AI frameworks and in emerging regulatory initiatives across Latin America, ultimately underscoring the urgent need for mandatory AI regulations that integrate environmental protection at both the international and national levels.

1.1 Methodology

This chapter employs a mixed-methods approach to analyse the inclusion of environmental standards in AI governance at both international and national levels. To select international standards, a systematic review was conducted of legally binding and policy-driven AI governance frameworks. The study focused on five key international instruments that shape global AI regulation, including the Organization for Economic Co-operation and Development AI Principles (OECD AI Principles), the United Nations Global Digital Compact (UN Digital Compact), and the United Nations Educational, Scientific, and Cultural Organization (UNESCO) Recommendations on the Ethics of Artificial Intelligence (UNESCO Recommendation), the European Artificial Intelligence Act (EU AI Act), and the Council of Europe Framework Convention on Artificial Intelligence and Human Rights, Democracy, and the Rule of Law (Council of Europe's AI Convention). These instruments were selected based on their legal enforceability, policy influence, and explicit references to sustainability and environmental protection.

At the national level, a comprehensive analysis of 77 AI-related legislative proposals currently under discussion in Latin America was conducted. These proposals were identified through a systematic search of official legislative databases in Argentina, Brazil, Chile, Colombia, Costa Rica, Ecuador, Mexico, Panama, Peru, and Uruguay. The legislative texts were examined to determine whether they included provisions addressing environmental risks associated with AI technologies. The analysis categorized these proposals based on their regulatory focus, distinguishing between general AI frameworks and sector-specific regulations, while also assessing the extent to which they incorporated sustainability considerations. This methodology ensures a thorough evaluation of AI governance developments, allowing for a comparative analysis between international regulatory trends and emerging national approaches in Latin America.

---

[10] Gudynas (2023).

[11] Nuñez (2022).

The importance of this chapter lies in its unique contribution to understanding how AI regulations in Latin America engage with environmental concerns. While existing studies have analysed AI governance from a technological, economic, and human rights perspective, there has been little examination of the environmental impact of AI in the region and its regulatory responses. By assessing whether emerging regulations incorporate sustainability measures and comparing them to international frameworks, this chapter highlights whether Latin American countries are shaping their own approach or adopting existing global models. Furthermore, it examines the potential influence of these regulations on broader AI governance debates and whether Latin America's environmental priorities are being adequately represented in international discussions.

In doing so, this chapter aims to examine the intersection of AI governance, environmental sustainability, and Latin America's evolving regulatory landscape. The second section, after this introduction, begins by recognizing the existing voluntary and mandatory international AI regulations, analysing how they incorporate environmental standards. It highlights that while several international initiatives acknowledge AI's environmental impact, most of them fail to develop a comprehensive analysis of these effects, with the notable exception of UNESCO. The third section examines the 77 AI regulations currently under discussion across Latin America, assessing how these national legislative initiatives engage with environmental concerns and whether they reflect international governance trends. The fourth and final section presents the conclusions, considering the implications of Latin America's regulatory developments and the potential influence of its emerging frameworks on global AI governance.

2 A Fragmented AI Governance Landscape: Wins and Losses for Environmental Protection Across the AI Life Cycle

While the introduction outlined the environmental consequences of AI development and the global governance challenges surrounding them, a deeper examination of the regulatory landscape reveals a stark imbalance in priorities. Many existing AI governance initiatives primarily emphasize ethical concerns, human rights, and economic development, often treating environmental sustainability as a secondary or overlooked issue. Despite increasing recognition of AI's environmental footprint, regulatory frameworks remain fragmented, with voluntary guidelines outpacing binding commitments. This section evaluates key international governance initiatives to assess how AI regulations integrate—or fail to integrate—environmental protections throughout the AI life cycle. By analysing policy-driven and legally binding initiatives, it explores whether the current governance frameworks provide meaningful safeguards against AI-driven environmental harms or merely perpetuate a regulatory patchwork that enables corporate evasion and regulatory arbitrage. The study focuses on five international initiatives, including non-UN and UN international initiatives.

The selection of the five international initiatives and their analysis involved a process of considering the seven interregional non-UN AI governance initiatives mentioned in the final report of the UN High-Level Advisory Board on AI[12] and considered the latest statements and recently updated or adopted regulatory and policy frameworks. Notably, the Council of Europe Drafting Group on Human Rights and Artificial Intelligence was not considered, as this study focuses on the two most recently adopted regulatory frameworks that originated in Europe.

After identifying 12 initiatives, we categorized them into policy initiatives and regulatory binding initiatives.[13] The main distinction between these two categories lies in their legal nature: regulatory binding initiatives impose legally binding obligations on signatory states, whereas policy initiatives represent voluntary commitments without enforceability. These last were also divided into statements and principles.

An initial analysis of the 12 initiatives focused on the keywords "climate change", "environment(s)", "environmental", "consumption", and "sustainable" to determine whether they establish purposes, principles, or action-oriented recommendations aimed at addressing environmental impacts. A key takeaway from the initiatives is that AI development is primarily framed as a tool to address global challenges such as health, food security, and sustainability. In fact, "sustainable" is one of the most frequently mentioned aspects linked to AI development, appearing in 10 of the 12 reviewed initiatives. However, while many initiatives acknowledge the need for AI to be sustainable, most policy frameworks that take the form of statements—such as those from the Group of 7, GPAI, and AI Summits Declarations—fail to address the need for environmental protection in the development, use, and deployment of AI.

Although the term "sustainable" is frequently used, its connection to specific environmental objectives remains vague in most policy frameworks, as they do not operationalize the concept or provide specific guidance on environmental protection. There is a clear need for explicit calls to develop legally mandatory actions and well-defined positions on the measures required to assess and mitigate AI's potential harms and risks to biodiversity and ecosystems.[14]

Notably—as highlighted in Table 1—of the 12 initiatives, only 5 explicitly mention climate change or climate crisis, primarily to highlight AI's potential role in

---

[12] UN High-Level Advisory Board on AI (2024), p. 9.

[13] The policy initiatives we considered include the G20 AI Principles (2019), the Global Partnership on Artificial Intelligence (GPAI) Ministers' Declarations (2022 and 2024), the Hiroshima AI Process G7 Digital and Tech Ministers' Statement (2023), the G7 Italia Ministerial Meeting on Technology and Digital (2024), the Bletchley Declaration (2023), the Seoul Ministerial Statement for Advancing AI Safety, Innovation, and Inclusivity (2024), the OECD AI Principles (initially adopted in 2019 and updated in 2024), the UNESCO Recommendation on the Ethics of Artificial Intelligence, and the UN Digital Compact. On the other hand, the regulatory binding initiatives we considered include the European Artificial Intelligence Act and the Council of Europe Framework Convention on Artificial Intelligence and Human Rights, Democracy, and the Rule of Law.

[14] Laville (2025) and Green Screen Coalition et al. (2025).

Table 1 International standards regulating AI

Initiative	Type	Mentions climate change/crisis	Environmental protection approach
G20 AI Principles (2019)	Policy	No	Yes
GPAI Ministers' Declarations (2022)	Policy	Yes	No
GPAI Ministers' Declarations (2024)	Policy	No	No
G7 Hiroshima AI Process International Guiding Principles for All AI Actors (2023)	Policy	Yes	No
G7 Italia Ministerial Meeting on Technology and Digital (2024)	Policy	No	No
Bletchley Declaration (2023)	Policy	No	No
Seoul Ministerial Statement (2024)	Policy	Yes	No
OECD AI Principles (2019, updated 2024)	Policy	No	Yes
UNESCO Recommendation on the Ethics of AI	Policy	Yes	Yes
UN Digital Compact	Policy	No	Yes
EU Artificial Intelligence Act (EU AI Act)	Regulatory	Yes	Yes
Council of Europe Framework Convention on Artificial Intelligence and Human Rights, Democracy, and the Rule of Law	Regulatory	No	Yes

Source: processed by authors, 2025

addressing this global challenge, while only 2 frameworks acknowledge AI's potential negative contributions to climate change. Furthermore, none of the initiatives reference the United Nations Framework Convention on Climate Change (UNFCCC) or the Paris Agreement, both legally binding treaties that establish obligations for states to combat climate change (see Table 1).

Although the scenario may seem discouraging, the principles and regulatory frameworks that have emerged so far have begun to incorporate environmental considerations in AI governance. Therefore, after the initial review of these 12 initiatives, this study focuses its analysis on the 5 key instruments that attempt to address AI's environmental risks and harms. These include three major policy initiatives: the OECD AI Principles, the UN Digital Compact, and the UNESCO Recommendation, as well as two legally binding regulatory frameworks, the EU AI Act and the Council of Europe's AI Convention. An in-depth analysis of the G20 AI Principles was not conducted, as they are based on the OECD AI Principles (2019), making a detailed review redundant. The analysis of the five key initiatives will show that due to the fragmented and noncoherent landscape of AI regulations, there is a risk of losing opportunities to effectively operationalize environmental protection as a core value. Thus, first, we will focus on AI policy frameworks to highlight how AI policy frameworks have been preparing an AI governance policy framework to protect the environment and how ambitious regulatory binding frameworks fail to effectively protect this core value and human right.

2.1 AI Policy Frameworks: Human Rights and Environmental Protection as Core Values to Attempt to Protect the Environment

As previously discussed, policy frameworks around AI have often focused on the sustainable development of these technologies, which are increasingly recognized as tools to tackle significant global challenges. However, the three key policy initiatives identified as having environmental protections in the previous discussion establish core values and principles that aim to protect the environment.

One of the most frequently cited guidance in non-UN interregional governance initiatives is the 2019 OECD AI Principles, which were recently updated in 2024.[15] The OECD AI Principles emphasize the importance of ensuring sustainable AI developments, particularly in Principle 1, which highlights the importance of environmental protection. This vision, stated in the OECD principles, calls for actions to ensure that AI's transformative potential is harnessed in ways that protect humanity and the environment. Furthermore, Principle 1.2(a) reinforces the call for a rights-respecting development across the life cycle of AI systems. However, while this principle demands respect for human rights, it does not explicitly mention environmental rights as values that should be respected throughout the entire AI system life cycle. Moreover, Principle 1.2 (b) refers to the measures that AI actors should implement to manage risks, but it focuses primarily on AI's uses rather than its entire life cycle.

Despite this, the OECD Principles emphasize in their principle of accountability that AI actors should be responsible for the proper functioning of AI systems. They further require AI actors to apply a systemic risk management approach at each phase of the AI system life cycle on an ongoing basis and to adopt responsible business conduct to address AI-related risks. This includes, as appropriate, cooperation between AI actors, suppliers of AI knowledge and resources, AI system users, and other stakeholders. At this point, the OECD seems again to limit the scope of the risks by saying that they encompass harmful bias, human rights concerns—including safety, security, and privacy—as well as labour and intellectual property rights.

The OECD Principles provide a general recommendation to address various risks associated with the AI life cycle, which could include environmental risks. However, since these principles remain broad and vague recommendations, adopting and implementing such measures rely entirely on individual states' efforts or international cooperation. Moreover, the OECD Principles do not provide concrete guidelines on mitigating these risks or ensuring that AI actors uphold environmental protection as a core value.

The UN Global Digital Compact (Digital Compact), adopted in September 2024 by the UN General Assembly as part of the Pact for the Future resolution,[16]

[15] OECD (2024).

[16] UN General Assembly (2024).

establishes a set of guiding principles for international digital cooperation, including provisions that explicitly address environmental sustainability and responsible governance of emerging technologies, including AI. Thus, this initiative does not have a specific focus on AI, but as it establishes complementary dispositions and a specific section for AI, it was considered for this study.

The Digital Compact in its paragraph 8, specifically principles (e) "Digital technologies unlock new capabilities and opportunities for advancing environmental sustainability" and (i) "Safe, secure, and trustworthy emerging technologies", highlights two interrelated dimensions of AI governance: first, the potential of digital technologies to drive environmental sustainability, and second, the imperative to ensure that emerging technologies, including AI, are developed and deployed in a responsible, accountable, transparent, and human-centric manner across their entire life cycle. Furthermore, Principle 8(c) of the Digital Compact explicitly anchors these commitments in international law, including international human rights law. It mandates that all human rights and fundamental freedoms must be respected, protected, and promoted both online and offline.

It should be noted that, as in the OECD AI Principles, the Digital Compact does not explicitly refer to environmental rights when referring to respecting human rights. However, the Digital Compact's broad human rights commitments, particularly those outlined in its "Objective 3: Foster an inclusive, open, safe, and secure digital space that respects, protects, and promotes human rights", create a foundation for interpreting environmental rights protection within the wider human rights framework. In this sense, the Digital Compact emphasizes the need to uphold international human rights law throughout the life cycle of digital and emerging technologies, and its Objective 3 sets a commitment to establish safeguards, conduct human rights due diligence, and ensure effective oversight mechanisms. Notably, Objective 3 includes an express call for digital technology companies, developers, and social media platforms to respect human rights online, be accountable, take measures to prevent and mitigate abuses, and provide effective remedies in line with the UNGPs and other relevant frameworks.

Additionally, the Digital Compact refers expressly to AI and its international governance in its "Objective 5", recognizing the need for a balanced, inclusive, and risk-based approach to AI governance. It also underscores the urgent need to inclusively assess and address AI's risks, as well as advancing equitable and inclusive approaches to mitigating these risks in full respect of international law, including international human rights law, and considering other relevant frameworks, citing the UNESCO Recommendation.

These commitments recognize the need for proactive governance that anticipates and mitigates potential adverse impacts, including those on the environment. Furthermore, although not yet expressly recognized in binding treaties, developments in international human rights law have increasingly acknowledged the interdependence between human rights and environmental protection.[17] The UN General

[17] Symonides (1992), p. 22; Weston and Bollier (2013), p. 123; Varvastian (2019), p. 12.

Assembly and the UN Human Rights Council adopted resolutions that recognize the right to a clean, healthy, and sustainable environment as a universal human right, reinforcing this connection.[18] In this context, the Digital Compact's commitments to prevent human rights violations arising from digital technologies, strengthen legal and policy frameworks, and ensure compliance with international law can be interpreted as extending to environmental considerations, particularly regarding AI's socio-ecological impacts.

The UNESCO recommendations adopted in 2021 provide valuable guidelines by establishing values and principles for states and companies to apply across the AI life cycle, becoming one of the most influential policies shaping AI regulations in Latin America, as discussed in the next section.

In the Preamble, UNESCO highlights ethical concerns, including threats and their broader impact on issues such as human dignity, human rights, gender equality, animal welfare, and the environment. Specifically, the "Environment and Ecosystem Flourishing" value urges the recognition, protection, and promotion of the environment throughout the AI life cycle, focusing on reducing environmental impact by preventing the unsustainable exploitation of natural resources.

UNESCO's operational principles reinforce these environmental commitments. The "Proportionality and Do No Harm" acknowledges that AI does not inherently guarantee the flourishing of humans, the environment, or ecosystems, urging the application of proportionality when choosing and using AI systems. The "Responsibility and Accountability" principle urges states to implement ethical and legal frameworks that balance innovation with environmental sustainability, requiring AI actors and states to respect, protect, and promote human rights, fundamental freedoms, and the environment throughout AI's life cycle. Closely linked is the "Transparency and Explainability" principle, emphasizing the importance of transparency for holding AI actors accountable for environmental impacts. The "Safety and Security" principle mandates AI development with human and environmental safety in mind, preventing environmental harm, such as energy overconsumption and non-biodegradable waste. The "Sustainability" principle urges to assess AI's human, social, and cultural impact and its potential effects on the environment, aligning with the United Nations' Sustainable Development Goals (SDGs). Additionally, the "Awareness and Literacy" principle ensures that AI development is based on informed decisions that prioritize sustainability. The "Fairness and Non-Discrimination" principle reinforces AI compliance with international law, ensuring social justice and requiring efforts to minimize and prevent discriminatory or biased outcomes throughout the AI life cycle.

To operationalize these values, UNESCO provides policy actions to embed accountability, environmental protection, and human rights, aligned with the UNGPs, into AI governance and development. A key action is the ethical governance and stewardship, which calls on states to develop, review, and adapt regulatory frameworks to achieve accountability and responsibility for AI systems at all

[18] UN General Assembly (2022) and UN Human Rights Council (2021).

life cycle stages. It calls for states to adopt clear liability frameworks that attribute responsibility to natural or legal persons rather than the AI systems themselves, emphasizing human oversight in the development, deployment, and monitoring phases.

The "Environment and Ecosystems Policy" action recognizes AI's ecological impact, urging comprehensive assessments of the direct and indirect impact through the AI life cycle, providing an open list of examples that include energy consumption, carbon emissions, and raw material extraction. States and businesses are urged to take proactive steps to mitigate these effects by complying with environmental laws and sustainability commitments. To achieve this, UNESCO emphasizes the inclusion of local and Indigenous communities in AI decision-making processes. The principle of proportionality is embedded within this policy action, ensuring that AI adoption is justified relative to its environmental costs, with the precautionary principle guiding the restriction of AI deployment when sustainability cannot be assured.

In addition, the ethical impact assessment action urges states to ensure that AI actors and their systems align with fundamental rights and sustainability goals. States are encouraged to adopt impact assessment frameworks that identify impacts on human rights and fundamental freedoms, incorporating an intersectional approach. This includes developing and adopting due diligence and oversight mechanisms to identify, prevent, mitigate, and account for risks to human rights, rule of law, and inclusive societies. The action also stresses the importance of assessing the socio-economic impact of AI systems to prevent widening the gap between wealthy and poor populations and reducing the digital divide within and between countries.

The growing international recognition of AI's environmental and socio-ecological impacts underscores the urgency of establishing governance frameworks that prioritize sustainability, accountability, and human rights. While existing policy instruments, such as the OECD AI Principles and the Digital Compact, lay important foundations for responsible and sustainable AI governance, the UNESCO Recommendations emerge as the most comprehensive and action-oriented framework. By integrating environmental protection and embedding risk-based and proportionality principles, they provide a concrete pathway for aligning AI development with ecological and social justice imperatives.

2.2 AI Binding Regulatory Frameworks: Gaps Addressing Environmental Protection

After analysing the three policy recommendations, we now move the analysis to examine the two already identified legally binding AI regulatory frameworks assessing how they integrate environmental objectives and obligations for signatory states. Both frameworks recognize AI's dual role as a tool for promoting sustainability and as a source of environmental risks. However, the operationalization of environmental protection as a core value falls short, as it will be discussed.

On June 13, 2024, the EU AI Act (Regulation (EU) 2024/1689) was adopted as the first legally binding framework governing AI systems across the EU. It integrates environmental protection as a core value,[19] and its principle of societal and environmental well-being calls for AI systems to be developed and used sustainably and in an environmentally friendly way. The principle also emphasizes the need to ensure that AI benefits all of humanity while monitoring and assessing its long-term impact on individuals, society, and democracy. The Act expressly recognizes that AI systems can impact fundamental rights protected by the EU Charter, including the right to a high level of environmental protection, particularly when assessing the severity of AI-related harms. Its Article 1 highlights environmental protection among its overarching purposes, stating that the regulation seeks to promote innovation and trustworthy AI while ensuring health, safety, democracy, and environmental protection.

The EU AI Act establishes a risk-based approach that regulates AI systems based on their potential harms, prohibiting unacceptable AI practices, setting requirements for high-risk AI systems, and imposing transparency obligations on certain AI deployments. However, this risk-based classification focuses primarily on deployments of AI systems and loses the opportunity to extend to harm throughout the AI life cycle that could compromise natural environments, biodiversity, and ecosystems. Thus, while the Act prohibits AI systems that manipulate human behaviour or exploit vulnerabilities of a person or a specific group of persons, it does not explicitly categorize AI-driven environmental harms as high risk or unacceptable risks.

Moreover, key measures in the EU AI Act remain voluntary. For instance, it establishes a voluntary code of conduct that encourages best practices in AI governance, providing a framework for adopting specific requirements for AI systems other than high-risk ones. The AI Office and member states are responsible for promoting the development of these codes, aligning governance mechanisms with the industry's best practices and available technical solutions. Among the elements mentioned as the basis of clear objectives and key performance indicators, the Act refers to the Ethics Guidelines for Trustworthy AI, which identifies societal and environmental well-being as a core principle. In line with this, it explicitly calls for assessing and minimizing AI's environmental impact, including energy-efficient programming and techniques for the efficient design, training, and use of AI systems.

Additionally, the EU AI Act promotes AI regulatory sandboxes, controlled environments for testing AI systems under real-world conditions while ensuring

[19] The EU AI Act references in its recital 27 the seven non-binding AI ethics principles developed by the High-Level Expert Group on Artificial Intelligence in the Ethics Guidelines for Trustworthy AI of the European Commission and recognizes that those principles provide a foundation for trustworthy, human-centric AI, aligning with the EU Charter of Fundamental Rights and the Union's core values.

compliance with legal and ethical standards. Competent authorities are responsible for providing guidance, supervision, and support within these sandboxes to identify risks, particularly those related to fundamental rights, health, and safety, as well as to test and evaluate mitigation measures in accordance with the EU AI Act and other relevant Union and national laws.

The most direct reference to environmental mitigation appears in Article 40, which establishes a framework for developing harmonized standards to enhance AI systems' resource efficiency. This includes reducing energy consumption and resource use across the lifecycle of high-risk AI systems and promoting energy-efficient development of general-purpose AI models. However, this provision is linked to the European Commission's authority to issue standardization requests, which primarily guide reporting and documentation rather than mandating concrete environmental improvements. One positive aspect of this measure is that these requests must undergo consultation with the AI Board and relevant stakeholders, including the advisory forum. Furthermore, Annex XI requires that general-purpose AI models maintain technical documentation, including their estimated energy consumption. Notably, the estimated energy consumption for the training of the model could be part of the criteria for considering a general-purpose AI model as a systemic risk.

While the EU AI Act acknowledges AI's environmental impact, its mechanism for requesting measures, imposing penalties, and overseeing measures falls short of imposing specific obligations to enforce AI sustainable development obligations. The Act represents an important step in recognizing AI's role in sustainability. However, without mandatory efficiency standards, life cycle impact assessments, or enforcement mechanisms, it remains unlikely to drive significant reductions in AI's environmental footprint.

On September 5, 2024, the Council of Europe's AI Convention on AI was opened for signature. This convention, open to Council of Europe member states, the European Union, and non-member states worldwide, aims to ensure that AI-related activities align with human rights, democracy, and the rule of law. Its preamble explicitly acknowledges environmental protection, underscoring the importance of considering the broader risks and impacts of AI technologies, including those related to human health, the environment, and socio-economic aspects such as employment and labour.

Among its core objectives and purposes, the Council of Europe's AI Convention seeks to ensure that AI systems activities throughout their life cycle align with human rights, democracy, and the rule of law. To achieve this, it requires parties to adopt or maintain appropriate legislative, administrative, or other measures to enforce its provisions. These measures must be graduated and differentiated based on the severity and likelihood of adverse impacts on human rights, democracy, and the rule of law, regardless of the specific AI technology used. Additionally, to strengthen its implementation, the Council of Europe's AI Convention establishes a follow-up mechanism and promotes international cooperation.

The Council of Europe's AI Convention provides general obligations and guiding principles for parties when adopting or maintaining measures to implement its provisions. It requires states to ensure the activities within the life cycle of AI systems are consistent with the obligation to protect human rights and do not compromise the integrity, independence, and effectiveness of democratic institutions and processes. Among its core principles, it emphasizes transparency and oversight, requiring measures to be tailored to specific risks and contexts. It also reinforces accountability and responsibility for the adverse impacts of AI on human rights, democracy, and the rule of law, which is related to its provision of remedies and procedural safeguards that require they are accessible and effective. Furthermore, it upholds the principles of equality, including gender equality and the prohibition of discrimination, ensuring that AI systems do not exacerbate existing inequalities. Additionally, it promotes safe innovation, encouraging AI development while mitigating potential harms. To support this, the Council of Europe's AI Convention calls on states to facilitate the creation of controlled environments where AI systems can be developed, tested, and evaluated under the supervision of competent authorities.

Additionally, the Council of Europe's AI Convention stablishes a risk and impact management framework that requires states parties to adopt or maintain measures for identifying, assessing, preventing, and mitigating risks posed by AI systems, particularly regarding their actual and potential impacts on human rights, democracy, and the rule of law. This framework requires that risk management measures to be graduated and differentiated based on the context and intended use of AI systems, the severity and probability of potential impacts, and the perspectives of relevant stakeholders, in particular persons whose rights may be impacted. Furthermore, the risk management measures must be applied iteratively throughout the AI life cycle, incorporating monitoring, documentation, and testing, particularly before first deployment or following significant modifications. Moreover, state parties are required to ensure that adverse impacts on human rights, democracy, and the rule of law are adequately addressed and documented, feeding into ongoing risk assessment efforts. Additionally, the Convention obliges states to evaluate whether a moratorium, ban, or other regulatory measures may be necessary for certain AI applications deemed incompatible with fundamental rights, democratic governance, or the rule of law.

In terms of stakeholder engagement, the Council of Europe's AI Convention mandates that states must ensure that important issues related to AI systems are duly considered. This includes engaging in public discussions and conducting multi-stakeholder consultations on the social, economic, legal, ethical, environmental, and other relevant implications of AI systems, as appropriate. This commitment to inclusivity is also reflected in the international cooperation obligations, which require states to exchange relevant and useful information concerning AI-related developments that may have significant positive or negative effects on human rights, democracy, and the rule of law.

Despite the above, the Council of Europe's AI Convention scope is heavily limited by its exclusions and to whom they apply. Specifically, it applies primarily to AI life cycle activities carried out by public authorities or private actors acting on their behalf. The Convention grants state parties discretion in determining whether and how to regulate other private actors. In this regard, the Explanatory Report acknowledges that some states may initially choose not to apply the Convention's principles and obligations to private actors, expecting their regulatory approaches to evolve. However, it does not impose any binding obligation on states to apply this framework to other relevant AI private actors.[20] Furthermore, the scope also excludes certain activities, such as AI systems related to national security interests, national defence, and research and development activities; these last when the AI system has not been made available for use, and the testing and other similar activities do not pose a potential for interference with the Council of Europe's AI Convention core values.

Despite their ambitious objectives and explicit recognition of environmental concerns, both the EU AI Act and the Council of Europe's AI Convention fall short of operationalizing environmental protection as a concrete and enforceable obligation. The EU AI Act acknowledges AI's environmental impact, but it tends to focus only on resource consumption; it relies on risk-based classifications that overlook environmental life cycle harms and risks and suggests voluntary measures that may not translate into binding sustainability commitments. Similarly, the Council of Europe's AI Convention incorporates environmental considerations within its broad human rights and governance principles but lacks strong enforcement mechanisms and leaves significant discretion to state parties, particularly regarding private actors and certain high-impact AI applications. These gaps are inconsistent with states' international human rights duties. For instance, Principle 1 of the UNGPs establishes that states must protect against human rights abuses by third parties, including businesses, by taking appropriate steps to prevent, investigate, punish, and remedy harms through effective policies, legislation, and regulation—measures that necessarily extend to addressing the ecological and social impacts of the AI life cycle.

2.3 The Limited Scope of AI Protections in a Fragmented Regulatory Landscape: Risks for the Global South

The Council of Europe's AI Convention negotiations were marked by significant tensions. Notably, countries, including the United States, the United Kingdom, Canada, Israel, and Japan, advocated for limiting the treaty's scope to public bodies and introducing an "opt-in" mechanism for signatory countries regarding their private companies.[21] In contrast, some EU countries and the EU Commission tried to expand the scope to private entities while also pushing for the exclusion of AI systems developed exclusively for national security, military, and defence purposes.[22]

[20] Council of Europe (2024).

[21] Bertuzzi (2023) and Bertuzzi (2024c).

[22] Bertuzzi (2024a).

Ultimately, the political imperative for broad international agreement prevailed, resulting in a text that prioritizes maximum signatory participation.[23] Consequently, the final adopted version narrowed the scope of this landmark international binding AI treaty. Critics during the negotiation not only highlighted valid concerns on potential challenges in effectively safeguarding human rights[24] but also how the Council of Europe's AI Convention could potentially fail to address local realities and instead primarily serve the interests of the Global North.[25]

This is particularly problematic for the following reasons. First, as highlighted by the UN High-Level Advisory Board on AI, many international AI governance initiatives at the interregional level show a lack of representation from Global South countries.[26] As a result, these regulations, mainly designed by and for the Global North, fail to account for the unique interests of Global Majority regions and countries, which continue to be viewed as zones of indiscriminate exploitation for the benefit of extractive industries, including AI.[27]

Second, in the current context, the absence of binding and robust regulatory frameworks endangers both human rights and the environment. The signatories of the Council of Europe's AI Convention are exclusively from the Global North, while Latin American observers such as Mexico, Argentina, Costa Rica, Peru, and Uruguay have yet to endorse it, highlighting a potential geopolitical disconnect in AI regulation on sustainability and human rights.[28]

This issue is further complicated by the fact that some of the Convention's signatory countries, such as the United States and the United Kingdom, have publicly refused to sign the States Declaration at the Paris AI Action Summit 2025[29] for inclusive and sustainable AI for people and the planet.[30] Their criticisms and reasoning for not signing are consistent with their advocacy work during the Council of Europe's AI Convention negotiations, reflecting a policy approach that prioritizes economic growth over environmental and social responsibility.

The path towards human rights-based and sustainable AI requires inclusive and representative international governance that considers environmental impacts across the entire AI value chain. While the two binding regulatory frameworks mark progress in recognizing AI's environmental footprint, their provisions fail to embed environmental protection as a core regulatory pillar. This highlights a key lost opportunity and a potential risk in case these two regulatory frameworks are widely adopted.

---

[23] Bertuzzi (2024b).

[24] Babická and Giacomin (2024).

[25] Global Partners Digital et al. (2023).

[26] UN High-Level Advisory Board on AI (2024), p. 8.

[27] See, for example, Urquieta and Dib (2024) and Barber (2024).

[28] See signatory states in Council of Europe (n.d.).

[29] See Elysée (2025).

[30] Milmo and Courea (2025).

3 Analysing AI Bills in Latin America: An Environmental Perspective

The fragmented nature of international AI governance, as discussed in the previous section, underscores the challenges of ensuring environmental protections within AI regulatory frameworks. While some policy initiatives, such as the UNESCO Recommendations, offer a more comprehensive approach to AI's environmental impact, legally binding frameworks like the EU AI Act and the Council of Europe's AI Convention fall short of establishing enforceable obligations. This regulatory gap has left countries in the Global South, particularly in Latin America, to navigate AI governance independently, often with limited influence in shaping global standards. In response, Latin American legislatures have begun developing their own AI regulations, attempting to balance innovation, human rights, and environmental concerns. This section examines the region's legislative landscape, analysing how emerging AI bills engage with environmental protection, whether they align with global governance trends, and to what extent they reflect local sociopolitical and ecological realities. The data collection process involved a systematic search of official legislative databases across the region, encompassing Argentina, Bolivia, Brazil, Chile, Colombia, Costa Rica, Ecuador, Mexico, and Panama. For countries with bicameral systems, searches were conducted in the databases of both chambers of parliament, such as the Chamber of Deputies and the Senate.

The analysis used the term "inteligencia artificial" (artificial intelligence) as the primary keyword. Non-legislative documents, such as resolutions and communications, were excluded to focus exclusively on legislative projects and approved laws. This approach yielded a total of 77 legislative projects (updated to January 24, 2025). The analysis primarily considered the original texts of the legislative projects, excluding amendments introduced during parliamentary discussions. Exceptions were made for a few projects that have been enacted into law, such as Peru's Law 32082, titled "Law for Interoperability and Use of Artificial Intelligence in Foreign Affairs Services", and Peru's Law 31814, titled "Law That Promotes the Use of Artificial Intelligence in Favor of the Economic and Social Development of the Country", the only two laws currently in force at the Latin American level.

The data reveals a significant increase in the number of legislative proposals since 2023, marking a distinct shift in legislative priorities. From 2019 to 2022, the number of bills proposed annually remained modest, with only 1–2 bills introduced each year. However, 2023 saw a dramatic surge, with 29 bills proposed. This upward trend continued in 2024, with an additional 44 bills introduced, underscoring sustained legislative interest. The boom in activity since 2023 likely reflects growing urgency among lawmakers to address emerging challenges, possibly spurred by advancements in technology, shifting sociopolitical demands, or increased awareness of sector-specific issues. These years mark a pivotal period of heightened focus, indicating a broader effort to establish comprehensive regulatory frameworks responsive to evolving needs.

The identified legislative projects were categorized by their regulatory focus. Some proposals addressed general frameworks for AI regulation, while others concentrated on specific sectors, including healthcare, elections, education, transportation, and security. This classification provided a nuanced understanding of legislative trends in the region. Special attention was given to whether the legislative texts included environmental considerations. Each project was reviewed to determine whether it explicitly addressed environmental impacts or sustainability concerns. Projects were then classified as either incorporating environmental considerations or lacking them. This categorization enabled the identification of patterns and the extent to which environmental issues are integrated into AI-related legislation in the region.

Given the broad scope of general AI regulations, it is expected that such frameworks should address overarching issues, including environmental sustainability. In contrast, sector-specific proposals, such as those dealing with AI in enhancing crime detection or applications in the health sector, tend to focus narrowly on operational or ethical considerations relevant to their field. As a result, environmental considerations are more likely to be embedded within general regulations rather than within specific use case contexts.

Out of the total 77 projects analysed, 44% (34 bills) addressed AI regulation in general terms, and among these, 61% (21 bills) incorporated environmental considerations. This highlights the limited but emerging recognition of the environmental dimensions of AI within the legislative frameworks of Latin America. The ways in which these bills address environmental protection will be further analysed.

It is noteworthy that three sector-specific projects also include provisions regarding environmental sustainability. These are:

1. **05182/2022-CR (Peru)**: A legislative proposal promoting the use of AI in the country's land transportation system. The proposal emphasizes that implementing AI in the transportation sector can improve efficiency, safety, and user satisfaction, thereby having a positive impact on both the economy and the environment. This project is currently under discussion.
2. **2405/24 (Argentina)**: A proposal to establish a permanent bicameral commission within the National Congress for the strategic and comprehensive regulation of AI. The commission is tasked with incorporating environmental perspectives into its strategies. This project is also under discussion.
3. **PL 3018/2024 (Brazil)**: Brazil stands out as the only country in the region currently discussing regulations specific to AI data centres. This proposal outlines detailed requirements for energy efficiency and environmental sustainability, specifying:

   - **Article 3, Clause IV**: AI data centres must implement practices of energy efficiency and environmental sustainability.
   - **Article 5, Clause I**: Requires the adoption of technologies and practices for energy efficiency, such as the use of renewable energy sources, efficient cooling systems, and hardware optimization.

- **Article 5, Clause II**: Mandates periodic energy audits to identify opportunities for energy consumption reduction and the implementation of recommended improvements.
- **Article 5, Clause III**: Obligates data centres to publish annual reports on energy consumption and measures adopted for efficiency, including achieved and future goals.
- **Article 5, Clause IV**: Calls for the development and adoption of environmental management plans, including greenhouse gas emission reduction targets.
- **Article 5, Clause V**: Promotes recycling and the proper disposal of electronic equipment.

As we have already highlighted, there are 24 bills that aim to regulate AI from a general perspective. We will now analyse the legislative techniques used to incorporate environmental issues in each of them. Having established the context of the legislative boom since 2023, we now turn to an analysis of how artificial intelligence (AI) regulations are addressing environmental concerns. This exploration focuses on four key approaches. First, regulations often emphasize the risks and obligations placed on AI developers and deployers, ensuring accountability for the environmental impact of their technologies. Second, many frameworks integrate principles, values, or foundational ideas that explicitly consider environmental sustainability, embedding these concerns within the broader ethical landscape of AI governance. Third, some regulations are specifically targeted at addressing climate change, showcasing a direct alignment between AI's transformative potential and urgent global environmental challenges. Lastly, there is a subset of laws that cite international standards dealing with environmental issues, leveraging existing frameworks to enhance the coherence and effectiveness of their regulatory efforts. These four approaches highlight the multifaceted ways in which AI governance is intersecting with and advancing environmental objectives.

3.1 *Risk-Based Approaches to Environmental Protection in AI Regulation*

The inclusion of environmental risks and obligations for developers and deployers in AI legislation demonstrates a concerted effort across jurisdictions to address potential ecological harm caused by emerging technologies. A common trend is the use of risk-based frameworks to identify and mitigate these risks, with a particular focus on high-risk systems that could significantly affect the environment.

In Peru, the bill 07033/2023-CR addresses environmental risks explicitly in Article 12, which outlines prohibitions and restrictions on AI systems. It states that AI applications with the potential to cause severe harm to the environment fall under restricted or prohibited use, signalling a clear prioritization of ecological safety alongside societal and individual protections. This provision aligns with a broader trend in the region of categorizing AI risks and linking them to tangible obligations for developers and deployers. Similarly, Argentina's FAMA bill (2285/24) incorporates environmental risks into the definition of grave incidents in its core framework. While its provisions integrate ecological harm as part of the broader risk landscape, Argentina's AVILA bill (1368/24) goes further by elevating environmental responsibility to a guiding principle for AI regulation. This dual approach reflects a commitment to embedding sustainability into both operational standards and the overarching ethical governance of AI systems.

Brazil's PL 2338/2023 reflects another facet of this trend, focusing on accountability and transparency. In Article 31, the bill mandates AI operators to notify competent authorities about incidents involving severe environmental damage. This emphasis on reporting aligns with a growing recognition that effective environmental governance requires robust monitoring mechanisms and a proactive approach to risk management. In Chile, the legislative proposals take a more detailed and structured approach to environmental risks. Bill 16821-19 includes multiple provisions addressing environmental concerns:

- Article 3 defines grave incidents to include environmental harm, ensuring these risks are formally recognized.
- Article 4 emphasizes the principle of "social and environmental well-being", mandating sustainable development and requiring long-term impact assessments for AI systems.
- Article 7 classifies high-risk AI systems that pose significant environmental threats and establishes compliance obligations, including human oversight to minimize risks. This multifaceted framework positions Chile's legislation as one of the most comprehensive in addressing environmental risks.

Colombia's bill 200-2023 incorporates environmental risks under Article 13, which excludes AI systems that could cause significant harm to the environment from development or deployment. This exclusion mirrors approaches seen in other jurisdictions, emphasizing the need for regulatory boundaries to prevent environmental degradation. Costa Rica's 23919 builds on this trend by integrating continuous risk evaluations of AI technologies. In Article 26, it requires responsible parties to present risk assessment certifications for high-risk projects, explicitly incorporating environmental dimensions. The alignment of these evaluations with sustainability goals and international norms further strengthens its commitment to ecological concerns.

In Ecuador, Article 7 of AN-2024-2928-450889 categorizes high-risk AI systems, explicitly mentioning environmental harm as a criterion. Article 18 mandates environmental impact assessments as part of broader human rights evaluations, ensuring that ecological considerations are systematically addressed before implementation. Finally, Panama's P0-A162 follows a similar trajectory, categorizing AI systems based on risk in Article 6. It establishes obligations for developers and deployers in Article 7, requiring them to avoid algorithms that could compromise environmental safety, among other societal values. This highlights a broader trend in Latin America of coupling risk classification with concrete obligations for AI stakeholders.

Across jurisdictions, the trend is clear: environmental protection is increasingly integrated into AI regulation through risk-based frameworks. These laws commonly establish categories of high-risk AI systems, require environmental impact assessments, and impose obligations for transparency and human oversight. This convergence underscores a shared understanding of the critical need to align AI development with sustainable practices, reflecting a regional commitment to safeguarding the environment in the face of rapid technological advancement.

3.2 *Environmental Sustainability as a Core Principle in AI Governance*

Across Latin America, AI regulation increasingly emphasizes environmental protection as a core value and foundational principle, reflecting a regional commitment to aligning technological progress with ecological sustainability. Several countries have embedded environmental considerations into their legal frameworks, ensuring these are integral to the development, deployment, and governance of AI systems.

Brazil's PL 2338/2023 establishes environmental protection and sustainable development as key foundations for AI governance, emphasizing in Article 2 that AI systems must be implemented in ways that promote sustainability. Similarly, Chile's 16821-19 links environmental and social well-being, highlighting in its message the potential of AI to optimize resource use, combat climate change, and enhance sustainable operations. This bill mandates that AI systems not only avoid environmental harm but also actively contribute to long-term ecological benefits, underscoring the need for sustainable development as a guiding principle.

Colombian legislation takes a values-driven approach, with Bill 200-2023 incorporating "environmental prosperity and ecosystem protection" as central tenets, inspired by UNESCO's recommendations. It requires developers to minimize carbon footprints, address climate change risks, and prevent unsustainable exploitation of resources. Building on this, Bill 154-2024 includes a proportionality principle, requiring evidence-based justification for AI projects to ensure they benefit humanity and the environment, integrating ecological considerations into decision-making processes.

Costa Rica's 23919 reinforces the ethical responsibility of AI developers, mandating in Article 5 that they actively protect ecosystems and promote sustainability throughout the AI lifecycle. The law aligns national AI regulation with international standards, including the Sustainable Development Goals (SDGs), ensuring global coherence. Ecuador's AN-2024-2928-450889 similarly incorporates environmental sustainability into its core principles, linking AI governance to the SDGs and emphasizing the use of clean technologies. Both countries highlight the importance of designing AI systems that reduce environmental harm and foster ecological preservation.

Mexico and Panama frame sustainability as both a potential benefit and a risk. Mexico's 6464-II and 6495-II stress the obligation to protect ecosystems for present and future generations, embedding these concerns into public policy to ensure that AI does not harm biodiversity or environmental stability. Meanwhile, Panama's P0-A162 and PL-14 recognize AI's potential to enhance sustainability across various sectors, from healthcare to resource management, while cautioning against the misuse of technology that could compromise ecological goals.

Across these jurisdictions, a consistent trend emerges: environmental protection is no longer an auxiliary concern but a central pillar of AI regulation. By embedding sustainability as a value and principle, these frameworks ensure that ecological considerations guide AI development, fostering technologies that not only advance innovation but also contribute to a sustainable and equitable future.

3.3 International Influence: The Role of UNESCO in Shaping AI Regulations in Latin America

International frameworks, particularly UNESCO's 2021 Recommendation on the Ethics of Artificial Intelligence, have significantly influenced the development of AI regulations in Latin America. These international standards provide ethical and operational benchmarks that guide national governments in addressing the multifaceted implications of AI, including its impact on society, individuals, and the environment.

In Colombia, UNESCO's recommendations serve as a cornerstone for legislative efforts. Bill 200-2023 explicitly cites the 2021 UNESCO agreement as a foundational document, emphasizing the need for strict personal data protection, prohibiting AI use for social classification or mass surveillance, and mandating supervision of AI's societal and environmental impacts. Similarly, Bill 154-2024 highlights the importance of these international ethical principles, reflecting Colombia's commitment to aligning its AI governance with global standards. Both bills stress the need for continuous evaluation and oversight of AI systems to ensure their alignment with human rights and sustainability.

Mexico's legislative initiatives also underscore UNESCO's influence. Bills 6464-II and 6495-II reference the 41st UNESCO General Conference, which approved the 2021 recommendations. These laws acknowledge AI's profound and dynamic impacts on human thought, decision-making, and social interactions, emphasizing the need to adopt regulatory frameworks that balance the benefits and risks of AI. By incorporating UNESCO's ethical principles, these bills seek to safeguard human dignity, promote fairness, and mitigate the environmental impacts of AI.

In Costa Rica, international standards extend beyond UNESCO to include European Union frameworks. Bill 24484 references the EU's 2024 AI Act, integrating a risk-based categorization of AI systems and prohibiting certain high-risk activities, such as using AI for environmental crimes or profiling criminal suspects.

While the EU's regulatory approach is central, UNESCO's ethical principles remain implicit in the bill's emphasis on sustainability and social responsibility, aligning with global norms.

UNESCO's influence is also evident in the broader framing of AI governance in Latin America. The recommendations advocate for a holistic approach, emphasizing AI's dual potential to positively or negatively affect ecosystems, societies, and human lives. Countries like Mexico, Colombia, and Costa Rica reflect this perspective, embedding mechanisms for ethical evaluation and oversight while encouraging the adoption of sustainable and human-centric AI practices.

The alignment with UNESCO's recommendations illustrates a regional trend towards integrating international human rights principles into local legislation. These frameworks not only provide a shared foundation for addressing AI's global challenges but also enable countries to tailor their regulations to national contexts, ensuring that AI serves as a tool for equitable and sustainable development. By adopting and adapting these international guidelines, Latin American nations are establishing themselves as proactive players in the global discourse on AI ethics and governance.

3.4 The Missing BHR Dimension in Latin American AI Bills

Although the analysis of the 77 AI bills in Latin America has focused primarily on environmental considerations, these issues intersect closely with business and human rights (BHR). AI-related environmental impacts (such as water extraction by data centres, increased energy demand, and upstream mineral requirements) directly affect rights recognized in international law, including the rights to health, water, land, and a clean and sustainable environment. Under the UNGPs, companies are expected to identify, prevent, mitigate, and remedy adverse human rights impacts across their entire value chains. In this sense, environmental governance of AI is inseparable from corporate human rights responsibilities.

Across the 77 bills analysed, none explicitly situate their regulatory approach within the UNGPs or related BHR frameworks. However, various legislative initiatives contain implicit components of responsible business conduct. Brazil provides the clearest example: the Brazilian AI Bill (PL 2338/2023, and subsequent unified drafts) expressly references human rights due diligence and allocates responsibilities to developers, suppliers, and deployers. Panama's Draft Law No. 014 similarly incorporates elements functionally equivalent to due diligence by establishing mandatory obligations across public and private sectors, including systematic risk assessment and ongoing oversight. Other countries integrate partial mechanisms:

- Chile's Boletín 15869-19 includes registration obligations and authorization requirements for high-risk systems, together with the establishment of a National Commission on Artificial Intelligence responsible for oversight and risk evaluation.

- Colombia's Bill 059/2023 introduces algorithmic impact assessments and procedural duties applicable to both public and private actors.
- Mexico's Gaceta Parlamentaria 6246-III foresees an ethics oversight council and requires entities to provide detailed information on the use of AI systems.
- Costa Rica's Ley 23771 and Peru's Ley 31.814 set out transparency obligations and administrative sanctions, which, although limited, represent building blocks of broader accountability structures.

Regarding the range of human rights addressed, there is significant variation. Brazil, Colombia, Mexico, and Panama adopt broader conceptualizations that include justice, equality, democratic participation, or labour rights. By contrast, Argentina, Chile, Costa Rica, Peru, and Uruguay tend to focus on narrower clusters, usually non-discrimination, privacy, and individual rights, without recognizing the wider spectrum of rights potentially affected by AI development, including environmental, collective, and territorial rights.

Three significant structural gaps emerge when the bills are examined against the pillars of the UNGPs. First, human rights due diligence is largely absent. Beyond Brazil and Panama, no jurisdiction establishes mandatory obligations requiring companies to evaluate and mitigate human rights and environmental risks linked to AI systems or related infrastructures. Many regulatory texts, such as Chile's Boletines 15935-07, 16021-07, and 16112-07, Colombia's digital transformation framework (Decree 1078/2015), or Argentina's Disposición 2/2023, rely on general ethical principles rather than enforceable due diligence duties.

Second, most bills fail to regulate the entire AI value chain, leaving upstream and downstream impacts unaddressed. Brazil is again the exception: the AI Bill acknowledges responsibilities across development, supply, deployment, and post-deployment phases. Panama similarly adopts a broad approach. By contrast, Argentina, Chile, Colombia, Costa Rica, Mexico, Peru, and Uruguay primarily regulate deployment or specific high-risk uses, overlooking upstream harms associated with data acquisition, extractive activities, energy usage, and material inputs.

Third, mechanisms for remedy and redress remain limited. Brazil provides the most explicit avenues, recognizing access to administrative and judicial bodies for individuals whose rights have been affected. In most other cases—such as Argentina's Bill 25.467, Chile's *Boletín* 15869-19, Costa Rica's Ley 23771, Mexico's 6246-III, Panama's Draft Law No. 014, or Peru's Ley 31.814—remedy mechanisms are either undeveloped, limited to sanctions, or absent altogether.

Alongside these gaps, a regional trend towards transparency and procedural obligations can be observed. Argentina's national AI policy mandates registration of AI systems; Brazil and Chile propose national oversight bodies; Mexico establishes ethical oversight functions; and Colombia and Costa Rica incorporate disclosure and reporting duties. These measures clarify expectations for algorithmic governance, but in the absence of explicit due diligence, enforcement mechanisms, and access to remedy, they fall short of constituting a comprehensive BHR framework.

Taken together, these findings show that while Latin American AI regulation incorporates early elements of responsible business conduct—such as transparency duties, oversight bodies, and limited risk management obligations—it remains significantly misaligned with established BHR standards. The absence of mandatory due diligence, partial treatment of the AI value chain, and insufficient remedy mechanisms are particularly important gaps, especially in a region where AI development intersects with long-standing socio-environmental inequalities. Stronger integration of BHR principles would enhance the region's capacity to govern AI systems in a manner consistent with international human rights obligations and with the environmental and social realities that characterize Latin America.

4 Conclusions

This chapter has explored the environmental implications of artificial intelligence (AI) governance, highlighting the fragmented nature of international regulatory efforts and the emerging Latin American response. While AI is often presented as a tool for sustainability, its life cycle—from the extraction of critical minerals to the energy-intensive training of models and the operation of data centres—poses significant environmental challenges. These challenges, exacerbated by weak or inconsistent regulatory measures, are particularly pressing for Latin American countries, which serve as resource providers for AI technologies but remain largely excluded from global governance discussions.

The first section of this chapter demonstrated that international AI regulations, while expanding rapidly, remain largely focused on ethical, human rights, and economic considerations, with limited attention given to environmental impacts. The analysis of key international initiatives, including the OECD AI Principles, UN Global Digital Compact, the UNESCO Recommendations on AI Ethics, the EU AI Act, and the Council of Europe's AI Convention, revealed that while some policy frameworks acknowledge the environmental risks of AI, few establish concrete, enforceable obligations to mitigate them. The lack of binding international agreements addressing AI's ecological footprint leaves significant gaps, allowing technology companies to engage in regulatory arbitrage, and avoid accountability for environmental harm. This regulatory fragmentation results in an uneven playing field, where AI's negative externalities disproportionately affect the Global South, particularly Latin America.

The second section examined the regional legislative response in Latin America, identifying 77 AI-related legislative proposals currently under discussion across multiple jurisdictions. While Latin American countries have largely been absent from global AI governance discussions, they have made strides in developing national AI regulatory frameworks. Our analysis found that 44% of these initiatives address AI governance in general terms, and among them, 61% incorporate environmental considerations. However, the integration of environmental concerns remains inconsistent and varies in depth across jurisdictions. Some countries, such as Chile and Colombia, have incorporated AI-related environmental risks into their legislative frameworks, whereas others have approached environmental sustainability as a broad guiding principle rather than a concrete regulatory requirement. Brazil's legislative proposal on AI data centres stands out as one of the few initiatives to explicitly regulate energy efficiency and sustainability in AI infrastructure.

A key finding of this chapter is the influence of international policy frameworks, particularly the UNESCO Recommendations on AI Ethics, on Latin American legislative efforts. Several AI bills explicitly reference these recommendations, incorporating principles of sustainability, transparency, and human rights protection. However, the extent to which these international norms translate into enforceable national regulations remains unclear. Latin American AI legislation is still in a formative stage, and while environmental considerations are increasingly being recognized, they have yet to be institutionalized into comprehensive governance mechanisms.

This chapter also raises important questions regarding the role of Latin America in shaping global AI governance. While the region has historically been excluded from major AI regulatory negotiations, its growing body of national AI laws presents an opportunity to assert a distinctive perspective on AI governance—one that prioritizes environmental sustainability and social justice. If Latin American states coordinate their regulatory efforts and push for stronger environmental protections at international AI forums, they could influence global governance structures and contribute to the development of a more inclusive regulatory framework. The recent AI Summit in France, which emphasized environmental considerations in AI governance, represents a potential turning point in this regard, but its long-term impact remains to be seen.

Despite the contributions of this chapter, certain limitations must be acknowledged. First, while our analysis identified 77 AI-related legislative proposals in Latin America, the evolving nature of AI regulation means that new proposals may emerge, and existing ones may undergo significant revisions. Future research should continue tracking these developments to assess how Latin American AI laws evolve over time. Second, while this chapter has primarily focused on legislative responses, it does not extensively analyse the enforcement mechanisms required to ensure compliance with environmental regulations. Many AI laws remain at the proposal stage, and their effectiveness will depend on the capacity of regulatory agencies to oversee and implement them.

Another key limitation is the lack of empirical data on the actual environmental impact of AI systems deployed in Latin America. While global estimates suggest that AI models contribute significantly to energy consumption and carbon emissions, there is little region-specific data on how these environmental costs manifest in Latin American contexts. Future research should seek to quantify the regional footprint of AI, examining factors such as energy usage, water consumption, and mining-related environmental degradation. Additionally, more work is needed to assess the extent to which AI could contribute positively to environmental sustainability in Latin America, particularly through applications in climate change mitigation, conservation, and resource management.

A final area for future exploration concerns the potential for regional cooperation on AI governance. While national AI regulations are developing at different paces and with varying degrees of comprchensiveness, there is currently no unified Latin American approach to AI governance. Regional initiatives, such as those led by the Organization of American States (OAS) or the Economic Commission for Latin America and the Caribbean (ECLAC), could play a crucial role in harmonizing AI regulations and promoting environmental standards at a regional level. Strengthening regional cooperation could also increase Latin America's leverage in global AI governance discussions, ensuring that its unique environmental concerns are adequately represented.

In conclusion, this chapter underscores the urgent need for stronger AI regulations that integrate environmental protection at both international and national levels. The fragmented nature of global AI governance has left critical gaps, enabling corporations to exploit regulatory weaknesses and externalize environmental costs onto vulnerable regions like Latin America. While some progress has been made through national legislative efforts, a more coordinated and binding approach is necessary to ensure that AI development aligns with sustainability goals, the UNGPs, and states' human rights obligations. Latin American countries have the opportunity to position themselves as leaders in advocating for AI governance frameworks that prioritize ecological responsibility and social equity. Whether they succeed in doing so will depend on their ability to collaborate, influence international governance structures, and implement robust regulatory mechanisms that move beyond mere principles towards concrete, enforceable obligations.

Annex: List of Bills Discussed in Latin American Parliaments

Bill Number	Country	Origin	Date	Environmental approach	General/ specific
1747/23	Argentina	Senate	14/08/2023	No	General
2469/23	Argentina	Senate	14/12/2023	No	Specific
959/24	Argentina	Senate	31/05/2024	No	Specific
992/24	Argentina	Senate	05/06/2024	No	Specific
1368/24	Argentina	Senate	08/08/2024	Yes	General
1370/24	Argentina	Senate	08/08/2024	No	Specific
2205/24	Argentina	Senate	07/11/2024	No	Specific
2285/24	Argentina	Senate	19/11/2024	Yes	General
6976-D-2024	Argentina	Chamber of Deputies	19/11/2024	No	Specific
7009-D-2024	Argentina	Chamber of Deputies	20/11/2024	No	Specific
7045-D-2024	Argentina	Chamber of Deputies	21/11/2024	No	Specific
7225-D-2024	Argentina	Chamber of Deputies	02/12/2024	No	Specific

Bill Number	Country	Origin	Date	Environmental approach	General/ specific
2405/24	Argentina	Senate	16/12/2024	Yes	Specific
PL 5051/2019	Brazil	Senate	16/09/2019	No	General
PL 5691/2019	Brazil	Senate	25/10/2019	No	General
PL 21/2020	Brazil	Chamber of Deputies	04/02/2020	No	General
PL 872/2021	Brazil	Senate	12/03/2021	No	General
PL 5721/2023	Brazil	Senate	27/01/2023	No	Specific
PL 2338/2023	Brazil	Senate	03/05/2023	Yes	General
PL 3592/2023	Brazil	Senate	19/07/2023	No	Specific
PL 146/2024	Brazil	Senate	06/02/2024	No	Specific
PL 210/2024	Brazil	Senate	07/02/2024	No	General
PL 145/2024	Brazil	Senate	07/02/2024	No	Specific
PL 370/2024	Brazil	Chamber of Deputies	21/02/2024	No	Specific
PL 1833/2024	Brazil	Senate	15/05/2024	No	Specific
PL 3018/2024	Brazil	Senate	01/08/2024	Yes	Specific
PL 4532/2024	Brazil	Senate	26/11/2024	No	General
15869-19	Chile	Chamber of Deputies	24/04/2023	Yes	General
15935-07	Chile	Chamber of Deputies	15/05/2023	No	Specific
16021-07	Chile	Senate	13/06/2023	No	Specific
16112-07	Chile	Chamber of Deputies	17/07/2023	No	Specific
16387-19	Chile	Chamber of Deputies	23/10/2023	No	Specific
16821-19	Chile	Chamber of Deputies	07/05/2024	Yes	General
17112-19	Chile	Chamber of Deputies	03/09/2024	No	General
17307-07	Chile	Senate	17/12/2024	No	Specific
21-2020	Colombia	Chamber of Deputies	04/08/2020	Yes	General
354-2021	Colombia	Chamber of Deputies	11/11/2021	Yes	General
253-2022	Colombia	Senate	05/06/2023	Yes	General
59-2023	Colombia	Senate	01/08/2023	Yes	General
91-2023	Colombia	Senate	09/08/2023	No	General
130-2023	Colombia	Senate	06/09/2023	No	Specific
200-2023	Colombia	Chamber of Deputies	08/11/2023	Yes	General
225-2024	Colombia	Senate	21/02/2024	No	Specific
154-2024	Colombia	Chamber of Deputies	08/10/2024	Yes	General
23771	Costa Rica	Legislative Assembly	30/05/2023	No	General

Bill Number	Country	Origin	Date	Environmental approach	General/ specific
23919	Costa Rica	Legislative Assembly	06/09/2023	Yes	General
24484	Costa Rica	Legislative Assembly	06/08/2024	Yes	General
AN-2024-2928-450889	Ecuador	National Assembly	20/06/2024	Yes	General
AN-2024-2990-454516	Ecuador	National Assembly	30/07/2024	No	General
LXV/2SPR-5/135000	Mexico	Senate	24/05/2023		General
LXV/3PPO-33/138776	Mexico	Senate	28/11/2023		Specific
6420-II	Mexico	Chamber of Deputies	05/12/2023	No	Specific
6420-II	Mexico	Chamber of Deputies	05/12/2023	No	Specific
6464-II	Mexico	Chamber of Deputies	14/02/2024	Yes	General
6468-II-3	Mexico	Chamber of Deputies	20/02/2024	No	Specific
6483-II-5	Mexico	Chamber of Deputies	12/03/2024	No	Specific
6495-II	Mexico	Chamber of Deputies	02/04/2024	Yes	General
LXVI/1PPO-83/145168	Mexico	Senate	13/12/2024		General
PL-14	Panama	National Assembly	06/07/2023	Yes	General
P0-A162	Panama	National Assembly	28/08/2024	Yes	General
07444/2023-CR	Peru	Congress	02/04/2024	No	Specific
05814/2023-CR	Peru	Congress	04/09/2023	No	Specific
06573/2023-CR	Peru	Congress	04/12/2023	No	Specific
LEY N° 31814	Peru	Congress	08/08/2022	No	General
07033/2023-CR	Peru	Congress	13/02/2024	Yes	General
08223/2023-CR	Peru	Congress	14/06/2024	No	General
Ley 32082	Peru	Congress	18/04/2024	No	Specific
05959/2023-CR	Peru	Congress	19/09/2023	No	Specific
08969/2024-CR	Peru	Congress	19/09/2024	No	Specific
07072/2023-CR	Peru	Congress	20/02/2024	No	Specific
07651/2023-CR	Peru	Congress	22/04/2024	No	Specific
07687/2023-CR	Peru	Congress	25/04/2024	No	Specific
05183/2022-CR	Peru	Congress	25/05/2023	No	Specific
05182/2022-CR	Peru	Congress	25/05/2023	Yes	Specific
05763/2023-CR	Peru	Congress	25/08/2023	No	Specific
06524/2023-CR	Peru	Congress	27/11/2023	No	Specific
06927/2023-CR	Peru	Congress	31/01/2024	No	Specific

References

Babická K, Giacomin C (2024) Understanding the scope of the council of Europe framework convention on AI. https://opiniojuris.org/2024/11/05/understanding-the-scope-of-the-council-of-europe-framework-convention-on-ai/. Accessed 11 Apr 2026

Barber H (2024) Battle lines redrawn as Argentina's lithium mines ramp up to meet electric car demand. https://www.theguardian.com/global-development/article/2024/jun/25/battle-lines-redrawn-as-argentinas-lithium-mines-ramp-up-to-meet-electric-car-demand. Accessed 11 Apr 2026

Bertuzzi L (2023) EU's AI ambitions at risk as US pushes to water down international treaty. https://www.euractiv.com/section/artificial-intelligence/news/eus-ai-ambitions-at-risk-as-us-push-to-water-down-international-treaty/. Accessed 11 Apr 2026

Bertuzzi L (2024a) EU prepares to push back on private sector carve-out from international AI treaty. https://www.euractiv.com/section/artificial-intelligence/news/eu-prepares-to-push-back-on-private-sector-carve-out-from-international-ai-treaty/. Accessed 11 Apr 2026

Bertuzzi L (2024b) EU Commission's last-minute attempt to keep private companies in world's first AI treaty. https://www.euractiv.com/section/artificial-intelligence/news/eu-commissions-last-minute-attempt-to-keep-private-companies-in-worlds-first-ai-treaty. Accessed 11 Apr 2026

Bertuzzi L (2024c) Tug-of-war continues on international AI treaty as text gets softened further. https://www.euractiv.com/section/tech/news/tug-of-war-continues-on-international-ai-treaty-as-text-gets-softened-further/. Accessed 11 Apr 2026

Council of Europe (2024) Explanatory Report to the Council of Europe Framework Convention on Artificial Intelligence and Human Rights, Democracy and the Rule of Law. https://rm.coe.int/1680afae67. Accessed 11 Apr 2026

Council of Europe (n.d.) The Framework Convention on Artificial Intelligence. https://www.coe.int/en/web/artificial-intelligence/the-framework-convention-on-artificial-intelligence. Accessed 11 Apr 2026

Cowen T (2023) Existential risk, AI, and the inevitable turn in human history. https://www.proquest.com/docview/2791065195/citation/4B63CAD31D9F4E84PQ/1. Accessed 11 Apr 2026

Elysée (2025) Statement on inclusive and sustainable artificial intelligence for people and the planet. https://www.elysee.fr/en/emmanuel-macron/2025/02/11/statement-on-inclusive-and-sustainable-artificial-intelligence-for-people-and-the-planet. Accessed 11 Apr 2026

Global Partners Digital et al (2023) The Council of Europe's AI treaty: perspectives from the global majority. https://www.gp-digital.org/the-council-of-europes-ai-treaty-perspectives-from-the-global-majority/. Accessed 11 Apr 2026

Green Screen Coalition et al (2025) Within bounds: limiting AI's environmental impact. https://greenscreen.network/en/blog/within-bounds-limiting-ai-environmental-impact/. Accessed 11 Apr 2026

Gudynas E (2023) El día cero. https://www.sinpermiso.info/textos/el-dia-cero. Accessed 11 Apr 2026

Laville S (2025) Call to make tech firms report data centre energy use as AI booms. https://www.theguardian.com/technology/2025/feb/07/call-to-make-tech-firms-report-data-centre-energy-use-as-ai-booms. Accessed 11 Apr 2026

Ligozat A-L, Lefevre J, Bugeau A, Combaz J (2022) Unraveling the hidden environmental impacts of AI solutions for environment life cycle assessment of AI solutions. Sustainability 14(9):5172. https://doi.org/10.3390/su14095172. Accessed 11 Apr 2026

Milmo D, Courea E (2025) US and UK resist Paris AI summit declaration. https://www.theguardian.com/technology/2025/feb/11/us-uk-paris-ai-summit-artificial-intelligence-declaration. Accessed 11 Apr 2026

Nuñez J (2022) Santiago to ration water as historic drought bites. https://www.theguardian.com/environment/2022/apr/11/santiago-chile-ration-water-drought. Accessed 11 Apr 2026

OECD (2024) OECD AI principles. https://legalinstruments.oecd.org/en/instruments/OECD-LEGAL-0449. Accessed 11 Apr 2026

Roff H (2019) The frame problem: the AI "arms race" isn't one. Bull At Sci 75(3):95–98. https://doi.org/10.1080/00963402.2019.1604836. Accessed 11 Apr 2026

Rolnick D et al (2019) Tackling climate change with machine learning. arXiv. https://doi.org/10.48550/arXiv.1906.05433. Accessed 11 Apr 2026

Saul J, Bass D (2023) Artificial Intelligence is booming—so is its carbon footprint. https://www.bloomberg.com/news/articles/2023-03-09/how-much-energy-do-ai-and-chatgpt-use-no-one-knows-for-sure. Accessed 11 Apr 2026

Schwartzentruber J (2023) Regulate AI before it's too late. https://nationalpost.com/opinion/jeff-schwartzentruber-artificial-intelligence-must-be-regulated-before-its-too-late. Accessed 11 Apr 2026

Spencer G (2018) AI for earth: helping save the planet with data science. https://news.microsoft.com/apac/features/ai-for-earth-helping-save-the-planet-with-data-science/. Accessed 11 Apr 2026

Strubell E, Ganesh A, McCallum A (2019) Energy and policy considerations for deep learning in NLP. arXiv. https://doi.org/10.48550/arXiv.1906.02243. Accessed 11 Apr 2026

Symonides J (1992) The human right to a clean, balanced and protected environment. Int J Leg Inf 20(1):24–40. https://doi.org/10.1017/S0731126500010842. Accessed 11 Apr 2026

UN General Assembly. (2022) The human right to a clean, healthy and sustainable environment, Resolution 76/300. https://digitallibrary.un.org/record/3983329?ln=en&v=pdf. Accessed 11 Apr 2026

UN General Assembly (2024) The Pact for the Future: resolution adopted by the General Assembly. https://digitallibrary.un.org/record/4061879?ln=en&v=pdf. Accessed 11 Apr 2026

UN High-Level Advisory Board on AI (2024). Governing AI for humanity: final report. https://digitallibrary.un.org/record/4062495?v=pdf. Accessed 11 Apr 2026

UN Human Rights Council (2021) The human right to a clean, healthy, and sustainable environment, Resolution 48/13. https://digitallibrary.un.org/record/3945636?ln=en&v=pdf. Accessed 11 Apr 2026

Urquieta C, Dib D (2024) The data center boom is wreaking havoc on local environments. https://restofworld.org/2024/data-centers-environmental-issues. Accessed 11 Apr 2026

Varvastian S (2019) The human right to a clean and healthy environment in climate change litigation. Max Planck Institute for Comparative Public Law & International Law Research Paper Series. https://doi.org/10.2139/ssrn.3369481. Accessed 11 Apr 2026

Vinuesa R, Azizpour H, Leite I et al (2020) The role of artificial intelligence in achieving the sustainable development goals. Nat Commun 11:233. https://doi.org/10.1038/s41467-019-14108-y. Accessed 11 Apr 2026

Weston BH, Bollier D (2013) Toward a recalibrated human right to a clean and healthy environment: making the conceptual transition. J Hum Rights Environ 4(2):116–142. https://doi.org/10.4337/jhre.2013.02.01. Accessed 11 Apr 2026

Sebastian Smart is a senior research fellow in Access to Justice, Law and Technology at Anglia Ruskin University, Cambridge. His work focuses on business and human rights, transitional justice, and the impact of digital technologies on human rights. He holds a Ph.D. in Human Rights and Latin American Studies from University College London and has worked with academic institutions and non-governmental organizations across multiple regions. He is also actively engaged in global human rights policy and advocacy.

Danny Rayman Labrin is a lawyer and international consultant specializing in corporate accountability, technology, and human rights. He has worked with the Business and Human Rights Resource Centre and several non-governmental organizations across Chile, Germany, and Switzerland. He leads the "Testigo en Línea" project, documenting human rights violations in Chile. He holds LL.M. degrees in New Technologies and in International Human Rights Law and Humanitarian Law and regularly teaches and publishes in the areas of business and human rights and digital rights.

Interweaving Economic Progress, Environmental Justice, and Social Equity: Case Studies from the Global South

Shuma Talukdar

Abstract This concluding chapter synthesises insights from case studies across Bangladesh, Kenya, Mexico, Brazil, Morocco, Indonesia, Thailand, and Latin America, examining the complex interplay of economic development, environmental sustainability, and social equity within Business and Human Rights (BHR) frameworks in Southern countries. The chapter situates these case studies within the broader context of systemic challenges such as financial constraints, lack of awareness, and infrastructure deficits, effective implementation of BHR norms, and environmental, social, and governance (ESG) mandates. It proposes actionable strategies, including standardised "co-developed" regulations, investment in rights-based infrastructure, financial incentives, and collaboration, to overcome these barriers.

By analysing diverse sectors, legal systems, and community struggles across Asia, Africa, and Latin America, the volume shows that corporate accountability is not merely a matter of implementing Northern standards but a dynamic, negotiated, and contextually shaped process. The conclusion, therefore, draws together the threads running across the chapters and outlines how this volume contributes to a more plural, equitable, and empirically grounded understanding of BHR.

1 Introduction

The case studies presented in this volume, from Bangladesh to Latin America, collectively illuminate the intricate balance required between economic development, environmental sustainability, and social equity within frameworks of BHR and corporate accountability. Each case reveals unique challenges and opportunities, yet they share common threads that underscore the necessity for a unified approach to sustainable development in the Global South. This concluding chapter synthesises

---

S. Talukdar (✉)
LexEd Research, Kolkata, Mahindra University,
Hyderabad, Telangana, India

S. Talukdar (ed.), *Law, Accountability, and Corporate Conduct*, New Approaches to Business, Human Rights and the Environment 1,
https://doi.org/10.1007/978-3-032-28714-4_10

these insights, situating them within the broader context of systemic legal and governance barriers faced by developing nations and proposing strategies to overcome them. By examining cultural sensitivity, legal enforcement, and global regulatory trends, this chapter aims to provide a comprehensive roadmap for advancing corporate accountability practices that prioritise equity and environmental integrity.

This volume, through its diverse case studies from Asia, Africa, and Latin America, collectively demonstrates that implementing BHR norms is not a uniform or technocratic process but a deeply contextual, contested, and evolving practice. The chapters reveal how local socio-economic realities, legal infrastructures, cultural values, and political economies shape the outcomes of corporate accountability in distinct ways. Rather than offering prescriptive models, the volume foregrounds grounded insights and critical tensions between economic growth and environmental limits, between international BHR standards and domestic legal capacities, and between aspirational policy frameworks and lived realities. In doing so, it advances a justice-oriented understanding of corporate sustainability that centres inclusion, participation, and accountability across jurisdictions.

This volume's findings can be situated within key theories of BHR. The UN Guiding Principles on Business and Human Rights (UNGPs), with their tripartite pillars, firstly impose a duty on states to protect against abuses committed by a third party, including companies, either within or outside the territory, against individuals or communities. Secondly, the guidelines made it obligatory for companies to respect the human rights (both environmental and social), and thirdly, they guarantee access to remedies for the right holders, who are victims of social or ecological abuse.[1] These guidelines provide a conceptual baseline for evaluating each chapter in the volume. However, the studies also reveal that the implementation of the principles is shaped by legal pluralism, where customary norms, informal governance, and sociocultural practices operate alongside formal law. This confirms that BHR norms do not simply "travel" to local contexts; they undergo processes of localisation, contestation, and adaptation.

2 Broader Context of Challenges in Developing Countries

Developing countries face significant barriers to effective BHR norms, including financial constraints, lack of awareness and expertise, conflicting economic priorities, limited regulatory capacity, weak rule of law, low bargaining power, and high enforcement costs.[2] High costs associated with infrastructure upgrades and technology adoption often limit access to green financing, as underdeveloped financial markets struggle to support responsible business initiatives.[3] Small and medium-sized

[1] United Nations (2011).

[2] Braithwaite (2006); Graham and Woods (2006); Giuliani (2016).

[3] Faracik (2017).

enterprises (SMEs) frequently perceive human rights due diligence as a compliance burden rather than a strategic investment, compounded by a shortage of qualified professionals in the field.[4] Governments often prioritise economic growth, poverty alleviation, and job creation, which can lead to reliance on high-pollution industries like coal and mining, further complicating efforts to align business conduct with human rights obligations.[5] Inadequate waste management systems, limited adoption of renewable energy, and weak environmental data governance exacerbate systemic challenges, while technical and institutional capacity for due diligence reporting remains underdeveloped.[6] These systemic issues provide a critical backdrop for understanding the studies presented in this volume. For example, Bangladesh's struggle with tannery relocation reflects both financial and infrastructural constraints,[7] while Kenya's flower farms highlight gaps in awareness and expertise.[8] Recognising these common barriers is essential for crafting effective regulations and strategies that can be applied across diverse contexts in the Global South.

From a BHR perspective, these challenges underscore critiques of human rights due diligence (HRDD) in the Global South. Scholars argue that due diligence requirements often assume resources, institutional capacity, and stable regulatory environments that many developing countries lack.[9] This gap between global expectations and local capacities exacerbates North-South power asymmetries.

3 Cross-Cutting Themes Across the Global South

The studies presented in this volume illustrate how legal, regulatory, and governance mechanisms shape corporate behaviour and community outcomes across diverse jurisdictions. From the judicial limitations observed in Bangladesh's tannery relocation[10] to the affirmation of participatory environmental justice in Mexico's mining litigation,[11] the volume underscores the centrality of enforceable legal frameworks and inclusive decision-making. Kenya's example highlights how labour rights and social inclusion can be embedded in business models aligned with international due diligence expectations, such as those under the EU CSDDD.[12] Brazil's judicial enforcement of constitutional environmental obligations demonstrates the potential of public interest litigation in holding both state and corporate actors accountable.[13]

[4] Partiti (2023).

[5] World Bank Group (2024).

[6] Haque (2021).

[7] Salekin and Kamal (2026).

[8] Sharon (2026).

[9] Wilhelm (2024).

[10] Salekin and Kamal (2026).

[11] Ramos Gómez and Ramos Gómez (2026).

[12] Sharon (2026).

[13] Bauer and Martins da Rosa (2026).

Morocco's tourism development case reveals the disjuncture between sustainability rhetoric and the absence of legal safeguards for community participation.[14] In Indonesia, legal fragmentation between state regulatory tools and voluntary certification schemes points to the need for harmonised human rights and environmental due diligence frameworks.[15] Thailand's reforms in fisheries governance offer a model of regional cooperation and institutional restructuring in response to international trade pressures.[16] In Latin America, the environmental implications of emerging technologies like AI underscore the urgency of developing legal frameworks that integrate sustainability and human rights principles into digital governance.[17] Based on these studies, the following cross-cutting themes across the Global South emerged.

3.1 Legal Pluralism as a Foundation for Accountability

Across the chapters, a consistent pattern emerges: accountability does not operate within a single legal system. Instead, domestic law, customary norms, judicial activism, community protocols, transnational corporate codes, and international human rights frameworks coexist and interact. Whether in the context of Indigenous environmental rights in Mexico, judicial interventions in Brazil, or hybrid certification systems in Kenya, plural legal orders shape how BHR norms are interpreted and applied. Legal pluralism as a non-state justice system[18] is not merely a descriptive reality but a source of innovative accountability pathways that global frameworks often fail to recognise.[19] In the absence of the rule of law, an experience common across much of the Global South, legal pluralism can meet the community's needs,[20] facilitate rights claiming, and effectively resolve disputes,[21] ultimately making states and corporations more accountable and injustice more remediable.

3.2 Community Agency as an Accountability Mechanism

Communities across the Global South are not passive victims of corporate harm; they are central actors shaping accountability outcomes when most states fail in their enforcement role.[22] The chapters illustrate how fishing communities in

[14] Bazzim and Edman (2026).

[15] Cetera and Hawari (2026).

[16] Kaewtong et al. (2026).

[17] Smart and Labrin (2026).

[18] Swenson (2018); Janse (2013).

[19] Swenson (2022).

[20] Tamanaha (2011).

[21] von Benda-Beckmann (2006).

[22] Chambers and Vastardis (2020).

Thailand, palm-oil-affected villagers in Indonesia, floriculture workers in Kenya, indigenous communities in Mexico, and leather workers in Bangladesh mobilise courts, customary dispute mechanisms, transnational advocacy networks, and social movements to defend their rights. Community agency, including that of NGOs,[23] as demonstrated in many other studies, identifies blind spots in corporate reporting[24] and due diligence tools, underscoring the importance of participatory and locally anchored forms of remedy.[25]

3.3 Judicial Activism and Regulatory Innovation

Many jurisdictions in the Global South demonstrate forms of judicial leadership that extend or reinterpret global norms. Brazil's courts expand environmental and human rights obligations, Mexican judges reinterpret indigenous governance norms, and many South Asian environmental courts, such as Pakistan and India, apply principles like the precautionary and polluter-pays doctrines in innovative ways.[26] These judicial developments show that Southern courts frequently advance international norms in ways not anticipated by global regulatory design and fill the justice gaps for the victims.[27]

3.4 ESG-Washing, Data Gaps, and Structural Inequalities

Several chapters reveal a mismatch between sustainability rhetoric and ground realities. Examples include Morocco's tourism sector, where ESG claims outpace actual disclosure and Indonesian palm oil, where state-backed certification systems coexist uneasily with global standards. These cases highlight the persistent data gaps, power asymmetries, and institutional capacity constraints that limit the effectiveness of global standards when transplanted into Global South contexts. Inequalities also persist because of the lack of UNGPs' enforcement power and the nexus between the state and businesses.[28]

---

[23] Brun et al. (2020).

[24] Angotti (2024).

[25] Garvey and Newell (2005).

[26] Hassan (2018); Antia (2024).

[27] Ahmad (2023).

[28] Macdonald (2020).

3.5 *Transnational Regulatory Pressures and Uneven Impacts*

The rise of EU-led regulations, particularly the CSRD, CSDDD, and EU Deforestation Regulation, creates profound ripple effects across Global South economies. Examples include Kenya's floriculture industry, whose most of the cut flowers are exported to the EU market, and Thailand's seafood industry, which became most responsible only after the EU issued a "yellow card", While these transnational laws can enhance transparency,[29] they also shift compliance burdens onto suppliers, risk excluding smaller producers, and impose reporting frameworks that do not align with local realities.[30] This often results in the Global South creating its own initiatives to deal with the sustainability crisis.[31] The chapters show that due diligence is not neutral; its meaning and consequences are shaped by global supply chain hierarchies, asymmetric powers, resource inequalities, and geopolitical dynamics.

3.6 *Capacity Constraints and the Realities of Implementation*

A recurring theme is that many Global South regulators operate under structural constraints: limited financial capacity, weak monitoring systems, restricted access to environmental and social data, and fragmented inter-agency coordination.[32] For overcoming these obstacles, NGOs were greatly relied on, primarily for monitoring and obtaining data. As seen in the case of Indonesia, NGOs were primarily relied on for monitoring. These constraints are not failures but contextual realities that global frameworks often ignore. Understanding implementation gaps thus requires recognising these structural conditions of the South countries, rather than attributing shortcomings to just a lack of political will.[33]

4 Strategies for Overcoming Challenges

The North-South struggle continues to deepen, partly because many Southern countries face slower progress in achieving sustainability goals.[34] This is not merely a domestic issue but a global one: when any region lags, it can impede the world's overall development trajectory, thereby creating a direct interest for the North in the

[29] Hale (2008); Jackson (2010).

[30] Narula (2019); Sarfaty (2015); Smit (2021).

[31] Van der Ven et al. (2021).

[32] Howes et al. (2017).

[33] Singh and Rajamani (2003).

[34] Iqbal and Pierson (2017).

South's progress.[35] Therefore, identifying the barriers faced by developing countries and formulating strategies for effectively implementing BHR norms become essential. Across the case studies in this volume, several strategies emerge to address these systemic barriers:

- **Standardised BHDD (Business and Human Rights Due Diligence) Frameworks**: Governments must implement enforceable due diligence laws that clarify business responsibilities for human rights harms and should make these requirements a mandatory part of corporate governance and operations.[36] Thailand's regulatory reforms and the Mexican judiciary's interpretation of "participatory rights" exemplify such legal evolution. Thailand's fisheries reforms exemplify how regulatory changes can drive BHR norms into businesses.
- **Incentives for Responsible Conduct**: Financial and tax incentives can encourage enterprises, especially SMEs, to adopt rights-respecting business models. For instance, India's Union Budget 2025–2026 allocates ₹150 billion for low-carbon steel and incentives for EV batteries and solar cells.[37]
- **Investment in Rights-Based Infrastructure**: Sustainable waste management, clean energy, and data governance infrastructure can support corporate compliance with legal obligations, as highlighted in the Brazil, Morocco, and Latin America chapters.
- **International Legal Cooperation**: Engagement with regional legal frameworks like Escazú and trade-linked sustainability requirements (e.g. EU CSDDD) can amplify national regulatory impact and create transnational accountability networks.

The effective BHR governance requires polycentric coordination among states, corporations, investors, civil society, and affected communities.[38] Thailand's fisheries reforms reaffirm how polycentric governance, rather than purely state-led regulations, can generate durable compliance. Moreover, regulatory reform, judicial interpretation, and creative use of law, such as treating external experts of companies as legal subjects (co-defendants)—as seen in several BHR litigations[39]—can also enhance corporate accountability.[40]

These strategies are increasingly reinforced by transnational regulatory developments, particularly those emerging from the Global North. The rise of EU regulatory provisions, such as the CSDDD, reflects theories of extraterritorial regulation, where home states regulate not only the overseas impact of their domestic companies but also the domestic impacts of on-scope foreign companies, thereby generating a transnational accountability network. This legal evolution challenges the traditional

---

[35] Walter and Ugelow (1979).

[36] Baxi (2020).

[37] The Economic Times (2025).

[38] Partiti (2021).

[39] Corporate Accountability Lab (CAL) v. Hershey and Rainforest Alliance (2021).

[40] McVey (2025).

notion that domestic laws are territorially confined within the national boundaries.[41] The positive impacts of such transnational accountability regulations are evident in the case of Thailand, where domestic reforms were undertaken to align with international standards and ensure BHR compliance. Although debates continue regarding the legitimacy and scope of transnational regulation, the Thai case illustrates that such frameworks can be necessary in certain contexts to mitigate the negative human rights impact of business activities and make them accountable.

5 Global South Perspective on BHR Scholarship

The significance of the Global South perspective in BHR scholarship has long been highlighted in the literature, for example, in challenging Northern-driven agendas, broadening the diversity of scholarship,[42] and examining intersectional issues such as digitalisation and gender.[43] This volume, in particular, demonstrates that a Global South lens enriches BHR in at least three key ways:

5.1 Norm Localisation

International law and transnational legal frameworks have historically ignored the knowledge creation capacities of Southern countries. As a result, human rights risks associated with business activities remain unevenly distributed, with Southern countries often bearing the greatest harm.[44] In the absence of meaningful Southern contributions to knowledge production, differences in opinion have also emerged between the North and the South regarding the legal nature of these frameworks: while the North often advocates for soft law approaches, the South tends to favour hard law, precisely because it disproportionately experiences the negative impacts.[45] Thus, the localisation of global norms becomes essential. Through this process, global standards acquire new meaning and, as they interact with local legal systems, cultural norms, and political contexts, become more adaptable.

As seen in the mining case in Mexico and tourism in Morocco, respecting local knowledge systems, traditions, and governance practices is key to achieving inclusive legal compliance. These cases demonstrate the relevance of decolonial BHR theory, which warns that Northern models of sustainability may sideline local epistemologies and governance traditions. Integrating cultural intelligence into BHR, therefore, aligns with the "norm localisation" approach, whereby global norms gain legitimacy only

---

41 Djelic and Quack (2018).

42 Köchli (2020).

43 Handl (2022); Mutung'u (2022).

44 do Amaral Vieira (2024).

45 Chiorean (2025), p. 25.

when adapted to local cultural and legal realities.[46] The volume thus advocates for the local adaptation of due diligence, remedy, and participation processes, which have the potential to transform imported standards into context-sensitive and effective tools.

5.2 Plural Knowledge Systems

Legal pluralism is a decolonising strategy that recognises relational, autonomous, and subjacent normativities that challenge monistic, state-centred legal frameworks.[47] It plays a crucial role in promoting justice by empowering local communities and recognising diverse normative orders.[48] This dynamic is visible in Kenya's cut flower sector and Thailand's seafood industry, where transnational legal frameworks interact with domestic regulations, customary practices, and local governance structures. These intersections create a plural legal landscape in which businesses are compelled to meet not only external regulatory expectations but also locally grounded environmental and social obligations, thereby making the global BHR framework more capable of producing sustainability outcomes that are both environmentally and socially responsible.

5.3 Resistance to Regulatory Universalism

Building on the critique that legal centralism is a Eurocentric construct that restricts political imagination and suppresses normative diversity,[49] the volume challenges the assumption that BHR standards can be uniformly applied across jurisdictions. The effectiveness of transnational frameworks becomes most visible when these laws, such as the CSRD and CSDDD, are operationalised in developing countries, where they intersect with distinct legal, social, and economic realities. While acknowledging the positive contributions of these instruments, the volume argues that their implementation must be locally grounded to avoid reproducing structural inequalities.[50] Experiences from the South reveal the unequal burdens, compliance costs, and systemic disadvantages embedded within Northern-designed standards, underscoring the need for context-sensitive adaptation rather than regulatory universalism.

By foregrounding these diverse contributions, the volume expands the epistemic geography of BHR, thereby advancing epistemic justice.[51] In doing so, it moves the BHR conversation beyond predominantly Northern institutional frameworks and corporate-centric reporting tools.

---

[46] Merino (2022).

[47] Wolkmer and Schumacher Wolkmer (2022).

[48] Dübgen (2025).

[49] Araújo (2025).

[50] Borghesi (2025).

[51] McDonnell (2023).

6 Co-Development of Standards: From One-Way Diffusion to Negotiated Governance

Laws made in the North without the participation of South stakeholders can perpetuate a colonial legacy.[52] Southern countries often become testing grounds for Northern regulatory ideas, enabling Northern actors to modify, refine, and influence the evolution of these laws. Some previous scholarship argues that BHR frameworks function as tools for Northern countries to control the South.[53] Conversely, other studies show that Southern publics do not necessarily perceive these frameworks as instruments of Northern control.[54] However, this volume's key contribution is the argument that global BHR standards are not simply exported to the Global South; rather, they are "co-developed", and when "co-developed", they make businesses more responsible. By this, I mean that:

- International and transnational frameworks such as the UNGPs or EU directives are interpreted, challenged, and reworked by Southern courts, regulators, and communities, thereby generating new meanings and applications.
- Domestic laws, such as "smart regulation" in Indonesia, Indigenous governance norms in Mexico, or certification hybrids in Kenya, shape how global norms materialise on the ground.
- Community-led resistance, as seen in Mexico, and judicial activism, as observed in Brazil, often reshape corporate behaviour more effectively than formal reporting standards.

Co-development is therefore a plural, iterative, and negotiated process in which the Global South actively contributes to the evolution of BHR standards. This contribution strengthens the understanding of human rights as an international responsibility.[55]

7 Towards a Shared Future

The burden of ensuring responsible business conduct within the field of BHR must be distributed equitably across all relevant actors. Such responsibility sharing should extend beyond mere acknowledgement of respective roles and encompass concrete remedial obligations.[56] Earlier scholarship has emphasised the need to transform traditional corporate models into "human rights corporations"[57] or to develop industry-specific human rights standards and metrics capable of strengthening

[52] Deva and Anand (2023).

[53] Gonzalez (2015); Imanaka (2019).

[54] Ron (2017).

[55] Beall (2022).

[56] Baumann-Pauly et al. (2016).

[57] Wolfsteller and Li (2022).

supply chain oversight.[58] Building on these insights, this volume endorses these approaches while proposing several additional forward-looking pathways.

First, community participation in due diligence processes should be enhanced through participatory monitoring mechanisms and the incorporation of Indigenous governance frameworks.[59] Second, regulatory design must embrace legal pluralism by integrating customary norms, community protocols, and culturally grounded understandings of rights and responsibilities. Third, effective implementation of BHR standards requires stronger support for Southern regulators, including capacity-building measures, improved data sharing, and adequate resourcing for environmental and social monitoring. Fourth, certification and reporting frameworks must be designed inclusively so that compliance requirements do not disproportionately burden small-scale producers or informal actors.

Moreover, the volume underscores the importance of cross-regional judicial dialogue to facilitate the exchange of jurisprudential lessons on environmental protection and social rights enforcement.[60] Finally, it advocates for an expansion of South-South cooperation on issues such as sustainable supply chain governance, digital rights, climate litigation, and labour mobility, areas in which collective learning and shared regulatory innovations are particularly valuable. Taken together, these pathways suggest a more balanced, context-sensitive, and justice-oriented approach to advancing the BHR agenda.

8 Concluding Reflections

The chapters from this volume collectively demonstrate that meaningful corporate accountability cannot be achieved through legal instruments alone. The effective implementation of BHR principles in developing countries requires a multifaceted approach that integrates community mobilisation, judicial innovation, plural legal systems, and regulatory experimentation rooted in a Global South orientation. Taken together, the chapters show that the future of BHR lies not in the universalisation of Northern standards but in co-developed, equitable, and culturally grounded norms that reflect the lived realities of affected communities.

They also illustrate that legal frameworks must not only mandate compliance but also ensure meaningful participation and access to remedy. As transnational obligations such as those under the CSDDD and Escazú Agreement expand in scope and global influence, Global South jurisdictions must be empowered to shape, adapt, and apply these norms within their legal systems. This volume thus contributes to an evolving legal conversation on the future of corporate accountability, rooted in justice, sustainability, and inclusive development.

---

58 Baumann-Pauly and Glimcher (2021).

59 Ramos Gómez and Ramos Gómez (2026).

60 Bauer and Martins da Rosa (2026).

These insights also open several pathways for future research. A key priority is assessing the long-term efficacy of mandatory human rights due diligence regimes and determining whether existing legal frameworks are robust enough to transform corporate behaviour. There remains an urgent need to refine enforceable methodologies that capture both quantitative and qualitative dimensions of business impacts on society and the environment. Comparative analysis, such as between the CSDDD and voluntary frameworks prevalent in developing economies, can illuminate best practices for harmonising global standards while preventing disproportionate burdens on suppliers. Further studies should examine how international instruments like the Escazú Agreement and the UNGPs reshape domestic legal obligations, especially in the areas of extra-activism, digital surveillance, and transnational supply chains.

Emerging technologies such as smart contracts, blockchain, and algorithmic governance present new opportunities for enhancing traceability and remedy mechanisms, warranting interdisciplinary research that bridges law, data science, and environmental studies. In resource-constrained settings, attention should also be given to the legal design of sustainable financial mechanisms capable of supporting rights-compliant business conduct. Together, these research trajectories can strengthen the legal foundations of BHR and contribute to the evolution of accountability regimes that are globally coherent yet locally responsive.

Theoretically, this study advances a justice-oriented understanding of BHR by emphasising that corporate accountability requires more than regulatory compliance; it depends on decolonial thinking, cultural intelligence, meaningful community participation, and effective state action consistent with the spirit of the UNGPs. From this perspective, the Global South is not a peripheral site of implementation but a key locus of innovation where some of the most urgent and transformative developments in BHR are emerging. By placing these contributions at the centre of global debates, the volume calls for a shared governance future grounded in pluralism, justice, and inclusive participation. In doing so, it challenges the persistent dominance of Global North frameworks in BHR scholarship and advances a more context-sensitive and equitable approach to corporate accountability.

References

Ahmad HM (2023) Judicial activism in transnational business and human rights litigation. Berkeley J Int Law 41:145

Angotti M, Ferreira ACDS, Eugénio T, Branco MC (2024) A narrative approach for reporting social and environmental accounting impacts in the mining sector–giving marginalized communities a voice. Meditari Account Res 32(1):42–63

Antia D (2024) Analysing the impact of judicial activism on human rights protection: a comparative review of Nigerian and Indian jurisprudence. Available at SSRN 4913442

Araújo S (2025) Legal pluralism as co-presence: Disobeying the hierarchies of the western canon. Oñati socio-legal series

Bauer L, Martins da Rosa RS (2026) The siege closes on self regulation, public rules and judicial precedents to implement ESG standards in Brazil. In: Talukdar S (ed) Law, accountability, and corporate conduct, this volume. Springer Nature, Switzerland
Baumann-Pauly D, Glimcher IW (2021) Seeking a 'Smart Mix': Multi-Stakeholder Initiatives and Mandatory Human Rights Due Diligence
Baumann-Pauly D, Nolan J, Posner M (2016) The future of business and human rights: challenges and opportunities. Bus Human Rights:316–320
Baxi U (2020) Nevsun: a ray of hope in a darkening landscape? BHRJ 5:241–251. https://doi.org/10.1017/bhj.2020.17
Bazzim RE, Edman H (2026) Ethical issues and the applicability of environmental, social and governance (ESG) standards in the Moroccan tourism industry: the case of the seaside resort Taghazout Bay (Agadir). In: Talukdar S (ed) Law, accountability, and corporate conduct, this volume. Springer Nature, Switzerland
Beall KM (2022) The global south and global human rights: international responsibility for the right to development. Third World Quart 43(10):2337–2356
Borghesi S, Costantini V, D'amato A, Dibattista I, Koundouri P, Li Q, Mazzarano M, Sterner T, Tiwari MM, Vis P, Xepapadeas A (2025) Reforming ESG: a European and global south perspective. Environ Dev Econ:1–15
Braithwaite J (2006) Responsive regulation and developing economies. World Dev 34(5):884–898
Brun A, Karaosman H, Barresi T (2020) Supply chain collaboration for transparency. Sustainability 12(11):4429
Cetera K, Hawari A (2026) Smart regulation in palm oil governance: enhancing the implementation of ESG principles in Indonesia. In: Talukdar S (ed) Law, accountability, and corporate conduct, this volume. Springer Nature, Switzerland
Chambers R, Vastardis AY (2020) Human rights disclosure and due diligence laws: the role of regulatory oversight in ensuring corporate accountability. Chicago J Int Law 21:323
Chiorean A (2025) A world where there are many worlds." Fragmentation of civil society advocacy for a UN business and human rights treaty. In Corporate accountability for human rights violations: civil society and transnational activism across the world. Springer Nature Switzerland, Cham, pp 21–48
Deva S, Anand P (2023) A global south perspective on labour rights and supply chains for a post-growth world. SSRN: 90
Djelic ML, Quack S (2018) Globalization and business regulation. ARS 44(123):143
do Amaral Vieira F (2024) The struggles for corporate accountability in the UN: a global south perspective. In: The wretched of the global south: critical approaches to international human rights law. Singapore, Springer Nature Singapore, pp 235–255
Dübgen F (2025) Horizons of justice in a Pluriversal World. Oñati Socio-Legal Series 15(5):1749–1757
Faracik B (2017) Implementation of the UN guiding principles on business and human rights. European Parliament. PE: 578
Garvey N, Newell P (2005) Corporate accountability to the poor? Assessing the effectiveness of community-based strategies. Dev Pract 15(3-4):389–404
Giuliani E (2016) Human rights and corporate social responsibility in developing countries' industrial clusters. JBE 133(1):39–54
Gonzalez CG (2015) Environmental justice, human rights, and the global south. Santa Clara J Int Law 13:151
Graham D, Woods N (2006) Making corporate self-regulation effective in developing countries. World Dev 34(5):868–883
Hale TN (2008) Transparency, accountability, and global governance. Glob Gov:73–94
Handl MN, Seck SL, Simons P (2022) Gender and intersectionality in business and human rights scholarship. Bus Human Rights J 7(2):201–225
Haque MS, Ramesh M, Puppim de Oliveira JA, Gomide ADA (2021) Building administrative capacity for development: limits and prospects. IRAS 87(2):211–219

Hassan P (2018) Judicial commissions and climate justice in Pakistan. In: Asia Pacific Judicial Colloquium on Climate Change: Using Constitutions to Advance Environmental Rights and Achieve Climate Justice, Lahore, Pakistan 4(31):26–27
Howes M, Wortley L, Potts R, Dedekorkut-Howes A, Serrao-Neumann S, Davidson J, Smith T, Nunn P (2017) Environmental sustainability: a case of policy implementation failure? Sustainability 9(2):165
Imanaka JL (2019) Global collaborative advantage: efforts toward decolonization of business ethics and management scholarship. J Manage Glob Sustain 7(2):4
Iqbal I, Pierson C (2017) A north-south struggle: political and economic obstacles to sustainable development. Sustain Dev Law Policy 16(2):4
Jackson KT (2010) Global corporate governance: soft law and reputational accountability. Brook J Int Law 35:41
Janse R (2013) A turn to legal pluralism in the rule of law promotion? Erasmus Law Rev 6:181
Kaewtong S, Kongmuang P, Jehpong P (2026) Illegal fishing in Thailand's food industry. In: Talukdar S (ed) Law, accountability, and corporate conduct, this volume. Springer Nature, Switzerland
Köchli SS (2020) International business and human rights in Brazil: an institutional perspective (Doctoral dissertation). Universität St. Gallen
Macdonald K (2020) Obstacles to implementing the UN guiding principles on business and human rights in Southeast Asia. Melbourne Asia Rev 3
McDonnell K (2023) Epistemic injustice and remedy: Can BHR ever really 'centre' rights holders? Aust J Human Rights 29(1):84–102
McVey M (2025) Outsourcing the responsibility to respect? 'Visibilising' the external expert in business and human rights litigation. BHRJ 10:363–378
Merino R (2022) The politics of localizing human rights: Chinese policies and corporate practices in Latin America. Bus Human Rights J 7(3):439–460
Mutung'u G (2022) The United Nations guiding principles on business and human rights, women and digital ID in Kenya: a decolonial perspective. Bus Human Rights J 7(1):117–133
Narula R (2019) Enforcing higher labor standards within developing country value chains: consequences for MNEs and informal actors in a dual economy. JIBS 50(9):1622–1635
Partiti E (2021) Polycentricity and polyphony in international law: interpreting the corporate responsibility to respect human rights. ICLQ 70(1):133
Partiti E (2023) Human rights due diligence and evolution of voluntary sustainability standards. In: Delimatsis P, Bijlmakers S, Borowicz MK (eds) The evolution of transnational rule-makers through crises. Cambridge University Press, Cambridge, pp 133–153
Ramos Gómez RA, Ramos Gómez AE (2026) Taking seriously the right of local communities to participate in environmental decisions in the context of damages caused by mining. In: Talukdar S (ed) Law, accountability, and corporate conduct, this volume. Springer Nature, Switzerland
Ron J, Golden S, Crow D, Pandya A (2017) Taking root: human rights and public opinion in the Global South. Oxford University Press
Salekin M, Kamal M (2026) Balancing economic growth and environmental justice: the challenges of Bangladesh's leather industry. In: Talukdar S (ed) Law, accountability, and corporate conduct, this volume. Springer Nature, Switzerland
Sarfaty GA (2015) Shining light on global supply chains. Harv Int Law J 56:419
Sharon M (2026) An analysis of Kenyan laws affecting environmental and social governance on and for the floricultural industry. In: Talukdar S (ed) Law, accountability, and corporate conduct, this volume. Springer Nature, Switzerland
Singh S, Rajamani S (2003) Issues of environmental compliance in developing countries. Water Sci Technol 47(12):301–304
Smart S, Labrin DR (2026) AI, Environmental damage, and regulatory divides: fragmented governance and the Latin American response. In: Talukdar S (ed) Law, accountability, and corporate conduct, this volume. Springer Nature, Switzerland

Smit L, Holly G, McCorquodale R, Neely S (2021) Human rights due diligence in global supply chains: evidence of corporate practices to inform a legal standard. Int J Human Rights 25(6):945–973
Swenson G (2018) Legal pluralism in theory and practice. ISR 20(3):438–462
Swenson G (2022) Contending orders: legal pluralism and the rule of law. Oxford University Press
Tamanaha BZ (2011) The rule of law and legal pluralism in development. Hague J Rule Law 3(1):1–17
The Economic Times (2025) Budget 2025: steel ministry seeks $ 1.7 bn to help mills cut emission. https://economictimes.indiatimes.com/industry/indl-goods/svs/steel/budget-2025-steel-ministry-seeks-1-7-bn-to-help-mills-cut-emissions/articleshow/117295097.cms?from=mdr. Accessed 14 July 2025
United Nations (2011) UN Guiding Principles on Business and Human Rights https://digitallibrary.un.org/record/720245?ln=en. Accessed 23 Nov 2025
Van der Ven H, Sun Y, Cashore B (2021) Sustainable commodity governance and the global south. Ecol Econ 186:107062
von Benda-Beckmann F (2006) The multiple edges of law: dealing with legal pluralism in development practice. World Bank Legal Rev 2:51
Walter I, Ugelow JL (1979) Environmental policies in developing countries. Ambio:102–109
Wilhelm M (2024) Mandatory due diligence legislation: a paradigm shift for the governance of sustainability in global value chains? JIBP 7:459–465. https://doi.org/10.1057/s42214-024-00193-4
Wolfsteller R, Li Y (2022) Business and human rights regulation after the UN guiding principles: accountability, governance, effectiveness. Human rights Rev 23(1):1–17
Wolkmer AC, Schumacher Wolkmer MDF (2022) The principle of the 'common', legal pluralism and decolonization in Latin America. Law Critiq 33(1):63–87
World Bank Group (2024) World Development Report 2024: The Middle-Income Trap

Shuma Talukdar is a corporate lawyer and governance professional with over 18 years of cross-sectoral and multi-jurisdictional experience across shipping, energy, infrastructure, and development. She holds dual master's degrees in Business Law and Public Administration and is currently pursuing a Ph.D. in law at Mahindra University, India. She is the co-founder of LexEd Research, a policy-oriented think tank. Her scholarship engages with sustainability law, corporate accountability, transnational law, and global governance, with a particular emphasis on Global South perspectives. Talukdar is the co-editor of *Judicial Responses to Climate Change in the Global South* (Springer Nature, 2023). She has presented her research at leading global institutions, including the Asian Institute of Technology, Max Planck Institute, Sutherland School of Law, UC Berkeley, University of Canberra, and University of Hamburg, and has published widely with leading international publishers.

Index

S. Talukdar (ed.), *Law, Accountability, and Corporate Conduct*, New Approaches to Business, Human Rights and the Environment 1,
https://doi.org/10.1007/978-3-032-28714-4

www.ingramcontent.com/pod-product-compliance
Ingram Content Group UK Ltd.
Pitfield, Milton Keynes, MK11 3LW, UK
UKHW020934180926
475692UK00003B/30
* 9 7 8 3 0 3 2 2 8 7 1 3 7 *